FUTURE ETHICS

CENNYDD BOWLES

 NowNext Press

© 2020, Cennydd Bowles

First published in 2018 by NowNext Press. NowNext Press is an imprint of Cennydd Ltd, The Old Casino, 28 Fourth Avenue, Hove, East Sussex BN3 2PJ, United Kingdom. nownext.press.

Cover image by Bernard Hermant. Typeset in Iowan Old Style.

ISBN 978-1-9996019-1-1

Calon lân yn llawn daioni,
Tecach yw na'r lili dlos:
Dim ond calon lân all ganu,
Canu'r dydd a chanu'r nos.

———

A pure heart full of goodness,
Is fairer than the pretty lily:
None but a pure heart can sing,
Sing in the day and sing in the night.

(*Calon Lân*, Welsh hymn)

Contents

Foreword

Ethics has rightfully earned its reputation as a ridiculously boring topic. Much of the existing canon on ethics sounds to the modern ear like theologians debating the number of angels in heaven. It's either not relevant, or its prose is turgid and prolix, or both. Contemporary practitioners find little traction in the world of conventional ethical thinking. Yet there is much of value, if only it could be couched in relevant ways. And that is exactly what you hold in your hands. Cennydd Bowles has accomplished much in this single, readable, and relatable volume.

The dawning ubiquity of software and its data in every aspect of our world has opened a Pandora's Box of ethical questions. The questions aren't new – they have been debated for centuries – but they are assuming new shapes in their digital manifestations, and they are assuming new, far greater magnitude in contemporary social, economic, and political spheres.

Like Moore's Law, the world of software grows at an exponential pace, rather than linear. Growth at that speed means that signposts far off in the distance will be whipping past us much sooner than our intuition would suggest. The ethical questions raised by software's new capabilities are legion, and they demand answers now.

Armchair ethicists in tech circles discuss the trolley problem. This is a hypothetical exercise where one must decide – by switching tracks – whether a runaway trolley should kill a young mother or an old man. It's true that makers of self-driving cars face a real world trolley problem, but average practitioners performing simple, day-to-day software design and development, are often blithely unaware of the ethical choices they make unconsciously. Yet these choices can have ramifications comparable to those faced by the inventors of poison gas or the atomic bomb. The frequency and consequence of ethical questions are far greater today than in the past.

In the industrial age, we allowed marketers to appeal to us with advertising design, product placement, and signage. The inherently sluggish atom-based world lulled us into believing this kind of persuasion to be harmless. Today, however, by analyzing your purchases and likes, Amazon can tailor its site for your personality and make you buy more stuff. While this is conceptually the same thing as cardboard signs in the grocer's aisle, its magnitude makes it a whole new world of morality. Some of the most fundamental questions about acceptable behavior are coming under scrutiny, and many of the answers need to change. And when the product being sold is a political party, or worse, a fear-based, totalitarian coup, change is imperative.

Software owned by someone else can gather data on you without you knowing it. Increasingly, it can do so without you even using it. Is that legal? Is that right? Who owns that data? What can they do with it? What rights do you have? What if that data is wrong? What if third parties make lasting decisions on that data? How do you even know?

Claiming that technology itself is morally neutral is a reassuring fig leaf worn by many technologists, but evidence against that idea has mounted to staggering proportions, and many digitally-savvy thinkers are confronting these apparently unprecedented moral dilemmas with fresh eyes.

Delegating authority to software without erecting robust feedback mechanisms is a common point of failure. Sure, the algorithm gives us an answer, but how do we know it's correct, and how do we fix it if not? For feedback loops to be effective, they have to be timely, and actionable, and some commitment has to be made to act on them. In pre-digital tech, the strong damping force of human participation in feedback loops helped to steady the process. Digital feedback loops may be too efficient, causing the system to oscillate and fail. Mostly, though, feedback mechanisms are non-existent.

With today's tech tools, software often makes decisions on data gathered by some far distant app, owned by some unaffiliated company, at some far off time. Even conscientious organizations may find it impossible to verify that the choices their algorithms make are correct, let alone update them to do better in the future. The victim, typically just a person asking for a loan, or applying for a job, or trying to get veterans help, simply falls through the net.

A backlash is brewing against the digital world, and we could benefit from the lessons of history. We need useful principles spelled out today more than ever. As our digital artifacts mature, they exhibit capabilities unimagined in arenas unpredicted. Products intended to sell books have morphed into the arbiter of our built environment. Products intended for young adults to meet each other have morphed into brain-washing tools and tribal drums driving us to war.

Worse than a backlash is its opposite. Companies like Amazon, Facebook, and Cambridge Analytica are enthusiastically applying digital tools on everyone. These organizations are willing to use your information to make a profit without any consideration of your inter-ests. And news outlets, whose industrial age distribution channels allowed some measure of detachment, are now virtual slaves to the click-through. Even mainstream news outlets like *The New York Times*, *The Atlantic*, and CNN have to exploit sensational 'news' in order to survive.

Governments, too, are playing this risky game. China is experi-menting with a social rating system, like a credit rating, except it rates whether or not you are a good person. The potential for abuse is clear. The next steps are police robots that autonomously peer into your bedroom and decide if you are behaving properly.

At the start of this book, Cennydd gives us a survey of the ethical landscape. He articulates these important ethical principles in the context of modern tech, so they make sense to the contemporary practitioner. He then draws out extended examples of the growing ethical binds in the real world, and shows us how to apply the frame-work. What's more, he makes it interesting and applicable.

Because this is not a deterministic problem, there are no black-and-white answers. But there are many useful techniques for the designer to master. The reader will be armed with a sense of mission, useful conceptual tools, and a map of the road forward.

We need good books about ethics now more than ever. Practitioners need guidance on how to think ethically, how to detect ethical choices, and how to resolve ethical dilemmas. That's exactly what this book is, and it's destined to become a well-thumbed classic.

—Alan Cooper,
21 August 2018,
Petaluma, California.

Acknowledgements

I'm indebted to:

My editor Owen Gregory, and my tech reviewers Thomas Wendt, Lydia Nicholas, and Damien Williams. No weak argument undented; no sweeping statement unchallenged; no scare quote unscrubbed.

Livia Labate, Eli Schiff, Paul Robert Lloyd, and Tom Hume for their invaluable reader feedback. Lou Rosenfeld, Richard Rutter, Abby Covert, Nick Disabato, and Brad Frost for publishing advice. Marcel Shouwenaar, Jeff Veen, Timo Arnall, Andy Cotgreave, and the Future of Life Institute for photo permissions. Christina Wodtke, Azeem Azhar, and Jon Kolko for the flattering blurbs, and Alan Cooper for his gracious foreword.

Attendees of the Juvet AI retreat for the inspirational conversations and childlike Borealis wonder, and everyone else working in the field of emerging technology ethics. Your work is vital and deep; I hope I've done credit to your ideas.

My family and friends. Thank you in particular to Sascha Auerbach and Andrew Fox for their ongoing (liquid) support.

Finally, my wife, Anna. My guiding star.

Chapter 1

Trouble in paradise

The utopian dreams of early cyberspace didn't come true. Eden was rezoned, walled off. The lemonade stands grew into colossal malls; disinformation and deceit polluted the global agora. After fulfilling their promise to demolish old hierarchies, technologists erected new towers and fiefdoms in their place.

Industry orthodoxy – the 'Californian Ideology' described in Richard Barbrook and Andy Cameron's influential essay – sees technology as the solution to any problem. To Silicon Valley's cheerleaders, technology is intrinsically empowering, so laden with good that harm is almost unthinkable. A spirit of exceptionalism courses through the community's veins: believers see themselves as beta testers of a brave new world, and regard existing social structures, norms, and laws as anachronisms, inconveniences best routed around. Technologists have learned to build first and ask questions later. Lean startup, tech's predominant ideology today, is vehemently empirical. It argues that we're so swept up in change it's futile to predict the future; instead, we should prioritise validation over research and learn through making. Build, measure, learn, repeat.

This approach has brought bold innovation to stagnant fields, but when technology becomes an answer to any problem, it should be no surprise that 'Can we?' overtakes 'Should we?' Just as promised, technologists have moved fast and broken many things. The industry's repeated missteps – racist algorithms, casual privacy abuses, blind eyes turned to harassment and hate – have eroded public faith and prompted the media to label technology a danger as often as a saviour. Tech employees may be surprised to find themselves in the crosshairs. Most genuinely want to improve the human condition, or at least tackle interesting problems, and have good intentions. The industry's problems are mostly down to negligence, not malice.

An ethical awakening is long overdue. Technologists are rightly starting to question their influence on a world spiralling off its expected course, and as the industry matures, it's natural to pay attention to deeper questions of impact and justice. As sociologist Richard Sennett points out, 'It is at the level of mastery [...] that ethical problems of craft appear.'[1]

This focus coincides with growing public disquiet and appetite for ethical change. Consumers want to support companies that espouse clear values: 87% of consumers would purchase a product because a company advocated for an issue close to their hearts.[2] Emerging technology raises the stakes further. Over the coming decades, our industry will ask people to trust us with their data, their vehicles, and even their families' safety. Dystopian science fiction has already taught people to be sceptical of these requests; unless we tackle the ethical issues that are blighting the field, this trust will be hard to earn.

Instrumentalism, determinism, and mediation

As our first ethical step, we should abandon the comforting idea that technology is neutral. This *instrumentalist* stance argues technology is just a tool, one that people can use for good or misuse for harm. Instrumentalists argue that since bad actors will always twist technology for evil, the only ethical recourse is to educate and plead for proper use. This deflects responsibility onto the user, allowing technologists to wriggle off the moral hook. We all know one popular instrumentalist refrain: 'Guns don't kill people; people kill people.'[3]

The opposing view – *technological determinism* – argues that technology is anything but neutral; instead, it's so powerful that it moulds society and culture, acting more as our master than our servant. Determinism pervades both science fiction and academia, and has even begun to seduce the media; gleeful reports on technology's brewing dominance over mankind litter today's front pages. Politicians are starting to catch the determinist bug too, declaring that technology will define the twenty-first century.

Instrumentalism is handy for shutting down critique: if technology is just an inert tool, it has no social, political, or moral effects. However, the industry has been obtuse in clinging to this view; tech marketing suggests the industry is well aware of its potential impacts. Technologists often describe their lofty goals with deterministic language – Democratise! Transform! Disrupt! – but fall back on instrumentalist defences to ethical issues: we truly regret this disturbing case, but we can't be held liable for misuse. In other words, technology will change the world, but if the world changes, don't blame us.

Technology's harmful impacts make instrumentalism unsustainable; even the supposedly benign search engine has reinforced bias and devalued trusted information sources. Opposing the neutrality myth is hardly a new stance. In 1985, tech historian Melvin Kranzberg presented six laws of technology. Law one: 'Technology is neither good nor bad; nor is it neutral.' But in rejecting instrumentalism we shouldn't necessarily leap to determinism. Putting technologists at the centre of the universe isn't healthy for an industry in dire need of humility, and determinism can curiously downplay technologists' ethical responsibilities. If we see technology as an unstoppable social force, we might conclude it's outside our control.

Tech philosopher Peter-Paul Verbeek suggests a third perspective – *mediation theory* – that neatly melds the competing views of instrumentalism and determinism.[4] For Verbeek, technology is a medium through which we perceive and manipulate our world. Glasses help us see and understand our environments; hammers help us build shelters and sculptures; cameras help us recollect and share our memories. Perhaps it's futile to separate technology from society. We don't fully control tech, nor does it fully control us; instead, humans and technologies co-create the world. An anecdote from Kranzberg about the violinist Fritz Kreisler shows this combination at work:

A woman came up to [Kreisler] after a concert and gushed, 'Oh, Maestro, your violin makes such beautiful music.' Kreisler picked up his violin (a Stradivarius, no less), held it to his ear, and said, 'I don't hear any music coming out of it.' You see, the beautiful music coming out of the violin did not come from the instrument, the hardware, alone; it depended upon the human element, the software.[5]

Only the violinist – a hybrid of the violin and the human – could create such memorable music (although we can blame Kreisler alone for the arrogant witticism).

Barriers to ethics

What does this mean for ethics? If humans and technology act in tandem, we can't claim technology is ethically inert, but neither can we separate it from human action. The ethics of technology becomes the ethics of everyday life. But as a conversation topic, ethics doesn't always spark enthusiasm. All those pointless thought experiments and dusty Greeks! Not to mention the definitional pedantry: what's the difference between ethics and morals, anyway? Perhaps your mind will wander back to high-school religious studies or civics lessons: isn't ethics about society's expectations and morality something more personal and innate? There's a deep philosophical rabbit hole here, but happily we can choose to sidestep it. Most (but not all) modern philosophers see no big difference between morals and ethics, and use the terms interchangeably. I will too.

Whatever the label, ethics matters more outside the classroom. Ethics is a vital and real topic, nothing less than a pledge to take our choices and even our lives seriously. This commitment is especially important for designers. Design *is* applied ethics. Sometimes this connection is obvious: if you design razor wire, you're saying that anyone who tries to contravene someone else's right to private property should be injured. But whatever the medium or material, every act of design is a statement about the future. Design changes how we see the world and how we can act within it; design turns beliefs about how we should live into objects and environments people will use and inhabit. In choosing the future they want, designers discard dozens of alternative realities, which pop briefly into existence through prototypes or sketches, but perish in the recycling bin. As one memorable quote proclaims, 'Ethics is the aesthetics of the future.'[6]

Bringing up ethics in the workplace often prompts two objections. First, some people claim ethics doesn't belong in industry, and that acceptable behaviour is for the market or the law to decide. This is a political idea, and its weaknesses should be clear to anyone who disputes its libertarian premise. A market that ethically self-corrects requires perfect information and full agreement on what's right and wrong. Customers can only punish ethical overreach if they know and understand what companies are doing, and if they agree it's unethical. But technology acts invisibly, often with dubious consent, and typically using a dialect only a few can speak. The general public has no idea what sorts of unwelcome acts are happening inside their gadgets. The idea of market self-correction is a fantasy.

The claim that the law is the best ethical arbiter is particularly wretched; it essentially argues we should allow all behaviour except the criminal. Ethics should be about living our best lives, not seeing how low we can sink. And laws themselves can be morally wrong; sometimes brave people have to disobey unjust legislation to spark ethical change: just ask Rosa Parks. Even if we ignore these arguments, for law to be an appropriate substitute for ethics in tech, we'd have to find legislators who deeply understand technology. History tells us these individuals are sadly rare.

The second common objection to business ethics is that it will hamper innovation. Sometimes that's true. Pausing to take moral stock will indeed extinguish some potentially harmful ideas, but an enlightened company should be grateful for the intervention. Ethics isn't just a drag on innovation; properly handled, it can fertilise new ideas as well as weed out bad ones.

This book

While it's heartening that technologists are finally taking ethics seriously, we shouldn't believe we're the first on these shores. Sadly, the philosophers, academics, writers, and artists who have studied the topic for decades aren't yet taken seriously within industry; tech culture prizes intelligence but is doggedly anti-intellectual. In turn, academics complain about practitioners' hubristic ability to run repeatedly into the same old walls, while being paid handsomely to do so.

As a working designer, not an ethicist, I'm writing this book for my peers in the tech industry. While the book owes deep gratitude to those who have paved the way, and won't shy away from complex ideas, I'll try to always translate theory into application. That said, a manual for ethics is an oxymoron; if you're after bullet-point instruction, you'll be disappointed. No one can answer ethical problems for us; we have to think them through for ourselves, and there's usually more than one answer. To paraphrase Caroline Whitbeck[7], ethical issues are like design briefs: there are often dozens of viable solutions, each with their own trade-offs. This doesn't mean there are no wrong answers, however. Ethics is beset with pitfalls and fallacies; we'll highlight the most common ones as we go.

Some politics is inevitable in a book like this, since ethics and politics are naturally entwined. The breadth of human opinion is reflected in the complexity of ethics; people's moral views tend to inform their political views, and vice versa. Those on the left might favour moral stances that prioritise social good, while those on the right may prefer perspectives that support individual sovereignty and autonomy. Personal experience also bears a strong imprint: a victim of robbery will probably feel more strongly about theft in future, whether consciously or not. It would be disingenuous for me to disguise my personal and political leanings in the name of false objectivity, but I'll try to avoid cheap point-scoring and instead give you tools to work through ethical arguments for yourself. You may even find that thinking deeply about ethics influences your views on broader society.

Thank you for taking an interest in forging a better tech industry; I hope this book will give you both the theory and practical advice you need to do just that. Let's get started.

Chapter 2

Do no harm?

As colonial rulers of India, the British grew concerned about the abundance of cobras in Delhi. Governors therefore proposed a simple economic remedy: a bounty for cobra hides. The policy was a hit; so much so, that enterprising Indians started breeding cobras just for the bounty. Seeing a suspicious uptick in bounties paid, the British eventually cancelled the scheme. Rather than keep the now worthless snakes, breeders chose to loose the surplus serpents, causing the wild cobra population to surge past its previous levels, and defeating the point of the programme.[1]

Unintended consequences and externalities

Even the most benign, well-intended acts can have unexpected impacts. The 'cobra effect' would be no surprise to the French cultural theorist Paul Virilio.

> When you invent the ship, you also invent the shipwreck; when you invent the plane you also invent the plane crash; and when you invent electricity, you invent electrocution... Every technology carries its own negativity, which is invented at the same time as technical progress.[2]

For Virilio, technology's every yin has a corresponding yang, a range of unintended consequences birthed when the technology fails, succeeds beyond expectations, or is simply used in unexpected ways. Philosopher Don Ihde argues that technologies have no fixed identities or meanings, and instead are *multistable*: people put tech to all sorts of uses beyond those the designer intended.[3] GPS was originally devised for the military, but since being released to civilians, GPS has spawned thousands of products and services, each with their own consequences. Satnavs have killed the road atlas and clogged village roads unwisely offered as shortcuts. Person-tracking software has both enhanced and eroded personal trust, saving lost children but ruining marriages and surprise parties alike. According to the *law of unintended consequences*, there will always be outcomes we overlook, but unintended does not mean unforeseeable. We can – and must – try to anticipate and mitigate the worst potential consequences.

A cousin of the unintended consequence is the *externality*. An externality is the economist's label for Someone Else's Problem, an effect that falls on someone outside the system. Passive smokers don't choose to smoke; instead they are victims of a negative externality, harmed by someone else's habit. Externalities can also be positive: one upside of public transport is that fewer pedestrians are killed by drunk drivers.

Unintended consequences affect familiar people in unknown ways, while externalities happen to people we've ignored. In other words, we overlook unintended consequences by not looking deeply enough, but we miss externalities because we were looking in the wrong places.

Externalities have been a sticky problem throughout the history of industry. A selfish, short-term focus has tempted many companies to harm their ecologies and futures. There's evidence, for example, that Exxon knew of CO_2's potential climate threat in 1977, but kept it quiet, preferring that society pay the cost.[4] Externalities also arise as a side effect of user-centred design. Focusing on fulfilling the goals and dreams of an individual user has caused tech companies to overlook impacts on non-users and wider society.[5] Airbnb is a dream for hosts and renters, but piles negative externalities onto the neighbourhood:

At least in the short term, [Airbnb] reduces stock available for long-term renting or purchase [...] Even then, though, a second externality remains: the impact on neighbors. Living next door to a permanent resident is very different than living next door to a constantly changing set of visitors that have no reason to invest in relationships, the neighborhood, or even a good night's sleep. To put it another way, small wonder hosts and guests love Airbnb: all of the costs are passed off to the folks who aren't earning a dime. —Ben Thompson[6]

The best way to quash externalities is, of course, to internalise them. Economists, as is their habit, typically suggest we do this with taxes or penalties. Many governments respond to environmental externalities with a *polluter-pays principle*, loading the cost onto the responsible party and nullifying the externality. Alternatively, they may choose to subsidise positive externalities, such as funding cycle-to-work schemes that also increase public fitness. If Airbnb chose to prioritise the neighbourhood's wellbeing – whether under consumer pressure, threat of fines, or as a result of some pang of social conscience – the externality would vanish. The community would become Airbnb's problem and neighbourhood-friendly policies would quickly follow.

Resolving externalities means we first have to recognise them, but often they lie in the shadows, falling on ignored minorities or existing only in a hazy future.

If somebody robs a store, it's a crime and the state is all set and ready to nab the criminal. But if somebody steals from the commons and from the future, it's seen as entrepreneurial activity and the state cheers and gives them tax concessions rather than arresting them. We badly need an expanded concept of justice and fairness that takes mortgaging the future into account. —Ursula Franklin[7]

Algorithmic bias

Algorithmic bias – when supposedly impartial algorithms encode implicit prejudice – is a textbook example of unintended consequences. Bias has become one of tech's most notorious ethical issues, evidenced by several ugly examples: predictive policing software that deems black people a higher reoffending risk than white people; YouTube's recommender system continually dragging people towards extreme content; networks that show high-paying job ads to men but not women.

Biased algorithms are clearly most dangerous when they rule over critical systems like justice or employment, but even a skewed commercial algorithm can have insidious effects. Individuals and groups can fall victim to *redlining*, denied products and services by biased software. The label comes originally from banking in the 1930s, when lenders drew on the city map to demarcate neighbourhoods (mostly home to black residents) they wouldn't lend to. Redlining today is less calculated but can be similarly damaging. Bloomberg found Amazon's same-day delivery service ignored majority-black neighbourhoods, such as Roxbury in Boston, despite all surrounding suburbs being eligible.[8] Even seemingly minor bias can stack up. Denied fast delivery, Roxbury residents may have to waste time and money buying from more expensive outlets: another brick in the wall of inequality.

None of these outcomes were planned; instead, they lay outside the scope of what technologists considered. No one looked deeply enough at the potential impacts on users, and no one thought to speak up for those who may be mistreated. This is still an industry failing. The public generally can't defend themselves against algorithmic bias or seek recourse. With no human in the loop, the decision rests in the hands of omniscient, unquestionable algorithmic gods. If your algorithmic luck is out, there's not much you can do except pray.

Sources of bias

AI ethicist Joanna Bryson claims algorithmic bias has three primary causes.[9] The first is poor training data. Data that's incomplete, unrepresentative, or improperly cleaned will always cause algorithmic blind spots. A facial recognition system trained only on white faces is guaranteed to be racist. This isn't just inconvenient, it's degrading: failing to recognise a face is failing to recognise someone's humanity.

Bias caused by patchy data typically hurts the underprivileged most. Rich people, with plenty of access to technology and detailed financial histories, cast large data shadows; the poor or marginalised usually don't. Although an extensive data profile can sometimes be a risk to individuals, systemic 'data poverty' causes creeping harms to whole communities. Subpopulations become algorithmically invisible and are therefore unfairly treated; oppression is digitally re-enacted and amplified.

Bryson's second source of algorithmic bias is intentional prejudice. Algorithms offer an appealing way to launder bias beneath the illusion of objectivity, and many bigots within our own companies and governments have the power to twist algorithms towards their preferred intolerance. Intentional prejudice is always unethical but often legal. Different countries and states diverge strongly in attitudes and laws; today, it's legal in Kansas to fire someone for being gay, but not so in neighbouring Colorado. Prejudice can also come from outside the team. Microsoft's notorious chatbot Tay was programmed to learn through Twitter interaction, leaving it vulnerable to manipulation. Trolls leapt at the chance to goad Tay into making outrageous remarks and, when word of early successes spread, abuse quickly spiralled.

This hints at the third, most fundamental, source of bias: even the most complete dataset is suffused with human prejudice. Since Verbeek's mediation theory tells us we shouldn't separate technological and human action, technologies will mirror social biases by default. These biases run deep. Bryson and two colleagues trained a basic machine-learning system on a standard corpus of text and found 'every linguistic bias documented in psychology that [they had] looked for.'[10] According to Bryson, word embeddings – essentially, mathematical mappings of language – 'seem to know that insects are icky and flowers are beautiful' simply because those types of word are frequently paired. No surprise, then, that sentiment-analysis algorithms have inherited prejudice, deeming European names (Paul, Ellen) more pleasant than African-American names (Malik, Sheeren)[11] and ranking the word 'gay' as negative.[12] Even amid changing public opinion, this bias will only drain out slowly. Data always looks backward, meaning historical prejudice is frozen into a training corpus.

Inequity goes beyond language, of course: almost any data can be imbued with implicit bias. Even if it's illegal to consider someone's race when calculating their credit score, every credit broker looks at the applicant's address, which is strongly correlated with race. Critics of the COMPAS crime prediction algorithm said it lent unfair weight to previous arrests and convictions. As law professor Ifeoma Ajunwa pointed out, 'If you're looking at how many convictions a person has and taking that as a neutral variable — well, that's not a neutral variable.'[13] It's well known that some populations are overpoliced and that ethnicity influences sentencing; these effects trickle into algorithmic logic. Even apparently innocuous decisions like where to build a distribution centre – presumably the root of Amazon's delivery bias – will depend on the local market, transport options, land values, and other factors heavy with implicit bias. Discrimination is already interwoven in the fabric of our tools and datasets.

Moral distribution

If bias is unintentional, is it really our problem? Surely it's not technology's job to fix every flaw in the human psyche? Again, remember mediation theory and its elegant dance of people and technology. At the scene of a crash, investigators will rightly ask whether the cyclist swerved, or whether the driver was fiddling with the stereo, but they may also check the car's brakes and ask who performed its last service. Technologies tend to spread moral responsibility between many actors.

As yet, we don't blame the technology itself, but if technology changes how users interpret the world, it follows that technologists influence people's moral choices. When things go wrong, the user and the technologist may both be to blame. Of course, technology is now a team sport: the era of solo hackers is long gone. Modern tech is made by teams of engineers, designers, product managers, and data scientists, relying on multiple underlying layers: AIs in apps on platforms, using shared libraries, plugged into various operating systems and protocols. Even if different teams or organisations have made each layer, all can be morally implicated. A team is only as trustworthy as its sleaziest partner. Build on a vulnerable platform, lock yourself into a disreputable social network, or share data with an abusive advertiser, and you will rightly bear some blame.

That's not to say we should blame technologists for every unintended consequence: given tech's multistable nature, there will always be some outcomes that couldn't have been predicted. It seems unfair, say, to blame the architects of GPS for rural traffic jams. However, we had advanced warning of the bias issue. Even in the 1980s it was a documented problem, after doctors at St George's Hospital Medical School discovered their admissions algorithm, trained on the previous decade's decisions, was discriminatory:

> The computer used [implied] information to generate a score which was used to decide which applicants should be interviewed. Women and those from racial minorities had a reduced chance of being interviewed independent of academic considerations. —Stella Lowry and Gordon Macpherson[14]

Algorithmic bias may not be intentional, but it is negligent. Technologists might not have seen it coming, but we didn't much care to look. Convinced that technology is neutral and objective, we mistakenly assumed bias was impossible; concerned only with the productivity of the primary user, we overlooked impacts on wider society.

In the end, blame may not matter. Causal responsibility and moral responsibility don't always coincide; it's perhaps more useful to ask who has the power to fix things. Even if technologists didn't directly cause an ethical mishap, we still have a duty to try to resolve it. Regardless of intent, we must try to reduce harmful bias for the good of society and, secondarily, for the sake of our own reputations.

Moral relativism

Here we hit a classic ethical problem: doing the right thing sounds appealing, but what is right? What makes an algorithm fair? This quickly gets political. Should we aim for equal treatment or equal outcome? Treat everyone the same and you do nothing to address the systemic issues that perpetuate inequality. But pushing instead for more equal outcomes leads to accusations of meddling and reverse discrimination. Should algorithms simply reflect today's society or help us achieve a fairer world? Who chooses? Come to think it, is anyone's moral point of view more valid than anyone else's?

This is the seductive territory of *moral relativism*. A relativist argues there's no one moral truth, no lone guiding star for behaviour; instead, ethical rules depend on social differences and vary across cultures.

Relativism usually stems from the well-meaning principles of tolerance and diversity. Holding all people accountable to the narrow values of a dominant culture – in other words, appointing a single party, country, or religion as the custodian of moral truth – has historically proved murderous, and relativists point out that people's individual beliefs are shaped by upbringing and evolve with experience. But conservatives typically decry moral relativism as postmodern flimsiness taken to dangerous extremes. Traditionalist philosopher Roger Scruton claims, 'A writer who says there are no truths, or that all truth is "merely relative", is asking you not to believe him. So don't.'

Globalisation is particularly challenging for relativism. Should we accept another society's choices that we find repellent? Should we do business with countries that actively discriminate, or where corruption is widespread? Moral relativism suggests a free-for-all: who are we to argue with the norms of another culture?

The philosophical debate rolls on, but for our practical purposes relativism is a dead end. If people can wriggle out of moral judgment by claiming their actions are culturally acceptable, morality itself becomes a questionable concept. Ad absurdum, if goodness is in the eye of the beholder, slave owners get to decide whether slavery is ethical. To make any kind of moral progress we need to be able to draw a line between acceptable and unacceptable behaviour. Fortunately, most cultures do agree on major rights and wrongs, such as murder and adultery. Forty-eight nations found enough common ground to encode basic moral principles into the Universal Declaration of Human Rights.

If we reject relativism, we have to reject it in the workplace too. Hardline tycoons might claim there's no room for personal morality in commerce: nice guys finish last. But if different cultures don't get to prescribe their own distinct ethical rules, nor does the business world. It's true that we all play many roles in life, and adapt our behaviours accordingly – a bruising tackle is acceptable on a football pitch, but not a wedding – but these roles are still underpinned by a common moral foundation, one that can't be substituted or switched off at will. Morality doesn't stop at the front door of the office; business is, after all, made of people.

The technocracy trap

If we're to make moral progress, someone has to define what our ethical standards should be. Ideally, that's a matter for society itself. Elected officials make laws; citizens slowly develop social conventions. But disruptive technologies often burst onto the scene without warning, before these social or legal norms can emerge. By default, new technologies bear the ethical fingerprints of their creators, not of wider society. Given how heavily technology shapes modern culture, this means technologists have significant influence over social norms: ethical decisions that should be democratic are instead technocratic.

This should worry us. No single group should have a greater claim over the future than the public, and technologists don't have the diversity and worldly wisdom to be natural ethical authorities. Governments are belatedly creeping into action, and the public are now paying more attention to their technological lives, but the industry must also become more responsible. We must show that we deserve society's trust by engaging the public in the moral decisions that surround technology, and prioritising the good of all, not just our revenue streams.

Defining fairness

What sort of moral lines can we draw on algorithmic bias? First, we need to be precise. The word 'bias' is useful to a point: it's broadly understood and admirably simple, but we soon need more detail. Bias is an umbrella term for several types of imbalance: are we talking about sampling bias, innate structural bias, or explicit prejudice? To be specific, we must also be bold and discard some perfectly viable definitions.

Imagine you work for Tinder. If you want to ensure your matching algorithms are racially fair, what would fairness actually mean? Perhaps fairness is about exposure, meaning we should show users potential matches that reflect the local racial mix. If 30% of people in the user's city are black, we could tweak the algorithm so 30% of a user's potential matches are black too. This sounds reasonable, but has an ugly flaw. The worlds of dating, sex, and love are riddled with human bias, meaning many people tend to stick to their own race when choosing a partner. So unless Tinder's users are bias-free, some people will be shown frequently to users who don't want to date someone of that race. We may achieve fair exposure, but certain races will be matched less often. One form of fairness forces another unfairness to the surface.

Should we aim instead for fair matching? Would it be better to declare that, whatever your race, you should have an equal chance of finding a partner through Tinder? This has the reverse problem. On today's online dating platforms, heterosexual white men give lower ratings to a woman if she is black.[15] To prioritise fair matching, the algorithm should actually *restrict* the racial mix by, for example, only showing black women to black men, who are more likely to respond positively. However, this is surely the opposite of racial fairness.

There's no way to square this circle. Thanks to the human biases surrounding dating, fair exposure can't be reconciled with fair matching. So perhaps we have to look elsewhere. Maybe a fair Tinder is one where people feel equally valued, or have similar levels of satisfaction with the service. This suggests we should care more about app usage patterns and satisfaction scores than the crude primary metrics of exposure and matching.

Any definition of fairness will be unfair from a different perspective. For some people, a fair algorithm is one that reflects today's society. For others, a fair algorithm must be an agent of social change. Some form of bias is logically, politically, and mathematically inevitable; nevertheless, someone has to make the call. Our decisions are the stars by which our algorithms will navigate. We must choose intelligently, considering the potential consequences and externalities of our choices.

Mitigating bias

Kate Crawford, NYU professor and co-founder of the AI Now Research Institute, is a leading expert in algorithmic bias. Crawford suggests teams invest in *fairness forensics* to mitigate bias. The first forensic step is simple: test your algorithms with a wide set of people and solid benchmark data to spot problems before they occur. However, some benchmarks are themselves imperfect: common open-source face databases have historically skewed white and male. So teams may also want to screen their training and testing data itself for potential bias. Google's Facets software, for example, helps teams probe datasets for unexpected gaps or skews.

If these tests find bias, the simplest debiasing strategy is to improve the training data. A machine-learning algorithm trained on patchy data will always struggle, but simply throwing more data points at the problem often won't work. If 500,000 points of training data contain implicit bias, 5,000,000 data points probably will too; more active intervention may be needed.

Startup Gfycat found its facial recognition software frequently misidentified Asian people. The team resorted to what amounts to an 'Asian mode', extra code invoked if the system believed the subject had Asian facial features. While improved accuracy probably justifies Gfycat's hack, this sort of solution – the algorithm warning itself it's about to be racist, like some woke Clippy – isn't exactly scalable. It's exhausting and inefficient to play whack-a-mole with each new discrimination you discover, and cramming people into categories ('Is this person Asian? Is this person female?') to spark code branching also feels somewhat distasteful. Society sees classifiers like race and, increasingly, gender as spectrums rather than discrete buckets; our algorithms should too.

An even more forceful way to debias algorithms is to explicitly overrule them, gouging biased data or offensive associations from the system. Google Photos fixed their notorious 'gorilla' blunder – when the software classified a group of black friends as such – by overruling the algorithm: the team simply tore the word off the list of possible categories. In this case, the price of diminished classification power was clearly worth paying. Google has also added stop lists to search, after researchers found some racial terms generated appalling auto-complete suggestions.[16] Potentially problematic search stems now get no suggestions at all.

This sort of direct interference shouldn't be performed lightly. It solves only the one visible case, and the idea of forcing an algorithm to toe the desired line will spark accusations that technologists are imposing their personal politics on the world. Vetoes are best saved for situations where the output is so clearly harmful that it demands an immediate fix.

Since bias can never be fully eliminated, at some point we face another tough decision: is the algorithm fair enough to be used? Is it ethically permissible to knowingly release a biased algorithm? The answer will depend in part on your preferred ethical framework; we'll discuss these shortly. A human decision will sometimes be preferable to a skewed algorithm: the more serious the implications of bias, the stronger the case for human involvement. But we shouldn't assume humans will always be more just. Like algorithms, humans are products of their cultures and environments, and can be alarmingly biased. Parole boards, for instance, are more likely to free convicts if the judges have just eaten.[17] After doing everything possible to ensure fairness, we might deem a lingering bias small enough to tolerate. In these systems we might release the system with caveats or interface controls to help users handle the bias, such as adding pronoun controls ('him/her/they') to translation software, allowing the user to override bias when translating from genderless languages.

While Crawford extols these forensic approaches, she also points out their shared weakness: they're only technical solutions. To truly address implicit bias we must consider it a human problem as well as a technical one. This means bringing bias into plain sight. Some academics choose to explicitly list their potential biases – a process known as *bracketing* – before starting a piece of research, and take note whenever they sense bias could be influencing their work. By exposing these biases, whether they stem from personal experience, previous findings, or pet theories, the researchers hope to approach their work with clearer minds and avoid drawing faulty conclusions. In tech, we could appropriate this idea, listing the ways in which our algorithms and data could demonstrate bias, then reviewing the algorithm's performance against this checklist.

Moral imagination

We can also pull bias out by the roots by getting better at spotting and addressing unintended consequences and externalities. For this, we need *moral imagination*: the ability to dream up and morally assess a range of future scenarios. Humans learn to use moral imagination throughout their lives – indeed, we're the only species that can – but it isn't always easy to imagine the real impacts of technology. Our work is used asynchronously across the globe; we can never directly see the joy or pain we cause others. Fortunately, moral imagination can be trained. Morality isn't a genetic godsend; it's a muscle that needs exercise.

We can kick-start moral imagination with some straightforward prompts. The question 'What might happen if this technology is wildly successful?' has spawned a thousand science fiction stories: Daniel Mallory Ortberg famously suggested TV series Black Mirror is a response to the question, 'What if phones, but too much?' Alternatively, we might indulge some pessimism: How could this technology fail horribly? or How could someone abuse this technology? (We'll talk in chapter 6 about the dangers of technology being used for intentional harm.)

We can also use analogy to encourage moral imagination. Has this situation happened before, or in another field? What happened next? Could it happen here? Economic historian Carlota Perez argues that every technological revolution follows a tight script.[18] First, an 'irruption' phase, when a technology showing both promise and threat attracts heavy speculative investment. Then 'frenzy', a period of intense exploration, in which new markets explode into life and companies often cut ethical corners to make a quick buck. Eventually the bubble bursts and high-profile failures force regulators to step in. The momentum swings from finance to production as the technology becomes widespread; a phase of 'synergy'. Finally the revolution is complete and 'maturity' dominates. The market is saturated, awaiting the next disruption. The Gartner hype cycle traces a similar route for emerging technologies, from innovation through inflated expectation, through the trough of disillusionment, toward eventual stability.

To exercise moral imagination we can simply track our chosen technology along these likely trajectories, imagining what life might be like at each point. Today, for example, cryptocurrencies and machine learning are in the frenzy or inflated-expectations phase. It doesn't take a vivid moral imagination to picture what might happen when these inflated expectations burst.

Futuring

These set forecasts can be useful, but the world doesn't always follow neat blueprints. To stretch our moral imaginations further, we can learn from the field of futures studies. The central principle of so-called *futuring* is to see the future as plural. In the words of famed robot ethicist and futurist Sarah Connor, 'The future's not set. There's no fate but what we make for ourselves.'[19] The future isn't a mark on a map; it's the map itself. Collectively we get to decide which coordinates to head to.

A common model in futures studies is the *futures cone*,[20] which uses the analogy of light shone from a torch.

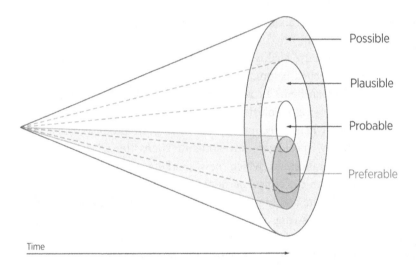

Possible

Plausible

Probable

Preferable

Time

The *x*-axis represents time, so the torchlight represents potential futures. Note that the beam diverges from the present: next week is predictable; next century, rather less. Each cone of light represents a different level of likelihood, sometimes known as 'the 4 Ps'.

At the bright centre of the beam are the *probable futures*, the most likely projections based on what we know today. Gartner's hype cycle sits here, as does most day-to-day design work. Moving outwards, we come to *plausible futures*. These scenarios are less likely but still foreseeable: some corporations pay millions of dollars for insight into them. At the outer edges of the beam lie *possible futures*. Lying in penumbra, these are harder to spot. Businesses typically aren't interested in these scenarios; instead, possible futures are the domain of what Anthony Dunne and Fiona Raby call 'speculative culture': science fiction, art, and games.

The final, and most important, cone depicts the *preferable future*. In a multitude of possible futures, some will be better than others. The preferable future is a value judgement; we have to consider the world we want and how we might get there. This ideal future might be highly probable, lying squarely in the middle of the beam, or an improbable wildcard found right on the edges.

Like any model, the futures cone has flaws. Design academic and critic Cameron Tonkinwise points out the direction of the beam depends on who's holding the torch: in an unequal world, everyone starts from a different 'now'. The idea of a preferable future is also loaded: preferable to whom? Nevertheless, the futures cone can be a useful prompt for strategy work and fostering moral imagination alike, illuminating various future trajectories and helping teams pick a preferred future to work towards.

Another tool for teasing out potential futures and unintended consequences is Jerome C Glenn's *futures wheel*. In Glenn's words, the futures wheel offers 'a kind of structured brainstorming' about the future. We start with a root trend, such as our chosen technology; then, in a ring around the trend, we write some of its potential consequences.

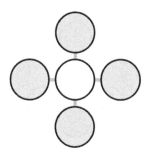

This first step tends to draw out the probable futures, which are often interesting but rarely novel. So we now go deeper, picturing some potential second-order consequences of each new scenario, and adding these in a second ring.

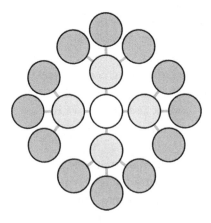

Finally, we pair together interesting nodes from anywhere in the diagram, and imagine what might happen if both futures come true, recording this in a third ring. As the horizon expands, the chains of causality sometimes stretch, the possibilities becoming more imaginative, unexpected, and even apocalyptic. This isn't always the case, however: a third-order node can still represent a probable future if its predecessors are highly likely.

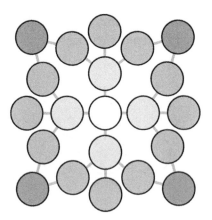

Running a futures wheel exercise with a tech team is usually as fun as it is eye-opening. It spawns some compelling stories about the possible impacts of our decisions, which makes it rich with ethical potential. Technologists don't often get a chance to think in this sort of speculative, even whimsical, way: the industry's focus on delivery tends to deter wild fantasies of the future. But futuring isn't about accurate prediction so much as opening a team's eyes to possibility. Conjuring up shared visions of the future is the cornerstone of moral imagination, and a crucial way to expose unintended consequences.

> So why try to predict the future at all if it's so difficult, so nearly impossible? Because making predictions is one way to give warning when we see ourselves drifting in dangerous directions. Because prediction is a useful way of pointing out safer, wiser courses. Because, most of all, our tomorrow is the child of our today. Through thought and deed, we exert a great deal of influence over this child, even though we can't control it absolutely. Best to think about it, though. Best to try to shape it into something good. —Octavia Butler[21]

Design as provocation

Abstract, theoretical futures are lifeless and hard to picture; we need to experience them too. Moral imagination should involve emotion, not just logic. To awaken people to the potential consequences of their choices, we need to paint a vivid picture.

> It is not enough for a virtuous person to *intellectually* grasp her moral duty to extend compassion, or even to understand that it would be irrational not to do so. We must also find ways to *feel* compassion, which is an experience that goes beyond the intellect. —Shannon Vallor[22]

How can we bring these theoretical futures to life? How can we portray convincing scenarios that spark reaction, emotion, and debate? With design, of course. This is the premise of *speculative design*, pioneered by Dunne & Raby at London's Royal College of Art. This emerging branch of design focuses on how things *could* be, asking what-if questions to spark conversations and decisions about the futures we want.

Speculative design builds neatly on our futuring approaches. We can tease out potential futures and then illustrate a snippet of life in those futures. These *design fictions* can take the forms of short films, stories, games, comic strips, role-play, or objects: anything that builds a believable world.

A design fiction often features a hypothetical artefact, some believable prototype of the technology in question. I call this (with apologies) a *provocatype*. A provocatype isn't 'good' design: it isn't a thorough response to the brief, nor does it address every user need. Instead, it's designed to provoke conversation among stakeholders and potentially users too, if introduced with caution, NDAs, and the appropriate caveats. A provocatype creates a curious wormhole between design and research: it's a designed product that nevertheless exists mostly as a research probe. The big difference from regular prototyping is we make provocatypes with not just a problem-solving mindset but also a problem-creating mindset. If we're successful, a provocatype will spark better reactions than a hypothetical discussion would.

Let's see a provocatype in action, created by design firm The Incredible Machine for two Dutch energy clients. Their chosen future featured energy scarcity and electric vehicles sharing public charging stations. These are reasonable extrapolations from today: we could confidently call this a probable future. The designers chose to design a high-fidelity provocatype of the charging point itself.

The Incredible Machine, 'Transparent Charging Station'. Reprinted by kind permission.

As the purported user, you plug your charging cable (provided with the provocatype) into a free socket, tap your ID card to authenticate, and request your energy using the dials. The dotted display shows the charging queue and estimated completion times. But how the cars get charged isn't the most interesting question. The provo-catype's main role is to explore how an algorithm might prioritise energy when demand exceeds supply. It gives us an insight into an algorithmically driven future – we might call it an *algocracy* – a decade from now. This all hinges around the ID card, which the designers also prototyped.

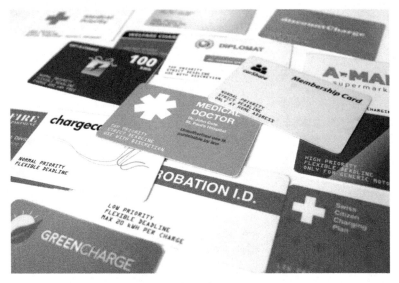

Reprinted by kind permission.

Each user is given a card that relates to their position in society. A doctor's card lets them jump the charging queue, but carries a penalty for misuse. A recently released offender gets a probation ID, which gives them low charging priority and caps their energy use.

The designers, Marcel Schouwenaar and Harm van Beek, aren't proposing this as the optimal solution; instead, they've created an object that gets the right conversations happening and stimulates our moral imagination. We can't help but imagine what life would be like when our social status is wrapped into a digital ID. We see the poten-tial positives – emergency services, for example, won't be unduly hampered by energy scarcity – but we also see how algocracy and the Internet of Things could reinforce social stratification and inequality.

Utopias and dystopias

Genevieve Bell points out a common pitfall with technological predictions: they often gravitate towards the extremes of utopia and dystopia.[23] We should be cautious of both.

Corporate vision videos usually depict a canonical capitalist utopia: gestural interfaces in gleaming offices, tediously perfect global collaboration. Ethically, these design fictions are empty: their provocatypes do very little provoking. But utopias can be dangerous, not just boring. The pursuit of a perfect society has at times been a gateway to extremism; the control required to make things just right can easily mutate into totalitarianism.

Dystopias are also seductive. Many designers will know the 'flip it' design game, in which participants imagine the worst possible solution to the brief, the idea being to then invert these ideas to uncover the principles of a successful design. Everyone has great fun drawing skulls and crossbones on things, and people often leave with surprisingly profound insights. Dystopias can indeed be powerful cautionary tales – Aesop's fables rarely had a happy ending – but dystopias can also be cynical and distant. They push away potential collaborators as much as engage them, and earn the ethically minded technologist a reputation as an obstructive fantasist.

The future usually follows a more nuanced path. When we're encouraging people to exercise moral imagination, we should steer clear of extremes. The ideal design fiction has a touch of moral ambiguity, hinting at good and bad alike. Speculative design intends to provoke responses, but it lets viewers construct those responses themselves, rather than forcing them to react in prearranged ways.

User dissent and crisis

Amid all this future-gazing we shouldn't lose sight of the human. Moral imagination should revolve around the people who'll live in our hypothetical futures and use our proposed technologies.

In *Design for Real Life*,[24] Eric Meyer and Sara Wachter-Boettcher recommend appointing a *designated dissenter*. This is a role of constructive antagonism, particularly useful in critique sessions. The dissenter's job is to challenge the team's assumptions, subvert decisions, and lob in the occasional grenade of defiance. They might role-play as a user who refuses to provide the demanded data, or one who's insulted by the tone of an error message. Meyer and Wachter-Boettcher stress, however, that the role is best rotated: teams have a knack of tuning out a repeated naysayer, and too long wearing the robes of dissent can sour even the most charitable soul.

Design for Real Life also highlights moments of user crisis. The smiling personas taped to tech office walls depict users as happy and productive, although always incredibly busy. But real people aren't wooden archetypes. Our users include those who are coping with a job loss or bereavement, whose relationship is breaking down, or who are struggling with physical or mental illness. These moments are loaded with ethical significance. How we treat people at their most vulnerable is our deepest moral test, and as our technologies reach yet more of the planet, we'll have to support more people through these periods of crisis. The designated dissenter can help us imagine how these crises might occur in our chosen future, but there's also room for careful research, such as interviewing people who've experienced similar adversity. This research has its own delicate ethical issues, and is best left to trained researchers, perhaps supported by qualified counsellors for the most sensitive cases.

Redefining the stakeholder

Futuring and speculative design can reveal unintended consequences, but what about the externalities, the effects on people we've overlooked? As discussed earlier, economists tend to argue externalities need regulation, but the tech industry can and should try to reduce externalities too, by catering to a wider range of stakeholders.

Every business textbook offers a step-by-step guide to stakeholder analysis, but most only cover teammates or suspiciously homogenous groups like 'users' or 'residents'. This perspective, reinforced by the individualist focus of user-centred design, means we often overlook important groups. Stakeholders aren't just the people who can affect a project; they're also the people the project might affect. To force ourselves to consider the right people, try using a prompt list (see appendix) to capture a wider range of potential stakeholders, and use this as an input to futuring exercises and the design process.

Not all stakeholders will be welcome. In some cases, it might be worth including, say, a criminal, terrorist, or troll as a negative stakeholder – a *persona non grata*[25] – so the team can discuss how to actively reduce the harm this person can do. He may even deserve full persona treatment, with a name, an abusive scenario, and listed motivations to increase his profile within the team.

Stakeholders could even include social concepts: things we value in society but rarely consider within our influence, such as democracy, justice, or freedom of the press. As we now know, technology has the power to damage these ideas; explicitly listing them as stakeholders, or at least acknowledging their potential vulnerability, might help us protect them.

A Hippocratic Oath?

Moral imagination, futuring, provocatypes, and designated dissenters are all far from business as usual. Isn't there an easier way? Couldn't we start by creating a Hippocratic Oath for technology? This is an understandable and common question from people new to the tech ethics field; a written pledge seems like an obvious starting point, taking a cue from other disciplines.

A code of ethics might be useful at the right time, but this isn't a clear-cut ethical fix. The simplest argument is that it's all been done before. Dozens of previous attempts haven't bedded in; why would another be different? Designers will already know, for example, the First Things First manifesto of 1964, which argued designers should use their skills for moral good, not just for commerce. To be uncharitable, the manifesto's reprise in 2000 suggested the first incarnation had little long-term effect. In the domain of emerging technology, several codification efforts are already underway. IEEE's Ethically Aligned Design initiative has involved hundreds of experts, and details several key principles like human rights and accountability. Similar efforts include the Asilomar AI principles and the Barcelona Declaration. Professional organisations like the Association for Computing Machinery (ACM) also publish a code of conduct they expect from members.

These efforts, usually spawned from heavy consultation processes or elite conferences, can be bulky but are preferable to codes written by a single author. The tech industry has seen a recent wave of what I call 'codes of reckons', simple bullet-point moral diktats from eminent technologists. These don't much help the cause of ethical technology. These codes' authors – unwittingly or otherwise – appoint themselves as ethical arbiters, projecting an unmerited stone-tablet authority. These documents lack public input and fall straight into the technocracy trap.

Ethical conventions don't themselves solve ethical problems: thorny moral questions still pervade medicine and engineering, despite the fields' prominent codes of ethics. Codes can offer some structure to ethical debate, but are usually too vague to resolve it. Consider two well-known maxims: the bioethics pledge 'First, do no harm' and Google's famous 'Don't be evil'. Although pithy, both statements are awkwardly imprecise in practice. What is harm? What is evil? Who decides? How do you resolve competing claims? To answer these questions we need more than a catchphrase; we need ways to properly evaluate ethical arguments. (We'll come to these in the next chapter.) Without this sort of moral framework, companies can choose any definition of evil or harm that excuses their chosen path. On its own, 'Don't be evil' means little more than 'Hey, ethics matters'. But we shouldn't be unfair. Acknowledging that ethics matters was itself something of a breakthrough at the time, and, while hardly a throwaway line, 'Don't be evil' was a small part of a Google staff manifesto rather than a formal corporate motto. In recent years it has become little more than a gotcha used by critics complaining about Google's mistakes. It's since been moved to the coda of a more detailed and more ethically useful code of conduct.

Codes of ethical technology also face enforcement problems. Professional bodies in many other disciplines have the power to disbar workers for malpractice, but since most technologists have no formal accreditation and membership of professional organisations is voluntary, codes of ethics in the tech industry are largely toothless.

Finally, codes are better at censuring bad behaviour than inspiring good. At worst, they can instil a checklist mindset, in which practitioners believe they can simply follow the numbered steps to pass ethical muster. Checklists have value but can be counterproductive if people fail to grasp the underlying spirit. In the field of web accessibility, the Web Content Accessibility Guidelines have been both a help and a hindrance. They provide clear advice on accessible development, but have also caused some teams to misrepresent accessibility as a downstream box-ticking exercise: check your contrast ratios, tweak a few font sizes, and you're fully compliant. Ethical technologists know better. They know accessibility is really about who we deem worthy of our efforts; a commitment to treat every person as a person. We shouldn't mistake an ethical code for ethics itself. The conversation and the outcomes are what matters, not the paperwork. Ethics must become a custom, a way of thinking, a set of values held by all in the industry: as Cameron Tonkinwise calls it, *ethics as ethos*.[26]

Ethical infrastructure and diversity

It can be easier and more productive to codify ethics within individual companies, particularly if we can piggyback on existing policies. *Core values* – essentially a list of the company's stances and commitments – are a widespread and important vehicle for ethics, and usually carry senior support. Project teams can also create more localised rules, such as *design principles* that govern the design decisions within a particular product line or project. Strong core values and design principles taken to heart are powerful tie-breakers for ethical dilemmas: in the event of moral emergency, consult the agreed tenets for guidance. This means core values and design principles need to be specific. Some companies choose single-word values: Adobe's are 'genuine', 'exceptional', 'innovative', and 'involved'. Reflecting on the traits and qualities of a moral life can be important – it's the cornerstone of a branch of ethics we'll discuss later – but single-word values are just too slippery for a whole company. They leave too much unspoken, meaning people can twist them for their own purposes in a debate: 'How can you object to this tracking software? It's *innovative!*'

Sentences are better. Twitter's 'Defend and respect the user's voice' is a sound principle, although morally ambiguous: does this include defending hate speech? Ben & Jerry's core values are highly specific and even political: 'We seek and support nonviolent ways to achieve peace and justice. We believe government resources are more productively used in meeting human needs than in building and maintaining weapons systems.' This may be *too* specific – it's hard to truly live by core values unless you can remember them – but it leaves no doubt about the type of company Ben & Jerry's wants to be.

According to researcher Jared Spool,[27] a good design principle is reversible. If you can flip the meaning and end up with a valid principle for a different team or time, you're being specific. 'Make it easy for users' is a platitude, not a design principle; the opposite would be absurd. The reversibility test doesn't fit core values quite so well. Sometimes it's helpful to explicitly support something that should be morally obvious – 'We care about the planet', for instance – but if in doubt, be specific.

Core values and design principles bolster a company's *ethical infrastructure*, as does team diversity. Homogenous teams tend to focus on the potential upsides of their work for people like them, and are blind to the problems they could inflict on a wider audience. The same divisions that pervade today's world are seen and even amplified in today's tech industry.

> If you live near a Whole Foods, if no one in your family serves in the military, if you're paid by the year, not the hour, if most people you know finished college, if no one you know uses meth, if you married once and remain married, if you're not one of 65 million Americans with a criminal record — if any or all of these things describe you, then accept the possibility that actually, you may not know what's going on and you may be part of the problem. —Anand Giridharadas[28]

Diversity and inclusion professionals often describe two dimensions to diversity: *inherent diversity* and *acquired diversity*. Inherent diversity refers to a group's innate traits, such as sex, orientation, and ethnic background, while acquired diversity refers to perspectives people have earned through experience. Both types of diversity can act as an early warning system for ethics. A team with broad inherent diversity will offer different perspectives and values, while people who are open to new experiences through, say, travel, literature, or languages generally find it easier to exercise moral imagination. While we should recognise the role of privilege – not everyone is lucky enough to see all the wonders of the world – actively absorbing new experiences typically strengthens one's ethical faculties.

Fortunately, our powers of imagination can be increased. Seeking out news, books, films and other sources of stories about the human condition can help us to better envision the lives of others, even those in very different circumstances from our own. —Shannon Vallor[29]

Simply befriending and learning from people unlike ourselves also helps, building our mutual understanding and hence a sort of second-hand acquired diversity. The quest for diversity suggests we should also embrace interdisciplinarity. Slowly, the tech industry is learning that people from non-technical backgrounds, such as politics, law, philosophy, art, and anthropology, can bring huge value, not just in terms of different professional perspectives, but in much-needed acquired diversity. Long may the trend continue.

Chapter 3

Persuasive mechanisms

In his influential essay 'Do Artifacts Have Politics?',[1] Langdon Winner concludes that yes, they do. He challenges the instrumentalist idea that objects are just inert products of the social forces that created them, and argues instead for a wider view: that objects themselves affect how power and authority are distributed, and how societies behave.

The essay examines, among other things, the overpasses that span Long Island freeways. Winner claims New York planner Robert Moses built these bridges unusually low to achieve 'a particular social effect', namely segregation. Poor residents, and non-white residents in particular, typically travelled by bus at the time; since these buses couldn't fit under the bridges, these people were effectively excluded from Long Island's beaches. Although Winner's account is now somewhat disputed, it still shows that even hulking masses of concrete and steel can enforce social change.

Designers are already well aware of the power of objects. For decades, graphic designers have tried to change public attitudes and behaviours, devising not only the appealing cigarette packet but also the calming hospital signage for the smoker's final days. Technological objects – computers, handsets, gadgets – can be particularly potent at kindling new desires and moulding behaviours: nothing so full of language, light, and energy could ever be inert.

Coercion vs. nudging

Designers sometimes embed moral decisions into the environment by force, meaning the user has to comply with the designer's wishes. Speed bumps force drivers to brake; safety catches make it harder to accidentally fire a weapon. Digital technology often similarly constrains user choice. We often hear that design is a conversation with the user; in tech, the conversation is woefully one-sided. In the words of former Google design ethicist Tristan Harris, 'whoever controls the menu controls the choices'. Short of learning a programming language, you can't make a computer do anything its interface doesn't allow. Design decisions, therefore, give technologies the power to enforce behaviour – and hence moral conduct – in the designer's absence.

Coercion might seem unethical since it limits people's free will, but plenty of our society relies on coercion and compliance, particularly our laws. Coercion instead affects where moral responsibility lies. You aren't responsible for behaviour that isn't freely chosen; we don't blame someone forced at gunpoint to commit a crime. Responsibility lies instead with the coercer: a designer must take responsibility for any decisions they force a user into. Military trials have made it clear, however, that orders from superiors don't count as coercion; soldiers can refuse to comply with unlawful or immoral orders, although they may pay a heavy price for it.

There are subtler persuasive arts than blunt coercion. *Nudge theory*, popularised by Richard Thaler and Cass Sunstein, tries to steer behaviour through simple changes to defaults and framing. Nudge has flourished in the public sector – opt-out policies for organ donations, electronic signs that smile or glower at a passing driver's speed – but Silicon Valley is also fond. Nudge doesn't trespass on individual freedoms the industry holds dear, but is still a potent technique for liberating people from their money or time.

Nudgers are quick to point out they merely massage available options, rather than reduce them. This paints nudge as a technique of persuasion, not coercion. However, persuasion still carries ethical concerns. As Daniel Berdichevsky and Erik Neuenschwander, early theorists of persuasive technology, note, 'Persuaders have always stood on uneasy ethical ground. If a serpent persuades you to eat a fruit [...] does culpability fall upon you or upon the serpent?'[2]

Even if persuasion isn't the explicit plan, design always influences behaviour. A design is successful if it steers the user to the right information or the next step in the process; enlarge a button to make it more visible and you'll find more people will push it. All target-driven design, therefore, is persuasive design. Any team with performance targets will try to manoeuvre user behaviour to reach company goals. This means we can't simply pledge to never practice persuasion: we'd have to quit design altogether. Instead, we have to dive in with intent, acknowledging our responsibilities and choosing how to address the ethical challenges.

Dark patterns, attention, and addiction

In a rational world, persuasion would be simple: outline the benefits and costs for each option and trust the user to make the right choice. No such luck. Persuaders must also appeal to bias and emotion, to what we may consider human weakness. Yet behavioural design often wears the cosy clothing of paternalism, faintly patronising but broadly beneficent. Nudge does exploit human weakness, but nudgers would argue they do it so we can overcome that weakness. Don't we all want to live healthier, more responsible lives? Persuasion itself is therefore positioned as a benign tool that elevates us all, helping people ascend the face of Mt. Maslow and reach an enlightened summit.

But persuasion can corrupt humanity as much as ennoble it: the techniques that can help people lose weight can also be used to encourage them to skip voting in the next election. In the tech world, unethical persuasion often takes the form of a *dark pattern*,[3] an intentionally deceptive interface that exploits cognitive weakness for profit. Most dark patterns today are extortive nuisances – fake scarcity on hotel sites, bait-and-switch subscriptions – but the dark pattern becomes more threatening as technologies become embedded in everyday life. Persuasive technology may fade from sight, but its force fields grow ever stronger.

Persuasive techniques can be pointed back at themselves: technology can persuade us to use technology more. Social media addiction has become a full-blown moral panic, fuelled by tabloid horror stories and pop-sci literature that reduces deep research to dopamine anecdotes and frontal lobe neurobollocks. Social media joins a rich canon of moral scourges: books, newspapers, and gramophones were all, in various centuries, linked to the certain downfall of social order.

It's common to blame Silicon Valley business models for the addiction crisis. Free services aren't really free, we're told; instead, users cough up an alternative currency – attention – which is monetised through advertising. In sectors like free-to-play gaming, this time/money equivalence is painfully literal: watch an advert and earn fifty coins. But we can trace a thirst for attention back through advertising, media, and even religion: the attention economy isn't just a consequence of search engines and social networks.[4]

The modern adage 'If you're not paying for the product, you are the product being sold' is facile. It implies that paying with attention is less ethical than paying with cash, a discriminatory position that suggests the poor are somehow less deserving of technology than the rich. It also ignores the market's habit of demanding paid and free services alike grab as much attention as they can. In July 2017, a 17-year-old boy in Guangzhou suffered a minor stroke after a forty-hour stint playing Tencent's mobile game Honour of Kings. Tencent responded bravely, announcing they would limit children's playing time. The company's stock sagged by 5.1%. Even subscription services, brimming with recurring revenue, brag in earnings calls about daily active users and time-in-app metrics. Even if you *are* paying for the product, your attention is still being sold. A cynic could go further, arguing that ensnaring the user in a business relationship is the whole point of experience design; an assertion sardonically illustrated by Jeff Veen.

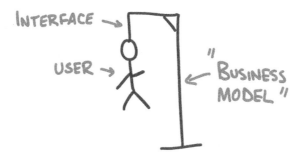

Redrawn and used with kind permission of Jeff Veen.

How harmful the attention economy is depends in part on whether its effects are zero-sum. Screens that only drag us away from other screens are relatively harmless, but if technology distracts us from what ethicists call 'the good life' – a vague concept, but one that might reasonably include family, friends, productive work, and self-improvement – technology becomes a force of alienation, as predicted decades ago by philosopher Karl Jaspers.

It now seems Jaspers' fears are being realised. Netflix CEO Reed Hastings has claimed 'we're competing with sleep';[5] the average American spends 3.1 hours on a mobile device each day, compared to just eighteen minutes in 2008, with no corresponding drop in desktop use.[6] We are all Sisyphus reborn, reducing unread counts each day until, in the words of Ian Bogost, 'conflict and exhaustion suffocate delight and utility'.[7] We are right to fear technology that erodes the rest of our lives.

Addiction concerns will grow as tech firms compete for long-term attention and the rich advertising seams dominated by TV and movies, and as more immersive technologies reach our homes. Virtual and augmented reality both offer the potential of an irresistible hyperreality, as foretold throughout science fiction. The common theme of these stories is, per Jaspers, alienation from authentic human experience: a science fiction character who gives up on the physical world rarely enjoys a happy ending. However, the threat is no longer purely fictional. The alarming phenomenon of *hikikomori* ('withdrawing inward') has seen hundreds of thousands of young Japanese men shrinking from society. Unlike the couch potato, the hikikomori does not embrace idleness for its own sake; rather, unable to cope with the stresses of the external world, he retreats into himself. Many hikikomori find themselves drawn into immersive media or games. Although we mustn't confuse causation and correlation, it's clear immersive technologies, along with automation, the collapse of local retail, and ageing populations, could cause people to withdraw from society.

Experimentation

Tech companies have so embraced behaviour change that they trial countless designs to find the most persuasive variants. Perhaps a larger Buy Now button will increase sales, or a different voice assistant script will encourage more queries. This empirical approach is reinforced by technologists' love of the scientific method, instilled in their STEMish undergrad days, and the rise of lean startup. Lean enthusiasts contend iteration is the best route to product–market fit: experimenting with, and on, users is celebrated as a natural step in this process.

Any project that learns from user behaviour is a user research project, yet the industry has tacitly chosen to exempt experimentation from research ethics. Users are given no right to withdraw from studies. Children are routinely included in experimental populations. Informed consent is brushed aside, supposedly replaced by an excusatory sentence in the terms of service. An institutional review board (IRB) would rebuff academic research this sloppy, but the industry argues this level of ethical oversight would neuter innovation. While regulators turn a blind eye, companies experiment recklessly on users. Experimentation can be a powerful way to test product improvements, but in some companies it has mushroomed beyond interface tweaks into psychosocial research, with sometimes shocking disregard for public wellbeing: Facebook's 'emotional contagion' study, which rigged the News Feed of 689,000 users to learn whether it affected people's moods, is a notorious example.[8] The research ran under the auspices of Facebook's own data policy rather than that of an IRB. Facebook presumes a user accepts the policy as a condition of using the service, but most users never open it, let alone read it. It's laughable to claim the policy ensures informed consent. No opt-out was offered, and the researchers seemed to ignore the study's potential impact on users with depression, despite the resulting paper mentioning the condition as a focus of prior research.

Many tech companies responded to the resulting outcry with a shrug, claiming this is simply how technology works. OkCupid boasted 'We Experiment On Human Beings! (So does everyone else.)', and the Facebook researchers expressed their shock at the reaction in keynote speeches. These blasé defences of experimentation are rooted in the dehumanising effects of scale and the industry's quantitative bias. Marry tech companies' enormous reach with a belief that progress must be measurable – that objectives and key results (OKRs), active users, or conversion rates are the only worthwhile barometers of success – and a culture of target-chasing often wins out. Gradually, users become not *raisons d'être* but subjects for experimentation, means for teams to achieve their own goals. We start to see not customers, but masses.

Persuasion and power

The dynamics of persuasion are often political. Even the ostensibly benign nudge has partisan effects. Citizens and politicians alike find the idea of nudging more ethical when the examples given align with the subjects' politics. Even libertarians, typically wary of nudge's overbearing tendencies, set aside their scepticism when they approve of the nudger's goal.[9]

At the height of the 2010–12 Arab Spring, technology felt emancipatory, a positive force for uprooting hierarchy and oppression. How naive that now seems. Today, the internet has become the key battleground for political persuasion, propaganda, and disinformation. By manipulating information channels like social media, parties and nations can jostle for narrative supremacy: a strategy sometimes known as *influence operations*.

The web's structure helps these efforts. Respected news sources, niche publications, and propaganda factories can all reach global audiences; all are a single HTTP request away. Modern conspiracies also look as legitimate as any respectable story. In years past, we could identify crank literature by its format – ugly scrawls and bad photocopying – but now templated publishers like Medium or Squarespace allow anyone to publish information in a credible format. Disinformation is aesthetically equivalent to a legitimate press release, and a social media post from an lone conspiracist looks the same as an official announcement from the BBC.

Hypertext represents knowledge in ways that encourage exploration, fragmentation, and reassociation. Hypertext therefore tends to break apart centralised, linear narratives and encourages instead *apophenia*, a habit of imposing relationships on unconnected things.[10] Conspiracies bloom in the dark, in the gaps between trusted information, allowing the powerless to explain away their lack of agency. In this battle of the timelines, no matter how outlandish the narrative, there are people ready to believe. Furries, flat-earthers, and fascists alike can stitch together their own narratives from the digital fragments of the web, and broadcast them into their communities.

From the 'paranoia tourism' of Pizzagate to Reddit's terrible unmasking of the wrong Boston bomber,[11] extremists and ideologues have smartly exploited the public using Silicon Valley's persuasive infrastructure. However, tech companies have denied any role in political persuasion, sticking to their instrumental excuse: we're neutral platforms, not media companies. This is a feeble defence. No industry that spends millions lobbying for deregulation can claim political neutrality. Facebook's denial of political influence particularly galls when their partnership puff pages boast of an 'audience-specific content strategy to significantly shift voter intent.'[12]

There are several reasons why tech companies have been slow to stamp out harmful and misleading information. Identifying this content is certainly difficult; no company will hire vast fact-checking teams, and automated efforts will throw up plenty of false positives. But social networks fundamentally didn't much care about the quality of information shared, so long as it was shared; almost anything that moved the needle was welcome. Companies only started paying due attention to the propaganda externality once politicians held them accountable and dragged executives in front of committees and tribunals.

In retrospect, the industry's failings on propaganda have familiar origins. In their rush to build, technologists didn't consider how the structures and affordances of their new systems might have unintended consequences. Tech teams failed to mitigate the risks, meaning society has to bear them instead, in the form of resurgent extremism and conspiracy.

Automated persuasion

Automated persuasion – artificial agents with their own forms of algorithmic inducement – may pose an even larger menace to truth and democracy. We mustn't repeat the same mistakes.

Bots are already a viable persuasive threat. Analysing the digital ecosystems of the 2016 US election, Berit Anderson and Brett Horvath uncovered 'a weaponized AI propaganda machine'[13] that hinged on Cambridge Analytica profiling, automated scripts, and a deep network of propaganda sites. Relying on disenfranchised people's appetite for conspiracy, disinformation accounts on social media whipped up dissent in sympathetic communities. Oxford academics observed a similar, albeit smaller, pattern during the Brexit referendum: Twitter propaganda accounts previously used to skew opinions on the Israel–Palestine conflict were given a coat of British nationalist paint and flung into the new debate.[14]

Reporting of the Brexit and Trump campaigns has been inconsistent: many so-called bots were instead paid trolls, apparently part of rival states' influence operations. Sloppy labelling is understandable – people are still scrambling to understand how our technologies are being turned against us – but automated persuasion has undoubtedly played a part in recent political upheaval. It will only become more influential.

Persuasion is an ideal candidate for machine learning. We can define simple metrics we want to maximise (more followers, clicks, and retweets seem like decent proxies for influence), offer a wealth of behavioural data to mine, and propose hundreds of potential parameters to tweak. Political bots can trial dozens of conversational approaches, hashtags, and slogans; a design bot can test countless interface permutations to induce a potential customer to buy. Amazon already employs automated nudges at vast scale.

Through our Selling Coach program, we generate a steady stream of automated machine-learned 'nudges' (more than 70 million in a typical week) – alerting sellers about opportunities to avoid going out-of-stock, add selection that's selling, and sharpen their prices to be more competitive. These nudges translate to billions in increased sales to sellers.[15]

Georgia Tech researchers found people were surprisingly susceptible to machine persuasion in an emergency.[16] Test participants were greeted by a crude robot and instructed to follow it to to the lab; half of the time the robot took wrong turns, to give the impression it wasn't exactly a competent navigator. Midway through the study, experimenters flooded the adjoining corridor with fake smoke, setting off a fire alarm. During the phoney emergency, not one participant escaped the way they'd come in, or rushed to an emergency exit: they all followed the robot's instructions to head for a back room, even if they'd seen the robot make mistakes or break down earlier. Participants probably knew the emergency was faked – an IRB would have ethical misgivings about a study that made people genuinely fear for their lives – but people still 'overtrusted' the machine far beyond the researchers' expectations.

Emotional, or affective, technology will further sharpen the persuasive toolkit. London's new Piccadilly Lights billboard uses hidden cameras to deduce the gender, age, and mood of people in the vicinity, so it can serve ads appropriate to the audience: the public realm becomes a data mine. The endgame for this scenario – an artificial agent that can not only read gesture, intonation, and body language but mimic it in its responses, adapting not just what it says but how it says it – will be a formidable manipulator.

Automated persuasion is structurally quite different from existing forms of mass persuasion like advertising. Persuasive algorithms can respond to change rapidly, learn from millions of successes or failures elsewhere in the network, and can be highly personalised. Given enough data and training, an algorithm can present a compelling, tailored message to every individual; one-size-fits-all marketing gives way to a system that pushes only your most sensitive buttons. Legal scholar Karen Yeung argues automated persuasion is so unlike its monolithic predecessors that it deserves a new name: *hypernudge*.

Hypernudges could transform persuasion into duress. In a 2017 study, researchers created a 50% purchase uplift simply by tailoring Facebook ads to users' inferred personality types.[17] Clearly, this profiling will become more sophisticated and tied to more persuasive messages in future. If we can exploit someone's weaknesses on cue, when does a nudge become a shove?

Perhaps the biggest ethical challenge of hypernudging is its invisibility. There's no way to tell whether a camera is feeding a persuasion engine; soon we won't know whether a help desk is staffed by humans or hypernudging algorithms. A power imbalance is implicit in connected technology: the public has no insight into the network's machinations and no recourse against exploitation. Historically, mass persuasion was homogenous and visible: everyone saw the same newspapers, ads, and political broadcasts. This meant they could be critiqued. People could object en masse to misleading or unethical persuasion, and authorities could demand a message be withdrawn. But invisible hypernudges allow less scope for protest. With persuasive content tailored to the individual and delivered on a personal device, it will be harder to unify in opposition, and authorities will struggle to take corrective action.

Price also has persuasive effects. Dynamic pricing is hardly new – airlines have been at it for years – but it could soon hit a wider range of industries. Algorithms will be able to fine-tune prices to preserve stocks, manipulate demand, and, of course, extract maximum profit. Networked electronic price tags allow retailers to adjust prices instantaneously, which reduces waste and point-of-sale admin, but also allows retailers to spike prices at times of peak demand: surge pricing at the gelato counter.

Demand is off the charts! Prices have
increased to preserve ice cream stock levels.

In theory, algorithmic pricing could have some social benefit. Matching price to someone's ability to pay could help address inequality, and explaining price variations could illuminate opaque supply chains: your latte's more expensive this week thanks to storms hitting production in Vietnam. But customers typically see price discrimination as unfair, meaning today it often meets fierce backlash. Just ask Orbitz, who were caught serving Mac users higher hotel prices, on the presumption of higher income.[18]

If algorithmic pricing does become widespread despite this opposition, the public's only recourse might be to collectively confuse or skew price signals: *price hacking*. Price hacking has already been recorded among Uber drivers: by colluding to go offline in unison, drivers create a supply deficit that instigates surge pricing. In a world of mundane algorithmic pricing, customers may find themselves following suit, abstaining from a product to crash prices, then stockpiling en masse. This might in turn spark secondary resale markets, or even some sort of futures trading. Friends will pool pricing information and ask whoever gets the best price to buy on others' behalf. Algorithmic pricing may even create de facto cartels by accident: if algorithms learn that competitors will immediately match price cuts, they'll soon learn to keep prices high. In 2011, duelling Amazon Marketplace algorithms responding to each other's price changes caused an out-of-print genetics book to be listed at $23.6 million.[19]

Price escalation and lock-in may become commonplace, even without criminal intent.

Evidence collapse

Two lynchpins of contemporary evidence – speech and video – will soon be falsifiable, further distorting the persuasive landscape. Convincing text-to-speech software already exists, although it's computationally hungry, and undetectable 'deepfake' videos are just a couple of years away. When we can simply import incriminating text and see an accurate rendition from our most hated politician, we will have to reconsider what we believe to be true. Photos are already useless as evidence: once audio and video follow suit, what can serve as an accurate record of fact?

Audio synthesis firm Lyrebird is among the few tech companies to publish an ethics statement.

> Imagine that we had decided not to release this technology at all. Others would develop it and who knows if their intentions would be as sincere as ours: they could, for example, only sell the technology to a specific company or an ill-intentioned organization. By contrast, we are making the technology available to anyone and we are introducing it incrementally so that society can adapt to it, leverage its positive aspects for good, while preventing potentially negative applications.[20]

That the statement exists is welcome, but the contents are lousy. (We'll discuss its flimsy ethical argument – 'If we don't, someone else will' – in chapter 5.) It's not enough for transformative technology companies to warn of ethical risk and leave society to figure it out. This is instrumentalism at its most dangerous; technologists must actively understand and mitigate the harms their products can do.

Evidence collapse threatens not only our understanding of facts and current affairs, but also our personal relationships. If we can't be sure whether the person on the phone or video call is who we think it is, the door is open for widespread manipulation. Trust-based technologies like cryptography or blockchain might help, but these will require excellent, consumer-grade design. If only a few techies can implement these safeguards, information anarchy will reign for everyone else.

Justifying persuasion: folk ethics

Clearly, persuasion has complex implications. We have to ask that evergreen ethical question: where should we draw the line? What divides the unethical dark pattern from beneficent persuasion? Let's start with some common ethical precepts.

The weakest justification for persuasion – or, indeed, anything else – is that everyone's at it. This is a classic ethical trap, identified centuries ago by David Hume and known as the *is-ought fallacy*. It's a theoretical error to derive what we should do (ought) from how people currently act (is). Our competitors' moral choices are irrelevant to our own. Just as a cheating peloton didn't excuse Lance Armstrong's drug use, OkCupid's blasé defence of persuasive experimentation as commonplace stumbles straight into the is-ought jaws.

The *golden rule* – do as you would be done by – is more helpful. This proverb of reciprocity is found in ancient belief systems from Leviticus to Confucius. Applied to persuasive design, the golden rule suggests we should only persuade someone to do something we'd do ourselves, or that we'd be happy for someone to persuade us of. The golden rule's biggest flaw is its egocentrism. It encourages everyone to see themselves as the ideal ethical arbiter, whether their interests align with others' or not. The golden rule ignores the variety of human desires and the role of context in ethical choices.

Perhaps we should instead treat others how *they* would like to be treated: the *platinum rule*. In other words, we should only persuade people to act in their own interests. We should pause here to distinguish individual interest from the public interest, an idea often found in journalistic ethics. Stories that operate in grey ethical areas, such as those that infringe privacy or involve deception, often undergo a public interest test. This decision weighs up potential harm to individuals against the wellbeing of society; an editor-in-chief will often deem stories that increase accountability and transparency at the expense of wrongdoers to be in the public good.

Some persuasive technologies have a public interest component. A weight-loss app could prevent thousands of obesity-related deaths.

But the common good is politically charged: attempts to specify how others should live often bear the taint of authoritarianism. The public interest is complex, and not always a helpful ethical focus.

If we should only persuade people to act in their own interests, who gets to decide what those interests are? Technologists probably aren't the right people for this decision; they typically favour the scientific over the spiritual, action over reflection, and progress over the status quo, values which may not be right for the individual in question. But simply asking people what their best interests are has its flaws too: people's stated opinions are unreliable, and at times everyone contradicts their own interests by seeking out things that limit their capacity to thrive, like tobacco and alcohol.

If we can't just ask people what their best interests are, and it's improper to specify interests on others' behalf, we're in a bind, torn between a paternalistic desire to help others and a tolerant respect for people's freedom to choose. These simple ethical guidelines – forgive the pejorative label, 'folk ethics' – don't solve the problem.

Persuasive theories

A few designers and scholars have proposed guidelines for persuasive systems. Daniel Berdichevsky and Erik Neuenschwander suggest, among other principles, we should judge persuasion on whether it would be appropriate in person, freed from technology.[21] This question has the valuable side effect of restoring the personal context technology so often strips away. In *Persuasive Technology*, BJ Fogg suggests that using negative emotions to persuade is ethically questionable.[22] Mass persuasion does plenty of this – advertisers play on envy; bitter politicians appeal to rank xenophobia – but we should be wary of the is-ought fallacy. Warnings on cigarette packets are perhaps more defensible; there's a case that the ends (saving lives) justify the means (using fear to persuade). If, however, we do reject the idea of tugging at the subject's negative emotions, we should prevent technologies from displaying these emotions too. An AI should never shout at its user for skipping an upgrade, no matter how improved the new firmware may be.

Almost all theorists agree it's unethical to mislead for persuasive purposes, including Richard Thaler, who includes it in his principles of ethical nudging.[23] But consider the *placebo button*, a functionless control such as the close door button in many elevators, or the save option in certain web apps. The motivation – giving users a sense of control – is benevolent, the means deceptive. Are placebo buttons unethical? They still respect the user's will – the door still closes, the settings are still stored – and perhaps a white lie is preferable to the truth: you aren't in control, the technology is. However, if in doubt, deceptive persuasion is best avoided.

Social design researcher Nynke Tromp suggests we classify persuasion by strength and visibility, creating four types of influence: decisive, coercive, persuasive, and seductive.[24] Let's say we're designing a smart energy hub and want people to conserve energy. Here are some potential design approaches, mapped to these four categories.

Strong

Decisive	Coercive
Adjust heating schedule (no notification)	Adjust heating schedule (with notification)
Undercharge car to match previous use patterns	Audit connected devices, suggest efficient replacements
Seductive	**Persuasive**
Move non-urgent energy tasks to off-peak times	Provide consumption summaries and tips
Recharge household batteries on abundant solar days	Display social proof comparisons

Hidden — Apparent

Weak

The ethical implications of the top-left quadrant seem the most significant. A cold house might be dangerous to the elderly, and an undercharged vehicle may prove disastrous in an emergency, but if the device takes unilateral, invisible decisions both could happen.

Strong forms of persuasion may at times be justified, but weaker forms usually place us on safer ethical ground. Luciano Floridi distinguishes informational nudges from structural nudges.[25] An informational nudge changes the nature of information available – labelling unhealthy snacks, for example – while a structural nudge changes the courses of actions available, such as moving these same snacks out of easy reach. The informational nudge is weaker than the structural nudge, but more respectful of free choice.

Persuasive objects in the physical world are usually visible or even highlighted, such as speed cameras, but digital constraints are often invisible. With a software volume lock in place, users will never know just how much louder and more harmful their headphones could be. Is disclosure the answer, then? Should persuasive technologies simply advertise their presence and methods? This is a promising idea, with two caveats. First, persuasion may require invisibility; disclosing persuasion might make it ineffective. Second, disclosing every single persuasive method would be messy and distracting. Explanations and warnings would litter our technologies; users would eventually just start to ignore them. Many persuasive techniques are just part of what we consider good design, such as ensuring labels are clear and calls to action are highlighted. There has to be some balance. Disclosing persuasive methods is a noble aim, but perhaps it's better to make this information available rather than prominent. We'll discuss an example shortly.

The role of intent

We should also consider disclosing our persuasive intent – the why behind the design. Intent comes up often in ethics, and is the corner-stone of the *principle of double effect*, which states that harm is some-times acceptable as a side effect of doing good. Double effect is often used in euthanasia cases: doctors may increase a dying patient's morphine dose to ease suffering, even in the knowledge the dose may prove fatal. If the intent were simply to kill the patient, the doctor would be morally and legally liable, but most authorities choose not to prosecute when a convincing double-effect defence (relieving pain) exists.

Most experts suggest ethical persuasion needs positive intent. In Thaler's words, 'there should always be a good and clear reason for why the nudge will improve the welfare of those being nudged.' We should be honest about our true intent when designing persuasive systems. Why do I want people to follow my advice? What's in it for them? What's in it for me? Unfortunately, intent is less useful when examining other people's choices. 'Did you mean well?' is vulnerable to all sorts of excuses; as Benjamin Franklin observed, being 'a reasonable creature [...] enables one to find or make a reason for every thing one has a mind to do.' An unscrupulous colleague can concoct a plausible upside for virtually any ethical transgression. The overpriced extended warranty? Invaluable to the small fraction of users whose product breaks. Sucking up the user's contacts without permission? Imagine how thrilled people will be when they learn their friends have joined! Suggest someone acted with impure intent and they'll often respond with twisted double-effect arguments and who-me gestures of mock indignation. Focusing just on intent also allows us to wriggle off the hook of unintended consequences. Users don't care whether we intend harm or not; they care whether we cause harm.

Introducing deontology

Persuasive theories and honest questions about intent are useful ethical tools, but perhaps we need something more rigorous, some set of moral rules to follow. This is the foundation of *deontological ethics* (or duty ethics), one of the three schools of modern ethics. Deontologists believe that ethics is governed by rules and principles, and that we have a moral duty to adhere to these rules. This can make deontologists somewhat rigid: if we believe we have a moral duty to always tell the truth, it's hard to justify lying to the secret police about where our family is hiding. Deontologists lead lives of principle, but also lives of self-denial and, occasionally, honourable suffering. That said, deontologists typically excel at resisting ethical pressure; their belief in rules and integrity mean they set clear boundaries and challenge bad behaviour.

Immanuel Kant, a pioneer of deontological thought, proposed a powerful idea: when faced with an ethical choice, we should universalise our thinking. Kant suggested we imagine whether our actions would be acceptable as a universal law of behaviour. *What if everyone did what I'm about to do?* This simplified version of Kant's most important theory[26] is an invaluable ethical prompt for technologists. It focuses us on the futures our decisions could create and forces us to see ethical choices from broader social perspectives.

Kant also posed another useful deontological question: *am I treating people as ends or means?*[27] This deserves some explanation. For our purposes, the question asks whether we're using people – users, stakeholders, wider society – for our own success, or treating them as autonomous individuals with their own goals. Designers usually don't struggle with the ends-or-means question, since they tend to believe deeply in the importance of users' goals. The question tends to be more difficult when we ask it about company-wide decisions, particularly those that affect millions of people.

While deontologists agree we should live according to moral rules, they don't specify those rules: the point is we have to figure them out as a society. The questions above are good prompts, but we still have to work hard to translate them into action. Let's see how our two ethical tests help us untangle our persuasive complications.

Should we ship a deceptive dark pattern that offers no user benefit but increases our profit? Well, what if everyone did what I'm about to do? If all technology were riddled with dark patterns, companies may earn more, but our technologies – and probably our lives – would be worse. Users would feel hoodwinked, and we'd squander the trust our industry urgently needs. So the deontological answer is clear: no, we shouldn't release this dark pattern.

How about the attention economy? A world in which we all paid for our beloved products with attention rather than cash wouldn't of itself be bad; although, as we'll soon see, there may be painful privacy implications. The problems arise when a user is truly addicted, to the point that it harms their overall wellbeing. If we encourage addicts to use our services, are we treating these people as ends or means? That's easy: means. We continually offer them something that harms them, while we profit. A deontologist will argue tech companies have a duty to intervene in cases of harmful use. Unlike a tobacco company, who can't cut off a specific smoker, tech companies could identify problem users from afar and take action. This could involve anything from a light touch – reducing notifications or showing a 'Time for a break?' fatigue alert – to total excommunication, banning a user's credit card and closing their account. A company that knowingly serves an addicted user is using that addict as a means for commercial success alone, and is crossing the ethical line.

Ethical experimentation

If we put experiments under the deontological microscope, there's plenty to improve. Our first deontological test – what if everyone did what I'm about to do? – suggests the idea of running experiments isn't itself too harmful; it's our methods that cause the problems.

First, users have no choice about whether to take part. Usually, every user can be co-opted into an experimental population; however, mandatory research doesn't allow for informed consent. This decision clearly reduces people's autonomy, and would make a bad universal law of behaviour. Second, experiments are opaque. People usually have no way to know which experimental groups they're in and when the tests will end. Opacity can't be a healthy universal principle either. Third, in some companies, the point of experimenting becomes not improving the product but hitting targets: teams throw out different approaches until people respond in the right way. This is the very definition of treating people as means, not ends.

Can we design a more ethical, deontological approach to experimentation, one we'd recommend as a universal method? Let's start by always considering users as ends, not means. We should pledge that we'll try to improve the user experience with every experiment, and decline to run experiments we believe will be neutral or harmful. Businesses often need to take decisions that users won't like, such as raising prices or pruning functionality; under this principle these changes aren't suited to experiments. If you want to raise prices, raise prices across the board. Pledging to always improve users' experiences would fix many of the problems with Facebook's emotional contagion study: researchers would have to ensure participants only saw happier updates, not more negative ones.

In recognition that experimentation is research, we should consider informed consent inviolable. Since children can't give consent, we should remove them from the experimental pool, unless we can also gain consent from guardians. We should also agree that users should be able to learn about experiments they're in, with some screen or notification that describes each experiment, tells the user who's running the research, and describes the goal, phrased perhaps in terms of the metrics we're tracking or the hypotheses we're testing.

Let's also draw from persuasive theory and pledge to avoid both negative emotion and deception in our experiments, and strive to use weak, visible forms of persuasion where possible, such as informational nudges rather than structural nudges. Finally, users should be able to opt out of individual experiments and the whole experimentation programme alike, with no negative effects. Users who opt out will still receive software updates once they're rolled out to all users; we just won't include these people in experiments.

For a hypothetical smartphone app, a single screen could satisfy many of these requirements:

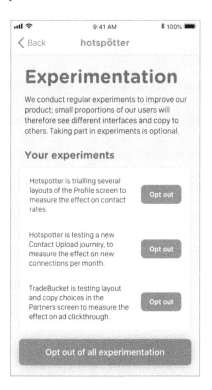

This more ethical approach to experimentation wouldn't be too onerous. We'd have to be more rigorous in selecting sample populations, add a new screen or notification, provide short metadata for each experiment, and build reliable opt-in and opt-out systems. These features needn't be highly prominent in the product, so long as they're available and findable. These small changes should help us treat users with respect, reduce the risk of regulatory wrath, and mean we run experiments in a way we'd be happy for others to follow.

The veil of ignorance

Another useful principle for designing fair systems is John Rawls's *veil of ignorance*. In *A Theory of Justice*,[28] Rawls contends that society – for our purposes we'll extend this to technological society too – is best structured as if its architects didn't know their eventual role in the system. Beneath a veil of ignorance, we wouldn't know our social status, our intelligence, or even our interests; but if the system is fair we should be satisfied wherever we ended up.

The veil of ignorance has some links with deontology; you wouldn't want to emerge from behind the veil into a role in which you're just a means for everyone else's ends. You may also recognise some parallels with the golden rule. However, this isn't just about treating people how you'd like to be treated yourself, but creating entire systems in which everyone is treated fairly. It's the you-cut-I-choose cake-sharing protocol from your childhood, stretched over an entire population.

Rawls's idea, focused on equality and redistributive justice, attracts criticism from predictable quarters when applied to politics, but for our purposes it's powerful. The veil of ignorance forces us to consider all the various roles people will play in our systems, and how our work might influence people from wide-ranging backgrounds. Applied to persuasion, the veil of ignorance suggests we should only create persuasive systems that would be fair to the persuader and persuaded alike.

Better persuasion

Some of our persuasive difficulties are direct consequences of our product development processes. The strategies that create desirable products also foster addiction. We use our phones 150 times a day; is that because they're designed to capture our attention, or because we genuinely love them? Probably both. That we find it difficult to tease these motivations apart speaks to the failures of the experience design movement. Designers haven't interrogated the difference between enjoyable and habitual use, and the rhetoric of designing for delight has directly contributed to addiction.

Some commentators argue that to counter manipulation, tech firms should actively expose people to conflicting views. The tech industry has plenty of tools at its disposal: fact-checking plug-ins and trust ratings to combat disinformation, and crowdsourcing, blockchains, and cryptography to fight evidence collapse. But counteracting people's biases is tough, thankless work. Early efforts to diversify the information environment have been exasperatingly crude: Facebook's attempts to warn users of suspect content actually made more people click on it, and I've only recently escaped an infuriating experiment that appended the most engaging reply (usually the most contentious or trollish) to every News Feed article.

Isn't this just more technocratic meddling, though? The idea that technologists should force-feed the masses balanced information diets should trouble us. Which harm is more severe: the threat of manipulation, or the authoritarian threat of controlling others' information environments? These questions are social, political, and legal as much as they are technical; as such, they aren't for us to answer alone. The technical fixes that would be most effective against disinformation, such as real name policies or better tracking of sources, would themselves endanger privacy. Perhaps our most important duty is to stimulate public discussion about persuasive technologies. The tech industry should look to boost information literacy at all levels of education and adult life, and play an active role in restoring a thriving, resilient press. Technologists may need to give users anti-addiction and anti-persuasion strategies, or even build counter-technologies that side with the user against the industry itself, such as persuasion blockers that scrub out manipulative advertising and bust people out of non-consensual A/B tests.

We should also eliminate the factors that have caused our persuasive woes. At the heart of the dark pattern, the addictive app, and the disinformation problem alike lies an undue fixation on quantification and engagement. Choosing new success metrics would smooth the route to more ethical persuasion. The Time Well Spent movement[29] asks how tech would look if it were designed to respect human values rather than capture attention. The movement taps into theories of calm technology and mindfulness to inspire designers to protect users' time and agency, and argues for new business models that subvert the attention economy.

Quantitative data should always be paired with accessible qualitative research, so human stories can claim their rightful place in decision-makers' minds. We can also select *mutually destructive targets*, metrics chosen in pairs such that one will suffer if we simply game the other. For example, dark patterns may well extract more revenue per user, but they'll also harm retention if users feel duped. Choosing both revenue and retention as mutually destructive targets provides a minor safeguard against abuse; if both measures move in the right direction, we can be confident things are genuinely improving.

Regulation and opt-out

If the industry fails to self-police, it should brace itself for consumer rejection. Until recently, society saw technological refuseniks as socially irregular, and it was mostly techies themselves who chose to abstain, deleting their apps, climbing mountains, and writing think-pieces about their experiences. These efforts reeked of privilege – after all, you need to be rich to need nothing – but amid growing concern about addictive technologies, a public temperance movement is brewing. Clinics are already treating self-described app addicts; perhaps a detox-as-a-service industry will emerge: hand over your devices and we'll lock you out for two weeks.

Where consumers lead, regulators will follow. Tech companies have already been sued and subpoenaed over unfair persuasion and dark patterns; in 2015, LinkedIn paid $13 million to settle a dark pattern class action suit. Regulation is likely to come first from the EU, given its historical opposition to tech monopolies and its citizens' sensitivity to corporate abuse. The German government is drafting a law that would impose €50 million fines on social networks that fail to curtail hate speech and disinformation. Regulators might decide to make platforms liable for hate speech, force tech conglomerates to split, or demand that social networks let users take their friend networks to competitor services. Online adverts might, and arguably should, be required to reveal their funders. Some philosophers and lawyers are even discussing whether there should be an enshrined legal right to attentional protection.

The early television age also spawned concerns about persuasion and disinformation. Many governments responded by establishing national broadcasting agencies and standards, creating a heavy top-down influence on the burgeoning industry. If this pattern is repeated for emerging persuasive technologies, the industry will have only itself to blame.

Chapter 4

The data deluge

Once upon a time, we talked about data using the language of the library. Data was collated and neatly catalogued, ready to be referenced and queried. But the explosion of online tracking, cheap sensors, and powerful computation has ushered in a new age – the era of big data – and caused a metaphorical shift.[1] Data now surges past us in liquid figures of speech. It has become a river, a torrent. Data is the new oil: immense, uncontrollable, and with a nasty habit of leaking.

The oil metaphor also portrays data as a precious fuel for digital industry. It suggests rapid prospecting, thirsty extraction, and occasionally dangerous exploitation. In chapter 6 we'll see how authorities such as governments, police forces, and militaries are taking advantage of the data revolution, but first let's explore new commercial uses.

The most obvious is advertising. The weightlessness of digital tech allows it to reach vast global audiences; knowing more about these users makes for better targeting and higher ad revenue. It's therefore in the interests of ad-funded platforms to gather as much information on as many users as they can. Harvard scholar Shoshana Zuboff describes this burgeoning trade as *surveillance capitalism*, a label that's attracted activists and data dissenters alike, among them security expert Bruce Schneier: 'In half a century people will look at the data practices of today the same way we now view archaic business practices like tenant farming, child labor, and company stores. They'll look immoral.'[2]

Any system that absorbs so much data about our lives has ethical implications, but the hyperbole of surveillance capitalism has clouded the debate. Labelling all ad-funded websites and social media as surveillance is a distortion that suggests users can neither consent to giving up data nor benefit from the technology that results. The trope that tech platforms harvest piles of data so they can sell it to advertisers is economically illiterate. It would be commercial suicide for, say, Google and Facebook to sell user data. Yes, these companies are motivated to gather information, but they do it so they can sell advertisers *access to users*, not the data itself. It's an important distinction. Facebook and Google's business models demand they protect user information zealously; relinquishing data would mean surrendering their competitive advantage. Far more deserving of the surveillance label are data brokers like Acxiom and Datalogix, who collect information from public records, purchase histories, warranties, and each other, and do indeed resell the lot. Data brokers have existed for decades, however; it's hard to argue they're a new phenomenon.

Data beyond advertising

It's not just the advertising industry that wants data, however. Data fuels analytics, helping companies understand their markets and measure product improvements, and allowing consumers to track their bodies and lives. But data's growing importance is chiefly down to AI.

Without data, there is no AI. Modern deep-learning systems study vast sets of training data, then compare new data against the models that result; what's known as *inference*. These systems already show exciting pattern-matching promise. Under controlled environments, AIs can spot pneumonia better than a radiologist,[3] evaluate NDAs faster than lawyers,[4] and answer trivia questions better than a human.[5] Data will train AIs that control the home, drive vehicles, and govern security systems. Today we can already unlock our devices and make purchases with facial data; banks use voice identification to reduce fraud. A Beijing park notoriously uses face recognition to ration toilet paper, ensuring visitors receive at most a two-foot portion every nine minutes.

Data is central to both the functionality and the user experiences of these technologies. Withholding personal data from a voice assistant will make it agonising to use, and it can never improve by knowing you better. A bot with total amnesia will quickly gather dust. Opt out of your bank's new security tech and you're thrown back in the old world of unwieldy passwords and code generators.

These diverse uses all carry some ethical risk. It's therefore a serious mistake to focus just on advertising when discussing data ethics. Those who argue that abuses flow naturally from advertising models overlook that *every* company now benefits from capturing more data. It hardly matters who's paying.

Raw data is an oxymoron

Although virtually everything we do casts a data shadow, we must remember that shadows are only ever outlines. Data is commonly interpolated, rounded, truncated, or just plain wrong. Anaesthesiologist Dr. Julian Goldman examined the clocks in 1,300 medical devices and found nearly 20% were off by more than 15 minutes, invalidating crucial timestamped dosage data.[6] Poke around any US marketing database and you'll discover a surprising number of customers hailing from Schenectady, NY; a bizarre finding until you spy the area's ZIP code: 12345.

The data-as-oil metaphor has one notable shortcoming: in describing data as a commodity, we ignore its origins. While we can simply tap into existing (albeit diminishing) reservoirs of oil, extracting data is not a passive act. The choice of what data to collect and what to omit, the technologies we use to collect and process it, and the techniques we use to analyse data are themselves laden with implicit assumptions and biases. Tracing a US gun owner, for instance, is intentionally taxing, involving an audit trail stretching from the nation's gun retailers to ATF shipping containers full of microfilm. Computerised search is prohibited, thanks to the NRA's efforts to keep the process as onerous as possible. The inability to separate data from its contexts of extraction and processing led Geoffrey Bowker to coin a memorable epithet: 'Raw data is both an oxymoron and a bad idea; to the contrary, data should be cooked with care.'[7]

Data representation also introduces connotation and bias. Designers know well how layout, type, and colour can bestow persuasive associations; here, Andy Cotgreave inverts the message of Simon Scarr's extraordinary Iraq war graphic with a new headline and a vertical flip.

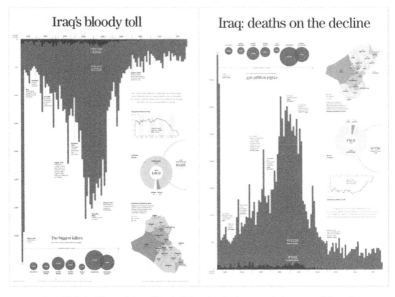

Republished with permission of South China Morning Post, permission conveyed through Copyright Clearance Center, Inc (left), and Andy Cotgreave (right).

We must therefore be mindful of data's power to mislead. This contradicts the dominant ideology surrounding data: ironically, that data has no ideology. Convinced that data is the heart of all knowledge, many technologists defend data as an an objective and accurate reflection of the world around us; seen from this hill, more information is more power, and the data is *the* data.[8] If data is irreproachable, the argument goes, so are the decisions based on it.

Resigned to insecurity

Even accurate data is harmful in the wrong hands. 2017's Equifax breach was the worst data catastrophe yet, surrendering the names, social security numbers, birth dates, and addresses of 145 million Americans. A further 209,000 credit card numbers were taken. After nudging a couple of executives towards retirement and offering credit monitoring to affected citizens, Equifax is still, at the time of writing, a $16 billion company, valued just 4% lower than pre-leak levels. The consequences of identity theft fall more on consumers than the companies responsible.

Rich data stores and poor security also invite blackmail. Attacks on sex websites Adult FriendFinder and Ashley Madison, provoked ostensibly by moral disgust, saw users extorted for hush money or further duped by the hackers to install malware, allowing further data siphoning.

Connected home devices are notoriously insecure, with many manufacturers competing on price alone and leaving gaping vulnerabilities as a result. Researchers hacked the Svakom Siime Eye, a teledildonic vibrator-cum-endoscope, allowing its streaming video to be watched anywhere within Wi-Fi range; the Mirai botnet, now attributed to three students trying to hamper rival Minecraft servers, zombified 600,000 devices by exploiting insecure admin passwords. As one anonymous wag commented, 'The S in IoT stands for security.'

Numbed by endless leaks, unreadable privacy policies, and aggravating consent forms, the public has grown resigned to insecurity: once more unto the data breach. It's hard to blame them. Even the industry's suggested user remedies – password managers, two-factor authentication, password rotation – place an unrealistic burden on non-technical users and unfairly individualise the problem.

Many data ethics issues revolve around privacy. Privacy is a complex idea, widely understood but poorly defined. It goes far beyond simple security, touching on important values like dignity and trust. A company employee browsing sensitive user data without due cause is violating people's privacy, even if the data is held safely and with consent.

Some theorists describe privacy as a right to choose seclusion, to decline a role in the public realm. Others define privacy as confidentiality, including legal scholar Richard Posner, who says what people mean by privacy is 'concealment of information about themselves that others might use to their disadvantage'.[9] These forms of privacy may no longer be sustainable. Someone who wants to fully conceal their personal data must essentially opt out of modern society: credit cards, mobile phones, and email already reveal personal information and permit tracking. Short of going off the grid, total information seclusion is impossible.

Perhaps it's better to understand modern privacy as control and self-determination. Where possible, people should be able to disclose whatever information they want, to whomever they wish, whenever they want, and be able to reverse those decisions too. Privacy, then, is a hand on the dial, not just a padlock.

The value exchange in practice

Giving people control of their data suggests they have a right to trade it. Privacy becomes a currency, something people can choose to swap for convenience. This is an important value exchange. In theory, if the trade-off is understood by and fair to both sides, there can be few ethical qualms; this is, after all, how trade is meant to happen. Done right, billions of people get innovative technology in exchange for an agreed amount of personal data. But is this trade fair today?

In truth, users have little power to negotiate compensation or opt out. Tech companies make fixed data demands in exchange for access: take it or leave it. The free-market defence that consumers can simply defect to competitors is unconvincing. Rival social networks are useless if your friends aren't on them, and it's difficult today to avoid the tech giants' ecosystems if you're after an affordable smartphone or voice assistant. Some digital services are so central to modern life they're practically utilities: users must either yield their data or live impoverished digital existences.

The terms of data exchange are usually murky. Byzantine privacy policies and curt OS pop-ups both do a poor job of explaining themselves: even a simple request like 'Grant access to browsing history?' can have many interpretations. How far back does it go? Does it log just domains or specific pages? Will it learn my search queries via URL parameters?

The public is also largely oblivious to how aggregation changes the data landscape. Companies can generate new insight by combining datasets; algorithms excel at reading between the lines. Tinder knows not just your declared romantic tastes but how attractive you actually find different racial groups. Facebook can deduce your politics from your in-app behaviour. Seemingly benign information requests can, if squeezed in the right way, yield highly sensitive second-order inferences.

Finally, people often end up making privacy decisions that affect others. Plenty of user data relates to multiple people: your calendar houses family birthdays; your friends are tagged in your photo library. Even emails have both a sender and a recipient. 320,000 people installed Dr. Aleksandr Kogan's notorious Facebook personality test, later used by Cambridge Analytica for political targeting; each 'seeder' also gave the app access to, on average, 160 friends. Similarly, an unnamed psychiatrist found Facebook's People You May Know algorithm suggested her patients befriend one another.[10] The most likely explanation? Each patient had added the psychiatrist to their phone's address book. Facebook then assumed that since these patients share a mutual friend, they might like to know each other; a grave privacy threat to the psychiatrist's patients, who included suicide survivors and people trying to escape violent relationships. By identifying other individuals mentioned in user data, tech firms can even construct shadow profiles of people who haven't signed up for the service.

In 2011, a World Economic Forum report labelled personal data 'a new asset class'. Tech companies' side of the data bargain is indeed growing, but users have yet to realise this new wealth. Search engines and social software are largely the same today as a decade ago, and while a few platforms like YouTube attempt revenue-sharing, only the most powerful users make any real profit. Compared to the utopian data-trading dream, users are no longer being fairly compensated.

Redefining public and private

For a fair data trade, both parties need similar views on what should be private and what is public. This isn't easy: the boundary shifts across cultures and generations.

> The concept of privacy, in anything like the senses in which we use it today, is a Western cultural artifact. The idea that it might be pleasant to be off the public stage was hardly meaningful in a society [...] Privacy was [once] the lot of the pariah.[11]

Privacy relies on a complex web of social conventions. Consumers who label a technology 'creepy' are complaining their expectations of the public-private boundary have been violated, that a technology knows more than they think it should. But this is an unstable border, perpetually redrawn and eroded. Tech companies typically benefit from rezoning private information as public; once data is in the open, it's easier to exploit. Many new technologies also have an innate tendency to erode private space, creating what we might call a *drift to disclosure*. Voice interfaces give human–computer interaction a broadcast radius, drones peer through high windows, and lip-reading tech will tear private conversation from the mouth of the speaker. Devices shared between users or installed in public spaces – the premise of the smart city – only accelerate this trend. Autonomous vehicles, for example, will continually record the street from hundreds of angles, creating footage that will prove invaluable to manufacturers and also the police, who will demand it for all sorts of investigations, not just road traffic accidents. This creeping colonisation of our cities prompted the *Economist* – hardly an opponent of technology or corporate power – to label autonomous vehicles 'panopticons on wheels'.[12]

Occasionally, the power imbalances inherent in today's technologies allow companies to annex private information by force. Many always-on products require users to acquiesce to new data demands, opening the door to abuse. In 2017, Sonos forced through a lopsided privacy update, and warned objectors they'd receive no future software updates, meaning their expensive devices would stop working over time. At worst, users aren't participants in the data economy so much as feedstock.

Unabated erosion of privacy could lead to real harm. This sort of *slippery slope argument* – a claim that a minor concession could precipitate more dangerous compromises – is common in ethics. Some privacy campaigners argue tech's appropriation of the private realm will, bit by bit, create a post-privacy future in which secrecy is an irregularity and the powerful can surveil anyone on demand. (We'll discuss this specific dystopia in chapter 6.) Slippery slope arguments rely on chains of cause and effect that don't always come to pass, but these claims still deserve attention. Slippery slope arguments are similar to the futures wheel exercise; sometimes even a slender risk demands preventative action.

Two effective ways to guard against slippery slope harms are imposing legal red lines – you may go this far and no further – and creating technologies that push back against the forces of gravity. In the data world these are known as *privacy-enhancing technologies* (PETs).

De-identification and re-identification

The most obvious privacy-enhancing approach is to scrub data of personally identifiable information. However, de-identification is increasingly easy to reverse. In 2006, two researchers combined Netflix and IMDb data to re-identify users on both services and deduce their political preferences;[13] and, by cross-referencing US census data with electoral rolls, Carnegie Mellon professor Latanya Sweeney was able to identify more than half of the US population using just gender, date of birth, and town of residence.[14]

Seemingly harmless data requests often become more dangerous when combined with other datasets. Many users willingly give up their locations, credit card histories, and heart rates, but anyone able to combine all three could easily assemble evidence of serious medical issues, or perhaps an affair. De-identified data therefore needs to be safe from not only current re-identification technologies but every dataset and every future algorithm that could be used for cross-referencing and analysis. Metadata that is harmless today may make you traceable tomorrow. This sobering prospect has led some tech insiders to claim de-identification is a doomed strategy.

> Uber is providing anonymized data on 2 billion trips. If you'd like the unanonymized dataset, just wait 6–12 months. —Maciej Cegłowski[15]

Recognising the threat, governments are now trying to legislate against re-identification. The UK proposes 'intentionally or recklessly re-identifying individuals from anonymised or pseudonymised data' should be a criminal offence. This sounds promising but lacks detail: will it, for instance, make it illegal to reveal who is behind a pseudonymous Twitter account?

Seamlessness and trust

Even public data can be used in ways that violate privacy expectations. In 2016, a controversial researcher called Emil Kirkegaard created a fake OkCupid account, then used a bot to scrape 68,000 dating profiles from the site. Kirkegaard then published this dataset, including usernames, and used it to try to demonstrate a link between intelligence and religious beliefs. He defended himself against the resulting uproar with a blunt claim: the data is already public, so what's the problem? *WIRED* magazine, in a remarkably understated denunciation of Kirkegaard's work, pointed out 'serious ethical issues that big data scientists must be willing to address [...] to avoid unintentionally hurting people caught up in the data dragnet.'[16]

It's no surprise technology is a key privacy battleground: the public generally has no idea what modern devices are up to behind the scenes.

> When a machine runs efficiently, when a matter of fact is settled, one need only focus on its inputs and outputs and not on its internal complexity. Thus, paradoxically, the more science and technology succeed, the more opaque and obscure they become. —Bruno Latour[17]

Latour is right that technologies naturally tend towards opacity, but hiding tech's inner workings has also been a conscious design choice. In the name of seamlessness, designers have convinced users they have no business looking under the hood. Data interchange has been treated as complexity, something best hidden via sleight of hand. This means the tech industry has to rely heavily on trust. Users must believe technologists' promises that voice assistants don't record until they hear the wake word, that cameras aren't turned on without consent, that no one is peeking in on intimate messages. The lower in the technology stack – think operating systems or browsers – the more dangerous potential violations of trust become.

Trust is an important ethical value, central to a healthy society. To trust someone with data is to be confident they won't disclose this data; trust is therefore a consensual security vulnerability. Most companies uphold this trust, although there's no easy way the user can be sure. However, some betray trust by using private data secretly for corporate gain. Verizon covertly modified users' web traffic to include a tracker described by the Electronic Frontier Foundation as 'an undeletable supercookie'.[18] The FCC's 2017 decision that ISPs no longer need consent to sell user data will doubtless encourage similar behaviour.

Whether an individual company is trustworthy is perhaps the wrong question; we should also ask what a bad actor could do with trusted information. Companies wax and wane, after all; they get bought out and hacked, meaning personal data frequently finds its way into the hands of untrusted or unknown groups.

Data regulation

With such potential for data misuse, and with opacity hampering fair data exchange, regulators are naturally taking an interest. Data protection law needs to walk a tight line, defending personal rights while accommodating the needs of innovation and the social good. Democracy, for example, needs an electoral roll, even though individuals may prefer not to have their information in a centralised database.

Different legal and social cultures have led unsurprisingly to contrasting approaches. The United States has, as usual, left the industry to self-regulate, seeing government intervention as a last resort. While there are hundreds of US privacy laws, many are limited and redundant, and there is no clear federal framework. Other nations are more exacting. India declared privacy a constitutional right in 2017, spurring a successful challenge to the country's long-standing ban on homosexuality. Campaigners argued sexual orientation and activity is private and hence newly protected. Regulations have unintended consequences too: in this case, happy ones.

Today, the sternest data protection regimes are in the EU.

Germany prohibits sales of smartwatches to children, classing them as 'prohibited listening devices', and, having suffered two totalitarian regimes in the last century, has deep cultural resistance to sharing personal data. Across the whole EU, 2018's General Data Protection Regulations (GDPR) have set a new landmark for data protection, covering any company, wherever they are in the world, that handles data on European citizens. GDPR broadens the scope of personal data, sets tough new standards for consent (a death sentence for data dark patterns such as opt-out boxes), offers new individual data rights, and restricts automated decision-making. Unlike their antecedents, these regulations can sting: fines mount to 4% of global turnover or €20 million for severe violations.

GDPR is probably just the first step of global data belt-tightening. We may soon see penalties for data leaks brought into line with those on industrial accidents, and laws that make tech companies liable for security defects. To keep industry onside, governments will presumably dangle incentives too, such as tax credits for safely sharing data that benefits new industries.

The *right to be forgotten* is an especially contentious legal and ethical debate. Digital data has a habit of lingering, freezing fleeting circumstances and beliefs into an icy snapshot. Is this fair, given the natural human tendency to forget? Should people be able to conceal their pasts? Withdrawing information from public view has legal and moral precedent. The UK's Rehabilitation of Offenders Act, for example, allows people to avoid declaring minor convictions if they don't reoffend. Alleged victims of sex crimes are granted automatic anonymity under UK law, a morally welcome decision, but one that can require some awkward redaction. When a British 15-year-old went missing with her teacher in 2012, the country's newspapers publicised calls for her safe return. Once it became known the two were in a (criminal) sexual relationship, the girl's name had to be immediately expunged from press coverage.

In 2014, the European Court of Justice ruled that Europeans can ask search engines to delist web pages about them; not so much forgetting as erasing the map. The ECJ ruling, praised by ethicist Luciano Floridi as 'the coming of age of our information society',[19] was nevertheless controversial, and is still disputed today. Journalists denounced the decision, claiming their scoops would vanish from the public eye and that crooks would erase history. Some newspapers have since fought back by posting their own lists of the pages Google has delisted. However, despite initial fears, the right to be forgotten hasn't just been used to hide wrongdoing. Applicants have included people wanting to renounce former political views, victims of crime making a clean break, and transgender people wishing to remove their 'deadnames' from record.

A deontologist might also be sceptical of the right to be forgotten, arguing that people have a moral duty to live with the consequences of their actions. If everyone asked to be delisted, our shared knowledge and trust would dissolve. However, it seems harsh to criticise someone on strict deontological grounds if they're making a request solely to help heal emotional trauma. The right to be forgotten also fits neatly with the idea of privacy as self-determination. Forgetting lets people live free from the stigma of minor mistakes. In *The Ethics of Invention*, Sheila Jasanoff argues the right to be forgotten is an important part of being 'a moving, changing, traceable, and opinionated data subject.'[20]

In practice, authority rests with the search engine, which can refuse a request on grounds of freedom of expression, legal necessity, and public interest. In three years of receiving requests, Google complied with just 43%.[21] Recent cases have at last shed some light on how the company makes these decisions. Google has a legal removals team and an advisory council on hand, but *The Register* reports software engineers sometimes contribute to or may even make the final call.[22] Although applicants can appeal to national data protection agencies, it's astonishing that a private company is forced to wield such influence over individual data rights, although Google arguably has immense power of this sort already, regardless of any right to be forgotten.

The right to be forgotten is still mostly a European phenomenon. A US version, for example, would be hard to reconcile with the first amendment right to free speech, so the outcome is highly territorial: links hidden in Europe are still visible elsewhere. New technologies may shake things up further. Good luck handling a right-to-be-forgotten request if you've already committed the data to an irrevocable blockchain.

Clearly, adapting to regulation isn't easy. Future data laws would force companies to change their algorithms, interfaces, processes, and policies: expensive changes that may hit small companies harder than large incumbents. Tech companies may have to make do with less customer insight and worse training data, and will doubtless have to discard some innovations as unworkable. Thanks to GDPR, Facebook can't offer Europeans a tool that proactively detects suicide risk, causing gleeful complaints from anti-EU and free-market campaigners. However, there's always a counter-framing. *Guardian* journalist Alex Hern reasoned Facebook's feature 'is literally illegal [...] because of the rampant privacy violations required to make it work.'

Tomorrow's data standards may be tighter but, if well managed, they'll also be clearer and better enforced. No longer will companies be able to compete on how much data they can stealthily grab and monetise; user trust will become paramount. Companies operating with shady consent out of public view will be the hardest hit. The digital tracking that's been hidden for years is finally being forced to the surface, causing panicked consolidation. Good legislation should mostly hurt the companies that made a clamp-down necessary: no flowers will mark the passing of ad tech data ransackers.

Introducing utilitarianism

Legislation should be a safety net, not an ethical baseline. The best way for the tech industry to avoid future regulation is to take better ethical decisions today. So let's look at another theory of ethics: *utilitarianism*.

Utilitarians aren't worried about moral law or duty; they only care about results. Utilitarianism is therefore called a *consequentialist* approach. It was proposed by the empiricists Jeremy Bentham and John Stuart Mill, who felt deontology was needlessly abstract and argued we should instead judge actions by whether they cause happiness. For utilitarians, happiness is the ultimate good, the main purpose of society and life. This doesn't mean we should just pursue hedonistic thrills, however; Mill, in particular, was keen to stress happiness should include intellectual and emotional fulfilment. Nor are utilitarians in it to boost their own happiness – an approach called *egoism*, generally seen as flawed in obvious ways – instead, they're interested in the happiness of a whole society. Utilitarians base ethical decisions on a simple but powerful question – *am I maximising happiness for the greatest number of people?* – and, by extension, am I minimising pain?

This approach feels intuitive; everyone would agree the world could use more happiness and less pain, and focusing on results makes utilitarianism more tangible than deontology's rules and duty. Since utilitarianism asks us to consider the overall sum of happiness, not just our own, utilitarians need a global and inclusive outlook. In the words of philosopher Henry Sidgwick, a utilitarian must consider 'the point of view of the universe'. Utilitarians also have to be flexible to the circumstances of each decision. An act that increases happiness in one context may cause harm in another; a utilitarian has to judge each case on its merits. This makes utilitarians versatile, willing to bend traditional moral rules if it increases the balance of happiness, and perhaps easier to get along with than their stern deontologist cousins.

So far, so promising, but there are problems too. Assessing everyone's future happiness and pain for every single action – *act utilitarianism* – sounds wholly impractical. Bentham proposed a 'felicific calculus', an equation for plugging happiness values into. Does morality condemn us to an eternity of number-crunching? Won't people skip the arithmetic and fall back on intuition, defeating the purpose? How do you even measure happiness anyway?

Utilitarians have therefore suggested some tweaks. *Rule utilitarians* agree with deontologists that we need some moral rules, but declare we should choose these rules on the balance of happiness they cause, rather than basing them on some mythical moral truth. So rule utilitarians still weigh up happiness and harm, but only to decide rules of behaviour. We outlaw fraud, say, because it harms both the victim and society; once we've made this rule we don't need to morally assess every single act of fraud. Alternatively, *preference utilitarians* say happiness is too hedonistic; better to act in accordance to everyone's preferences. (Preference utilitarianism is a valuable way to look at robot and AI ethics, as we'll see in chapter 8.)

Utilitarianism sometimes struggles to protect individuals and minorities from oppression. If 99% of a population wants to exile or execute a 1% minority, a deontological rebuttal is far easier than a utilitarian one. This 'tyranny of the majority' can be a sticky problem for utilitarians. Similarly, an act utilitarian may find it tough to argue against killing one person so their organs can save five, or pushing a criminal off a lifeboat to save a doctor.

Utilitarianism also seems to let dubious behaviour slide if it doesn't cause any harm. If schoolboys exchange compromising photos of a female classmate without her knowledge, is this wrong? Absolutely, says a deontologist: the girl is being treated as a means of titillation, not an end in her own right, and we have a duty to respect each others' privacy. But unless the girl finds out, a utilitarian may find it harder to condemn: the boys enjoy it, so surely the balance of happiness is positive? The typical utilitarian defence in these cases is that denying people justice is harmful overall, and makes us less happy as a society. But it's clear that utilitarianism sometimes leads us toward conclusions that seem morally counterintuitive.

Scientific morality

The tech community tends to be fond of utilitarianism, in part because it seems somewhat quantifiable. In a world where most decisions are subservient to data, why not morality? The idea of quantifying and proving human values – 'scientific morality' – has flourished in recent years. In *The Moral Landscape*,[23] Sam Harris claims advances in neuroscience and computing mean Bentham's felicific calculus may yet be within our grasp. For Harris, science is the saviour of ethics: big data and a few well-placed electrodes will soon tell us for sure which laws and lifestyles cause the greatest human happiness.

The idea of a rational, scientific approach to ethics isn't new, and many ethicists have criticised Harris as a dilettante. The biggest flaw with Harris's reasoning is the is-ought trap: you can't derive moral guidance by looking at the data of what *is*, which is precisely Harris's intention. But to me, seeing ethics as just another equation to be solved is a sad, solutionist point of view. It ignores the most important parts of ethics: dialogue, consensus, resolve. The idea that an fMRI scanner is some tool of moral enlightenment is an injustice to both science and ethics.

Utilitarianism or deontology?

Although utilitarianism has some awkward weaknesses and is prone to pseudoscientific delusions, it's an important ethical model. The idea of maximising happiness is more accessible than lofty ideas of moral duty, and utilitarianism tends to be a particularly useful way to think about the implications of the new. Government-backed ethics commissions, for example, often default to utilitarian perspectives when considering the impacts of innovation.

> Legislation must be broadly utilitarian in outlook [...] In trying to decide what it would be best to do, legislators must be consequentialists [...] each member of society should count for one, and no one should be given special consideration. —Mary Warnock[24]

However, a deontological stance may be more appropriate for stopping significant ethical breaches in communities that have previously overstepped the mark. At the cost of being seen as occasionally obstinate, deontologists draw a line in the sand, establishing clear ground rules.

Let's put these two ethical theories into practice by considering a near-future data-driven device. Imagine a smart home hub that connects your household appliances and your family's devices, monitoring things like energy use, media habits, locations, and health biometrics. The hub allows you to visualise this data and use it to automate your home, setting alerts, turning lights on, and so on. Let's assume the hub is operating with your full consent: you know exactly what it gathers and where that data goes. The manufacturer gives the device away for free. In return, its screen occasionally shows targeted ads, and advertisers pay the manufacturer whenever you respond to an ad.

You come across a hack that will disable the home hub's ads. It takes some specialist knowledge – you'll have to root the device – but you're confident you can get it working. Is it ethical to hack your hub?

There are some parallels with web ad blocking today, a debate beset with hyperbole. One side claims ad tech is so hostile it's effectively malware; the ad industry counters by claiming blocking is theft: 'Every time you block an ad, what you're really blocking is food from entering a child's mouth.'[25] Let's use our ethical theories to see through this ludicrous rhetorical fog.

From a utilitarian angle, we have to weigh up the likely happiness and pain of all concerned. Let's focus on three stakeholders: you (the user), advertisers, and the hub manufacturer. As the user, your main gain is privacy: your personal life retains a little more concealment and integrity, and you'll probably feel happier as a result. Since you're only blocking the ads, not the data capture, this effect is mostly illusory, but even perceived privacy can be valuable. You'll also benefit from your attention being protected.

> In the short term, distractions can keep us from doing the things we want to do. In the longer term, however, they can accumulate and keep us from living the lives we want to live [...] Thus there are deep ethical implications lurking here for freedom, wellbeing, and even the integrity of the self [...] The question should not be whether ad blocking is ethical, but whether it is a moral obligation. —James Williams[26]

For Williams, blocking ads is self-defence, something almost required if we're to regain control of our attention and lives.

How about potential negative impacts for the user? Since this is an advanced hack, it might be frustrating to implement, and you might break everything if you get it wrong. There's a risk of annoyance, but for the user this is a net utilitarian positive.

Your hack might save advertisers a few dollars – you can't act on the ads if you can't see them – but otherwise it's a net negative for them. Advertisers will lose brand awareness and potential sales, although if you're inclined to block ads, perhaps you weren't going to click anyway.

The impact on the manufacturer is mixed. You already have the device, and applying the hack will improve your experience and maybe increase your lock-in to their brand. The manufacturer keeps you as a customer and can still use your valuable data with your consent. However, they lose the chance to be compensated. It's probably a net loss, but not so clear a loss as for the advertisers.

Remember that utilitarians ask whether an action maximises society's net happiness, which means balancing competing interests. This tends to get political. If public happiness goes up but corporate revenue is damaged, is that a net good? In our ad-blocking case it's unclear, but since only a few people will install this demanding hack, the harm to advertisers and the manufacturer is negligible. A handful of ad avoiders won't cause cause the company's employees any real loss of happiness.

The complexity of business and capitalism can act as buffer for utilitarian discussions: it's hard to argue a multinational feels pain at losing a few hundred dollars, although things become more tangible if people start losing their bonuses or jobs. A broader question is whether society itself is hurt by people opting out of commercial agreements; either way, however, a utilitarian might decide the hack is just about ethically permissible. If the hack were easy to apply, things could well be different. The harms would escalate steeply if half the user base blocked ads: a technology's usability can change its utilitarian impact.

The deontological argument proceeds rather differently. Is there any moral duty at stake? Yes: you arguably have a duty to honour your promises. You agreed to give advertisers and the manufacturer your data and attention when you installed the device, but you now want to wriggle out of that agreement by withholding your attention. What if everyone did what you're about to do? If everyone blocked ads, the manufacturer would have to either withdraw the hub or charge consumers directly, potentially increasing technological inequality. Worse, you'd establish a precedent that it's fine to avoid paying your fair share.

How about our other deontological test: are we treating people as means or ends? Again, installing the hack is arguably treating others as means: you're using the manufacturer's technology for your own gain, and the advertisers as a means to get it for free, with no intention of reciprocation. Some activists would accurately counter that the ad industry has for years treated consumers as means rather than ends, but that's hardly relevant to this particular act. For a deontologist, hacking the hub is probably unethical.

The choice looks quite different from the two ethical perspectives. Utilitarians emphasise the consequences – pretty minor in this case – while deontologists are more concerned by the nature of the act itself and its contradiction of moral duty. Either view is valid, of course, although you might find yourself more convinced by one than the other. If so, you've taken your first steps towards understanding your preferred ethical stance. You might even disagree with my arguments and conclusions. This is the complex, often frustrating nature of ethics: there are often several plausible answers. Ethical theories aren't tools so much as lenses through which to see the world. It's not possible to simply crank the handle and see what results; ethics is more about asking the right questions and discussing the responses. The journey is often as relevant as the destination.

A fairer exchange

Let's return to our data utopia: a fair exchange in which people consent to swap a little personal data for access to valuable technology. How could this come about?

First, the tech industry has to be realistic about the true value of its work. It's unsustainable for companies to demand more data without offering more genuinely useful technology. Overestimating the value of technology will always threaten the prospect of fair exchange; a company that believes it offers something truly revolutionary will probably demand grave privacy sacrifices in exchange. Realism, humility, and a deep understanding of real-world benefit will reduce the risk of imbalance.

Technologists should also consider data and algorithms as inexorably entwined. Data collection can feel abstract, divorced from its effects, but any conversation about how data is gathered must also ask what the data will be used for. Although I've split the two topics across separate chapters, in practice algorithmic harms typically have their roots in data harms.

> When I hear 'is it ethical to build AI applications that do X on some massively aggregated database', I want to ask whether it was ethical to massively aggregate that database in the first place. —Matt Blaze[27]

But perhaps the key to fair data exchange is to treat data as a material, not as magic. Magic is a seductive metaphor for technology; designers are so eager to delight the customer and minimise user effort it's tempting to conclude technology should work almost supernaturally. But magic is about withholding information, concealing the mechanisms of a trick. The idea that technology should be magical dissuades people from investigating how it works; in the information vacuum that results, people can't make informed decisions. Artist James Bridle: 'Those who cannot perceive the network cannot act effectively within it, and are powerless.'

In a fair data exchange, users should know how their technologies extract data and move it through the network. Privacy policies aren't enough: they're legal tools, not communication tools. It's surely better to highlight data flows within the products themselves. Some people label this 'data transparency', but I think this is precisely the wrong framing. Instead of making data transparent, we should *materialise* it. Only by pulling data into the visible spectrum, by giving form to the previously spectral, can we help users understand it. Materialising data also makes it easier for people to intervene if the system is gathering unwanted or incorrect information.

Technology today does a poor job at materialising data. Voice assistants flounder with straightforward data protection questions like 'What do you know about me?' or 'Where do you store my data?' A simple summary, with a link to a more detailed explanation, would help build trust and data literacy. A lot of today's graphic visualisations are flattened, reducing complex data flows to a single icon or graph, or providing granular readouts only after the event.

Android Oreo's data usage screen (left) shows net consumption in megabytes; useful for predicting your phone bill, but no help in ensuring that data is fairly traded. The location history screen in iOS 11 (right) provides a more granular data breakdown, but only, of course, in retrospect.

Immaterials: WiFi Light Painting (2011) by Timo Arnall, Jørn Knutsen and Einar Sneve Martinussen. Reprinted with kind permission.

In their *Immaterials* project, Timo Arnall, Jørn Knutsen and Einar Sneve Martinussen materialise urban Wi-Fi through 'light painting'. The pattern is made by connecting a tall pole strung with LEDs to a Wi-Fi detector, and taking meticulous signal measurements at fixed intervals. Long-exposure photographs capture the field strength along city streets, creating a snapshot that beautifully exposes the complex, unseen data infrastructure that permeates our world, with its spikes, dead zones, and gradients. These photographs help us understand that digital space and physical space are one, and engage our curiosity about what else is happening beyond our thresholds of perception.

> As we increasingly inhabit technical systems, and enact society and culture through them, it seems dangerous to have so little idea about how these things work. Making visible material out of technological infrastructure is the first step towards understanding them. What we can't see, we cannot critically evaluate. —Timo Arnall[28]

Could we draw inspiration from this work, and iOS's granular location breakdown, to offer a real-time snapshot of data's status and movement? If users could see a representation of the data swirling around them at any moment – or an overview of the data exchanges they're about to enter into – they'd be better able to associate their actions to clear data consequences and make more informed choices.

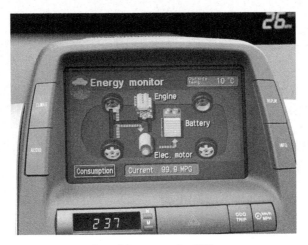

Toyota Prius energy monitor, 2003.

Perhaps the closest analogue to this snapshot today is a hybrid car's dashboard energy monitor. This view skilfully shows how another invisible entity – energy – moves through the car, showing direction of flow, rate of change, and reserves. The monitor gives instant feedback based on the driver's actions, helping the driver better understand how the car uses energy, and promoting a driving style that will improve economy. Let's try a similar layout for our imaginary smart home hub.

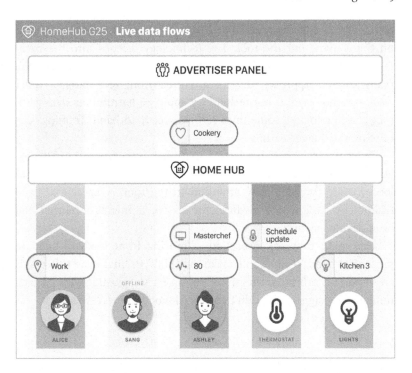

By showing how data worms its way through the system, this dashboard lets our hypothetical users know what data the system is collecting, what inferences the hub has made, and which data flows are active at present. It also depicts which devices are communicating with the hub – allowing debugging if things aren't working as expected – and lets family members drill down on individual data flows to quickly correct or remove them. The dashboard goes some way to ensuring a fairer exchange: users see exactly what data they are trading in exchange for the hub's utility. The hub can't simply grab as much data as it wants; instead, it relies on understanding and consent.

A screen may not be the best canvas for this materialisation; it may be better to overlay data on the real world using augmented reality. Whatever the interface, the ethical value of exposing data flows should be clear. Not only can users better understand the agreement they're entering, but they can also spot potential risks more easily.

Sometimes these risks deserve to be highlighted. In Martin Heidegger's elaborate terminology,[29] designers typically seek to make technologies that are *ready-to-hand*. In this state, the user is focused on the activity, not the tool. The technology recedes into the background: we think through the hammer to the nail. By its nature, a ready-to-hand approach diverts attention from technology's inner workings; however, if the technology could be harmful, as data-gathering technologies sometimes are, a ready-to-hand framing can obscure the danger within.

By contrast, a tool that is *present-at-hand* is (paraphrasing Heidegger) one we mentally bump into. If the head of the hammer comes loose, we're forced to pay attention to the tool. A present-at-hand technology isn't just a medium for action: it invites attention and even circumspection.

Designing to break user flow – moving from ready-to-hand to present-at-hand, from 'don't make me think' to 'make me think' – is an important ethical strategy. To stop users sleepwalking into a data minefield, designers shouldn't reduce friction but increase it.

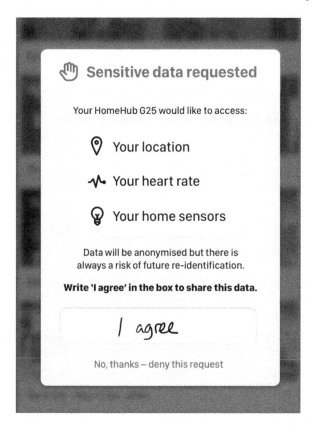

This consent interface contradicts basic usability principles by adding friction. The technology becomes present-at-hand, demanding attention and making it harder for the user to numbly surrender highly personal information.

High-friction transactions and real-time data snapshots might help level the data playing field, but simply exposing data flows doesn't necessarily make them equitable. A system can expose its data-gathering activities while those activities are still nakedly unfair. It's remarkable how many harmful data practices are already widespread in the tech industry. There can be no hope of fair data exchange while apps casually demand entire address books or ask people to share their locations even when the apps are closed. Even previous consent doesn't always ethically absolve a data harvester. The Cambridge Analytica scandal showed that practices that were once tolerated – such as giving apps access to your entire friend network – can be shocking in later years. As the public's data literacy has grown and data harms have become more obvious, privacy expectations have shifted, making Facebook's previous decisions look irresponsible. Consent notwithstanding, the company arguably failed in its duty of care towards users.

Rawls's veil of ignorance can be useful here. To design fair systems we should pretend we don't know the role we'll assume in the system. Would we be as happy with the user's end of the bargain as the advertiser's end? What if we were a user from an underrepresented group, or one who has previously suffered data discrimination and redlining?

Self-ownership and pocket AI

If we squint, we can see the course of computing as an oscillation between near and far.[30] The hulking mainframe begat the desktop PC, spawning the global internet; mobile then made the internet personal, before cloud computing took over. The cloud is, of course, a convenient euphemism, shorthand for 'other people's computers'. Wherever data originates, it's usually processed centrally, in data centres stacked with GPU-heavy servers.

This centralisation causes many of today's privacy risks: once data evaporates off a user's device, it tends to disappear in the mist. Perhaps the pendulum will swing once more to local technology. As portable devices become more powerful and machine-learning hardware gets cheaper, computing may start to decentralise again. Instead of pouring data into vast private reservoirs, users could hold it safely on their own devices, manage it with consumer-friendly wallet apps, and license it to others as desired. This would eliminate vulnerable central data repositories and instead give users the power to grant, withdraw, and audit data consent at will. Combine this with *pocket AI* approaches that promise all AI training and inference is handled on-device, and this starts to look like a privacy campaigner's utopia. The user has complete control, with minimal data transfer and less risk of invisible exploitation. Not only that, but the resulting systems will have lower latency and work offline too.

Data ownership and on-device processing is a beautiful dream, but one that may never fully come true. Ownership is rarely binary; the data drama inevitably involves many actors. Some transactions make it impossible to refuse data exchange – tax authorities and doctors, for example, need our information to treat us correctly – and swathes of personal data lie outside our control, in friends' contact lists, state-owned CCTV footage, or employers' files. Even simple tasks generate competing data claims. If I charge my electric car, does the charging data – kWh used, charge duration, capacity – belong to me, the car manufacturer, or my energy provider?

Decentralising data may also fragment it and decrease its utility. Data is far more valuable at scale, as analyst Benedict Evans points out:

> Any individual human probably only contributes a millionth of the data needed to be useful for any one task [...] These data points matter only in aggregate of millions, to 4–5 unrelated companies. How would I 'own' them? What on earth would I do with them?[31]

Pocket AI is still a way off. While there are encouraging moves towards on-device processing – face recognition in Apple's Photos happens entirely on user devices, and Google is placing it at the heart of its AI efforts – machine-learning tasks like speech recognition and computer vision are computationally hungry. Training a deep neural network can take days even on a powerful server. Until personal devices, limited by size and battery power, can do both inference and training themselves, decentralisation may hamper AI innovation. The best hope may lie in *federated learning*, which asks devices to combine forces for training, while keeping data on individual devices.

The data-ownership utopia could also spell trouble for ad-funded services. Data licensing would allow some users – likely the richest – to opt out of targeted advertising, crushing advertising rates and potentially threatening the whole model's viability. A bring-your-own-data world could precipitate a two-tier digital society in which the rich pay for privacy, while the masses have to hand over their data. To an extent, the smartphone market is already heading this way, with the iPhone positioned as a high-end privacy-first device and Android offering a more affordable but looser data ecosystem. The idea of privacy as a luxury good should worry us, since it helps only the already powerful.[32] Add the user experience challenges of a decentralised world – will mainstream users tolerate the storage costs and fiddly hygiene tasks for such nebulous benefit? – and full decentralisation seems implausible.

It's likely instead we'll end up with some combination of on- and off-device storage and processing. Android handsets already perform rough speech recognition locally, then send the audio to the cloud for increased accuracy. If training remains too tough for a mobile device, desktop-like machines may yet have a future as personal servers, processing data and training AI on behalf of the user's other devices. The tasks are better suited to the device, but everything still sits under the user's control, with no data going to the cloud.

Portability and differential privacy

For now, data portability may be a likelier bet than ownership. Offering users a way to download and reuse their personal data may help re-establish a sense of control and equality; however, it won't be an easy sell to the tech giants. Data portability makes it easier for consumers to switch providers, meaning businesses are generally reluctant to offer it. Portability will probably only gain traction if required by law; GDPR, for example, makes some basic data portability demands.

Most tech firms would rather retain valuable data centrally but reassure users that centralisation is safe. As such, they may use techniques like *differential privacy*, which adds a measurable amount of statistical noise by swapping out questions for others that have known response rates ('What month were you born in?'). User data is therefore blurred before it reaches the server and, since there's no way to know which users were asked which questions, re-identification becomes harder.

Apple is particularly keen on differential privacy, using it first to analyse keyboard and emoji use, and then to safeguard browsing history and health data. Some analysts, however, doubt whether Apple is living up to its differential privacy promises. The effectiveness of differential privacy depends on how much detail a company is willing to sacrifice, encapsulated by an 'epsilon value', essentially a measure of privacy loss. Researchers found Apple was using weaker epsilon values than expected and, unlike competitors, keeps these values secret, meaning it's hard to know just how well private data is obscured.[33] Frank McSherry, one of the inventors of differential privacy, was scathing: 'Apple has put some kind of handcuffs on in how they interact with your data. It just turns out those handcuffs are made out of tissue paper.'[34] Apple in turn has rejected the researchers' findings as incomplete.

Apple is at least making good strides with other privacy-enhancing technologies. Hardware and OS manufacturers are ideally placed to change the world's data and security practices. Software-based PETs, like password managers and two-factor authentication, are essentially failing as consumer technologies – fewer than 1% of Dropbox users, for example, are rumoured to use two-factor – but moving PETs to the device is enormously effective. Apple's Touch ID sensors helped iOS passcode use to leap from a paltry 49% to 89%,[35] and end-to-end encryption has become an essential component of iMessage and Face-Time, along with third-party services like Signal.

Almost every PET creates antagonism. Safari's intelligent tracking prevention protocols limit third-party cookies, to the delight of loyal users but to the rage of advertisers, who snarl that Apple has sabotaged the economics of the internet. Governments and police forces repeatedly beg tech companies to weaken their security measures in the name of national security; anti-encryption laws may follow. Privacy fights tend to require taking a side.

The nuclear no-data option

On-device processing and differential privacy are promising techniques, but like any technological approach, they carry the risk of whitewashing data practices that are still harmful. Jathan Sadowski gloomily predicts that cybersecurity 'only postpones catastrophic failure'. Zeynep Tufekci contends that meaningful individual consent is simply impossible, since people are clueless about how companies will manipulate their data now and in the future.

It's right to ask how we can handle user data safely, but there's a fundamental question: should we gather user data at all? Some companies have decided the costs and risks aren't worth it. If data becomes a toxic liability, the best strategy is to not handle it at all. In 2017, British pub chain Wetherspoons deleted its entire email database. This may not have been an entirely noble act, however: two years previously, the company lost 650,000 customer records in a data breach. Some analysts speculated that database problems had caused Wetherspoons to lose consent records, prompting the company to abandon email marketing altogether rather than go through the huge process of re-establishing consent.

The nuclear no-data option is easier for a pub chain than a tech firm, but choosing not to collect data is the best possible guard against re-identification, and, whether as an act of safety or protest, carries significant political meaning. Ethically minded technologists should consider refusing data collection if they think it will be used prejudicially, or could harm users if seized by authorities. For example, racial data can be used to perpetuate bias; there may be a case for not collecting this data – and any other data that could be used to re-identify or interpolate race – if it would reduce that risk. No one can hand over data they never had to begin with. Perhaps we should see data through the developer's lens of progressive enhancement: good software should work fine without data, and work even better with it.

Data refuseniks are essentially applying the *precautionary principle*. A formalised version of 'better safe than sorry', the precautionary principle reverses the onus of proof, and permits action only if we're sure it can't cause harm. High-risk fields like environmental protection, medicine, and food safety tend to default to precautionary stances, but the principle runs against the disruptive grain of the tech industry and would mostly be a needless drag on decision-making. However, where there's a significant prospect of harm, the precautionary principle may still have its place.

Privacy as strategy

It's important to see data ethics not just as a matter of reducing security or compliance risk, but also as a seed of innovation and a competitive advantage. This is Apple's approach today. By going long on privacy and placing PETs at the heart of their offering and marketing, Apple hopes to differentiate against Google and, to a lesser extent, Facebook and Amazon.

While it's about time a major tech firm positioned itself as a privacy advocate, some of Apple's rhetoric falls into tired surveillance capitalism traps, and it rather misrepresents their competitors' stances. It's hard not to be a touch sceptical of this weaponisation of ethics. As analyst Ben Thompson suggests, it's no accident Apple's ethical stance benefits its business, which is all about high-margin hardware sales rather than reach and data monetisation.

> I am far more impressed when a company does something according to its 'values' and 'principles' when it runs in opposition to its business model than I am when the company's business model makes it easy to score PR points.[36]

Apple and similar privacy-focused companies are the prime beneficiaries of data ethics scandals; the greater the public and press backlash, the easier a privacy strategy becomes. Today, Apple is seen as behind on AI; it must hope its design and technological interventions will, in the long run, show it's already on the other shore.

Treating privacy and data properly has PR and marketing benefits, but it's also just good strategy. This is the crux of the *privacy by design* approach, created by Ann Cavoukian, then privacy commissioner of Ontario. Privacy by design establishes seven design principles for weaving ethical data approaches into a business:

1. Proactive not reactive; preventative not remedial
2. Privacy as the default setting
3. Privacy embedded into design
4. Full functionality – positive-sum, not zero-sum
5. End-to-end security – full life cycle protection
6. Visibility and transparency – keep it open
7. Respect for user privacy – keep it user-centric

Privacy by design is well established as voluntary best practice; GDPR requires companies to follow a similar process, showing they've considered data protection for EU citizens in the design phase. It therefore makes sense for tech firms to adopt privacy by design as a global standard. The alternative – creating separate systems for EU and non-EU citizens, bifurcating codebases and policies accordingly – will surely only appeal to companies who are threatened by privacy protections. Unsurprisingly, some data brokers have chosen this route, desperate to protect the parts of their businesses that rely on lax regulation; some ad-tech firms have chosen to wind down their European operations completely rather than adopt privacy by design. But for the ethical tech company, privacy and data ethics should be an obvious strategic bet.

Empowering the public

All these proposals are industry-centric; they can't alone provide all the answers. It's only right that the public should help set the course of our data world. Sadly, consumer acquiescence contributes to the worst abuses. Unscrupulous companies (and governments; see chapter 6) get away with misusing data because they meet little popular resistance. This isn't the public's fault. Press coverage of data issues is so drab, the violations so endless, and the options for recourse so few that the public has shrugged off the issue. While there are lingering worries about what happens to personal data, most people aren't sure of the implications beyond identity theft, itself an abstract concept covering a range of frauds.

It doesn't help to believe the public ought to be furious at the modern data condition; while we should always guard against data abuse, fair and consensual data exchange can still put valuable tech in the hands of billions. Technologists would be shooting themselves in the foot if they caused a backlash against all data-driven innovation. It will be better to address the causes of public data lethargy.

Chief among these is lack of understanding; the most effective way to engage the public is to help build data knowledge and confidence. Materialising data will help, as will offering PETs and explaining their value. But we should also try to build awareness through education and news. Technologists need to highlight data issues beyond security; there's more to the topic than images of padlocks. We should try to build a convincing public and political narrative about the role of data in our future society, covering data's growing importance and value ('Are you being fairly compensated?'), the risks that implied and aggregated data can create, and the threat of algorithmic injustice caused by data abuse.

One way to do this is through the political process. Concerned technologists can help shape national data policy by contributing to consultations, writing to representatives, or even standing for office. For those less politically inclined, there's still plenty of technology to build. PETs such as ad blockers (if ethical!), anonymisers, burner accounts, encryption software, and tools for automating requests under data protection law will all boost public awareness and resilience. And there'll always be a need for alternatives to data-extracting services, to serve as shining examples of how data and privacy can be treated fairly.

Chapter 5

Seeing through new eyes

Until recently, we assumed that for machines to understand the physical world, the world would have to volunteer its information. We'd need both human mapmakers – information architects and other masters of taxonomy and labelling – and a range of self-describing, self-reporting objects ('spimes') that continually broadcast their status.

That no longer seems necessary. As mediation theory suggests, every innovation gives us new ways to interpret the world. Emerging technologies are increasingly able to unilaterally extract information from the physical world, dragging the previously unseen out of the shadows.

Computer vision

Cameras will be the next decade's most important input device, ever cheaper and smaller, mounted in personal devices, in our living rooms, on drones, and on our streets. One firm estimates there will be 45 billion by 2022, a 220% increase in just five years. Splash the cash and you can buy daily satellite footage of anywhere on earth; soon, wearable cameras will stream from millions of faces, and autonomous vehicles will record the city from every angle. We will soon have so many perspectives on almost any event that it'll be noteworthy to learn where cameras are not; likely the sites of society's darkest secrets: abattoirs, landfill sites, and the meeting rooms of the powerful.

Computer vision, the act of turning this footage into structured data, may prove to be the information era's killer app. Machines have known how to recognise barcodes, text, and numbers for years; they are now about to fully open their eyes.

Facial recognition is already remarkably accurate in the right contexts. Facebook's DeepFace system is 97% accurate when deciding whether two photos are of the same person, and many providers claim near-human levels of precision. Several facial recognition startups are valued at over $1 billion; some, such as Megvii, have privileged access to the Chinese government's dataset of 1.3 billion faces. There are still severe challenges to overcome, however. MIT researcher Joy Buolamwini found many facial recognition tools are biased, misidentifying 1% of lighter-skinned men, but 35% of darker-skinned women,[1] and accuracy rates touted by insiders only apply under specific conditions. Facebook's photo-tagging algorithms, for example, have the advantage of enormous training datasets and prior knowledge of people's friend networks, and face recognition systems sold for security often require users to stare directly into a camera. It's not yet possible to recognise faces across an entire city; the processing and storage capabilities are too great, and older CCTV cameras are too low-resolution. Nevertheless, recognition capabilities will only grow with time.

Many tech firms, seeing gold in the computer vision hills, are desperate to persuade users to consent to facial processing. GDPR treats biometrics as 'special category' data, meaning users must freely give explicit consent, except for a few cases in the public interest, like policing. Tech companies will therefore have to dangle particularly appealing benefits in front of users; fortunately for them, computer vision unlocks a wealth of innovative uses.

Of course, computer vision can codify not just faces but also entire environments. Lidar – essentially radar but using light pulses – can help machines map their surroundings, and is critical to most autonomous vehicle systems. In time, billions of artificial eyes will throw bounding boxes around road signs, ashtrays, and seagulls alike. Today, $249 will buy you 'The world's first deep learning enabled video camera for developers', with free shipping and some assembly required. The top customer question 'Will this detect hot dogs?' is answered simply: 'Yes'.

Listening machines

Machines are also becoming adept listeners. In 1952, Audrey ('automatic digit recognizer') could recognise digits spoken by its owner, but it took the advent of Markov prediction models and cloud processing for accuracy to really accelerate. Now that any device can access powerful processing and make an educated guess about what might come up next, major speech recognition platforms have accuracy above 95%.

In theory, speech is an excellent way to communicate with machines. It's fast – around 150 words per minute, compared to a typing average of 40 – and personal, well suited to the narrowing gap between humans and technology. However, speech has limitations. Voice interfaces force the user to remember commands, ambiguity is a problem, and accents, dialects, and intonation muddy the waters further.

Astonishingly, audio recognition doesn't need audio. A lip-reading algorithm from Oxford University and DeepMind researchers correctly recognised 46.8% of words in BBC news clips: far more accurate than a professional lip-reader.[2] Researchers have discovered that sensitive smartphone gyroscopes respond to external noise, allowing a snooper to eavesdrop on nearby conversations without requesting OS microphone permissions,[3] and a 2014 MIT study reconstructed a song played in a soundproofed room by analysing high-speed video of a pot plant twitching to the music.[4]

No surprise, then, that computer listening spawns some anxious conspiracies. The rumour that Facebook is snooping through our phones' microphones, listening for our darkest secrets so it can tailor better ads, is particularly resilient. Despite Facebook's denials and a gaping lack of evidence, it's an understandable neurosis. In 2017, security researchers revealed they'd discovered 234 Android apps 'constantly listening for ultrasonic beacons in the background without the user's knowledge';[5] two years prior, Samsung admitted their smart TVs were sharing audio with unnamed third parties. Manufacturers retort that they only process audio on request – usually following a wake word such as 'Alexa' or 'Hey, Siri', or a button press – and always provide feedback, such as a microphone icon or lit LED. In the invisible world of data interchange, it's hard to verify these claims. Users have to rely on blind trust.

The future for voice recognition, beyond reducing errors and colonising more homes with smart speakers, is recognition that's ubiquitous and seamless. No longer tied to a home device or handset, listening assistants become ambient services. Once technology can overcome the so-called cocktail party effect and learn to disentangle multiple voices, we can imagine assistants soon escaping their magic lamps and becoming disembodied avatars that follow us out of our homes into the public realm: the street, the office, the bar.

Talking with machines

Since machines are listening, we might as well strike up a conservation. Lab-generated machine speech is now barely distinguishable from humans, and conversational engines can make a computer whisper, pause, or vary its pitch on demand. As well as the implications for information credibility, fabricated speech also poses tough questions about the ethics of anthropomorphism. We'll get to these later.

Machine conversation can have curious effects on humans. Spend time with a voice assistant and you'll find that stilted phrases often work better than full sentences, and you'll quickly learn to set an alarm for forty-nine minutes, not the easily misheard fifty.

> People speak to machines differently than how they speak to people. They move into a different register. If you're standing next to somebody in an airport or at a bus stop or something, you can typically tell when they're talking to a machine rather than talking to a person. —Alan Black[6]

There's nothing new about humans moulding their behaviours around technology. For decades we've gesticulated at bathroom light sensors and grunted at call centre menus, and in search engine optimisation we've created a whole professional field that makes human communication more attractive to the algorithm. But verbal optimisation might also spread to human-to-human communication, particularly when it's conveyed through technology. Many messaging and email apps now offer prefabricated, predictive replies: 'Sounds good to me', 'Thanks for the info!' These are framed as convenient suggestions; a user has full control to write their own reply. But it's easy to imagine a voice-based system that, constrained by the medium, offers only these ready-made responses. It'll no doubt be efficient, but it could impoverish communication. These conversational systems will likely be trained on large corpora of text and replies from other users; unless this training data is linguistically and dialectally diverse, irregular phrases could be squeezed out of our speech. Over time, we'll learn to strip colloquialisms from our commands, and the machines will in turn respond in standardised dialects. Having trained ourselves to communicate in machine-readable ways, we may see the emergence of a Bay Area English lingua franca that slowly erodes linguistic diversity.

The datafied body

Our bodily data is also up for grabs. Networked scales, smart toothbrushes, and sleep-monitoring mattresses silently document the sins of the flesh, fitness wearables measure our vital signs like heart rate and blood oxygen, and our personal devices increasingly reveal our locations. A Facebook patent describes using phone accelerometers and gyroscopes to calculate not just when two people are standing together, but also who is facing whom.[7] In a 2016 trial, Transport for London tracked smartphones by MAC address to understand commuter routes through the London Underground, unearthing route information the entry-and-exit payment system couldn't determine. Some 0.1% of passengers, presumably gripped by dark spirits or mind-blowing psychotropics, travelled between King's Cross and Waterloo by way of the Central line.[8]

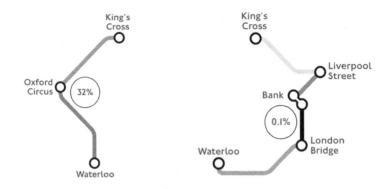

While these bodily data points may seem inconsequential in isolation, even trivial information becomes revelatory when combined with other datasets and tracked over a long time. And once more we may not need the devices for long. A fleet of facial recognition cameras will soon be all we need to track someone's location and, as a bonus, find out who they went for coffee with. It's already possible to detect someone's pulse[9] and extract their fingerprint patterns[10] from high-definition footage. As resolutions grow and specialist hardware creeps into the consumer market – basic thermal cameras now cost under $200 – cameras are increasingly looking into us, not just at us.

Our bodies are also vectors of emotional information. The distasteful promises of neuromarketing – using brain scans and skin probes to measure emotional response when someone sees a particular brand – get more intrusive when combined with algorithmic extraction. Dozens of tech firms claim they can quantify emotion from text, images, video, and speech, and the technology is already used widely in the gaming, advertising, and security industry. In 2017, a leaked Facebook Australia document claimed the company could detect when a young user felt 'worthless', 'stupid', or 'insecure'. The company's PR team defended the technology, arguing it was never meant to be used for ad targeting.

The hypermap

We can imagine ourselves soon being able to quantify the whole world, turning its people, objects, and properties into structured, actionable information. No need to stick QR codes or RFID patches on every physical object; computer vision and listening, combined with massive outpourings of device data, will map the world at a distance and by force. In a fully recognised, codified, and labelled world, we will know exactly what everything is, and exactly where everything is. We can even imagine some way to bounce, Matrix-like, between these two views: atoms and information. Let's call this environment of total metadata a *hypermap*.

A hypermapped world is swollen with potential. Nothing would ever be lost again, from car parts to car keys to car thieves. Our bodies will become our identification at our front doors, at the departure gate, and when moving money. Cameras will monitor drivers for fatigue and assembly lines for defects, and recognise illness before we even feel the symptoms. Unknown places will become immediately more familiar, overlaid with translations and context for the traveller. And the hypermap needn't be constrained to the present; by examining historical images, video, and audio, computers can structure the past. Stretching across time, the hypermap could redefine our histories in ways we'd never have dreamt up.

The possibilities are deeply ambivalent, and should inspire both excitement and fear. Every upside of the hypermap could be harmful in a different context: a technology perfect for catching criminals is also ideal for surveillance, and a world of perfect information is a world ripe for totalitarianism. Combine a hypermap with powerful persuasive technologies and we can imagine connected technologies that resist political dissenters in both dangerous and petty ways. Your devices report your every word to the police, of course, but your airfares are also tripled, and even your toaster burns your breakfast as punishment for your aberrant views.

The hypermap itself is, of course, never fully achievable; there will always be blind spots. But as a future object even partly realised, the hypermap poses profound ethical questions. Even a partially hypermapped world will feed predictive and autonomous systems: sensing the world is a necessary step before acting within it. While the label 'artificial intelligence' isn't always helpful – it mythologises tech as a new species, a self-directed moral agent outside our control – learning algorithms scouring the hypermap will doubtless transform our understanding of the world. Computer vision systems can already predict voting trends from Google Street View, using truck-to-sedan ratio as a political proxy;[11] similar systems are now making other, more damaging inferences.

Neo-physiognomy

In 2017, Stanford researchers Michal Kosinski and Yilun Wang made an astonishing claim: they had trained a machine-learning system to purportedly tell gay and straight people apart on sight. Kosinski and Wang claimed the system was 81% accurate for men and 74% accurate for women, and linked their findings with the controversial stance that orientation has a biological basis, rooted in prenatal hormone exposure.

> Gay faces tended to be gender atypical. Average landmark locations revealed that gay men had narrower jaws and longer noses, while lesbians had larger jaws. Composite faces suggest that gay men had larger foreheads than heterosexual men, while lesbians had smaller foreheads than heterosexual women.[12]

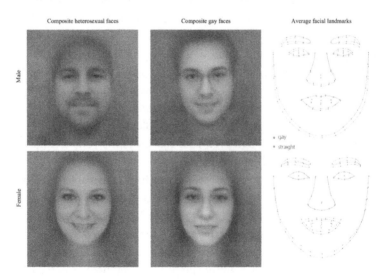

Composite faces of straight and gay people, from Kosinski and Wang's study. Reprinted with permission of the APA.

In centuries past, the idea that someone's face reveals their traits and character was known as *physiognomy*; today it's widely dismissed as bigoted pseudoscience. Kosinski and Wang's research – which quickly became known as the 'gaydar study' – attracted fierce criticism, with peers and activists alike decrying it as junk science and a regrettable revival of physiognomy. Some reviewers attacked what they saw as methodological flaws, such as the study's apparent disregard of grooming and self-presentation, while Oberlin College sociologist Greggor Mattson condemned the study's 'hermetic resistance to any contributions from the fields of sociology, cultural anthropology, feminism, or LGBT studies.'

> [Kosinski and Wang] think that nose shape and cheekbones are fixed landmark contours; if they'd ever met a drag queen, they'd know contour is a verb. There is a stunning assumption here: that dating site photos and profiles are unmediated, unmanipulated, accurate facsimiles of the real body (tl;dr they're not).[13]

Gay-recognising technology is patently dangerous. Dozens of countries still imprison people solely for their sexual orientation; some victims are put to death. Extremists in Islamic State-controlled territory and Chechnya have entrapped gay men and tortured and killed them: it is not hard to imagine the atrocities this technology could precipitate in the hands of homophobic militants.

The Diagnostic and Statistical Manual of Mental Disorders (DSM) listed homosexuality as a disorder until 1973, and prior to 1996 the Dewey decimal classification often caused library books on LGBTQ culture to sit under the headings of 'abnormal psychology' or 'social problems'.[14] The gaydar study marks a regressive step in sexual classification, undermining decades of effort to humanise gay people as valid members of society.

Kosinski is widely known in the world of profiling. He's part of the team behind the Facebook micro-targeting experiment mentioned in chapter 3, and has been linked to security firm Faception, whose site boasts about their recognition technology, asking, 'What if it was possible to know whether an anonymous individual is a potential terrorist, an aggressive person, or a potential criminal?' Although Kosinski has downplayed these links, he clearly sees other applications for neo-physiognomic technology. In a puff piece on the gaydar study, the *Economist* reported 'With the right datasets, Dr Kosinski says, similar AI systems might be trained to spot other intimate traits, such as IQ or political views.'[15]

The authors have robustly defended both their study and intentions, pointing out the research was cleared by Stanford's institutional review board. This is true. IRBs often underestimate the threat from machine-learning projects, since no humans are directly involved; this IRB decision is highly questionable, showing a lack of foresight into the technology's potential abuses. Kosinski and Wang also stressed they merely manipulated existing technologies rather than making anything new, and claimed they published their results to warn of the inherent dangers.

> We felt that there is an urgent need to make policymakers and LGBTQ communities aware of the risks that they are facing. Tech companies and government agencies are well aware of the potential of computer vision algorithm tools. We believe that people deserve to know about these risks and have the opportunity to take preventive measures.[16]

'If I don't do it, someone else will'

This takes us into classic ethical territory. Kosinski's argument is a variant of 'If I don't do it, someone else will', a common defence from people working on controversial projects. If the technology is going to get built regardless, is it better that Kosinski and Wang do it, rather than someone less ethically minded?

This is a fairly solid utilitarian defence. Some shady regime or company has doubtless built similar tools already, so perhaps we should be grateful for Kosinski's purported altruistic intent in bringing it to public attention: the harm to human happiness may be slightly lower. However, a deontologist will be sceptical. Surely it can't be right to celebrate the birth of harmful technology? We might reach for the generalisation test – what if everyone did what I'm about to do? – but philosopher David Lyons explains we have to phrase the question carefully. The world would certainly be worse if, say, we all started working for weapons companies, but Lyons claims a fair generalisation test would have to point out that if we refused, someone equally capable would accept.

Randy Cohen, former author of NYT column 'The Ethicist', is scathing of the 'If I don't...' defence. '"If I don't do it, someone else will" [does] not justify nefarious conduct. Someone else will do pretty much anything. I've met "someone else," and he's quite the little weasel.'[17] Cohen is right. We can't base our morality on a hypothetical other: our ethical choices are for us alone to make. To argue something will happen with or without you is to resign yourself to a sad position of preemptive powerlessness. Besides, the 'If I don't...' justification would surely excuse any heinous act.

> If we accept this as a justification, it is hard to see what acts, however otherwise wicked, could not be defended in the same way. The job of hired assassin, or controller of the gas supply at Belsen, or chief torturer for the South African Police, will surely be filled by someone, so it seems to make no difference to the total outcome whether I accept or refuse such a job. —Jonathan Glover[18]

We can also counter 'If I don't...' more generously by pointing to missed opportunities. If you're alert enough to be asking ethical questions, surely you can do something more positive than make dubious technology? Go ahead and leave the project for the next person in line; they'll probably do a morally average job, while you could do far more good elsewhere. The social signal of your principled refusal could in turn send ripples of positive influence through your peer groups.

A useful test we can apply to any questionable project is: 'Is there any situation in which this technology is beneficial?' I see no positive applications of the gaydar technology whatsoever. It offers potentially lethal side effects and zero benefit: as a pure harm, it should be obstructed on principle. Dangerous technology created as a warning is still dangerous technology. In the words of Bion of Borysthenes, two millennia ago: 'Boys throw stones at frogs in fun, but the frogs do not die in fun, but in earnest.'

If it can be dangerous to even discuss potentially harmful technology, doesn't this apply to speculative design too? Isn't there a risk that we introduce and normalise dangerous ideas to the very people capable of bringing them to life? There is indeed. In May 2018, a morally ambivalent design fiction escaped the walls of Alphabet's usually taciturn 'X' subsidiary, causing concern in the press.

> What happens when speculative design goes corporate? When the practice retreats behind the walls and NDAs of giant Silicon Valley companies, it loses its status as a public provocation and becomes instead something much more troubling. At its most disturbing, it's a way of giving a company's employees permission to think the unthinkable—to grapple with how omniscient and powerful that corporate entity might become. —Felix Salmon[19]

The could-it-be-beneficial test can be a helpful filter, and provides another reason to avoid pure speculative dystopias. But the episode should serve as a reminder that speculative design, provocatypes, and design fictions must be surrounded by proper ethical discussion and appropriately labelled as fiction, to avoid being confused for genuine plans in the event of a leak. Design fictions are not good artefacts to let loose unsupervised: the resulting conversation, not the artefact, is the point of the exercise.

The deadly seams

The hypermap will emerge piece by piece, and the algorithms that act on its knowledge won't spring to life fully formed. Automation will necessarily be incremental. Unfortunately, splitting duties between humans and machines can be fraught with danger. Particularly treacherous are moments of handover between the two: what I term the *deadly seams*. In *Designing Agentive Technology*, Chris Noessel dedicates a chapter to these handovers, calling them the 'Achilles heel of agentive systems'.[20] Let's look at the deadly seams in a modern context: self-driving cars.

Handover can happen in either direction. Passing control from human to computer is usually the lesser problem: the car can announce when it's ready to take over, ask the driver to confirm the switch if required, and confirm everything went well. There are a few failure states to consider, but this transfer should usually only happen in stable, safe conditions. The handover from computer to human, on the other hand, causes autonomous vehicle (AV) manufacturers profound difficulty. Recent data on California AV trials shows 'disengagements' per thousand miles ranged from an impressive 0.18 (Waymo, regarded as clear industry pacesetters) to an alarming 755 (Mercedes-Benz).[21]

The main danger with AV disengagements is they're slow and prone to catastrophic errors. University of Southampton academics found drivers took between 1.9 and 25.8 seconds to regain full control after a disengagement; drivers who were distracted took on average 1.6 seconds longer still.[22] It's worth noting that the first person killed in the driver's seat of a semi-autonomous vehicle, Joshua Brown, had ignored repeated warnings to keep his hands on the wheel.

The aviation industry is all too familiar with the dangers of disengagements. The mysterious crash of Air France 447, which dropped into the Atlantic in 2009, was finally explained as a chain of pilot errors following an unexpected disengagement. The plane's autopilot switched itself off while travelling through a heavy storm, putting the plane into a different mode of behaviour.

> Once the computer lost its airspeed data, it disconnected the autopilot and switched from normal law to 'alternate law,' a regime with far fewer restrictions on what a pilot can do. In alternate law, pilots can stall an airplane. —Jeff Wise[23]

Misreading their instruments, the pilots didn't adapt to this new mode, adamant a stall was impossible despite audible stall warnings. Human error may have brought down the aircraft, but the bungled transition to human control set off the spiral of mistakes.

The human on the receiving end of a disengagement might lack critical information or have even forgotten how to properly control the system. As Marshall McLuhan taught us, 'every extension is also an amputation'.[24] Surrounded by cosy automation, drivers' skills may wither with time. Without time at the wheel, drivers can't sharpen their situational awareness, their feel for the rhythm of traffic and the rules of the road.

Making the deadly seams safer is no easy task. There's a strong case that driving tests should focus more on disengagements in a semi-automated era, but we won't always be able to train the user. Some AV projects are exploring handing control to a supervision centre, where a trained human operator can handle emergency transitions remotely. But most of the focus is on designing safer handover. Noessel suggests phasing preemptive warnings if possible: an AV might first warn conditions are getting tricky, then announce it's nearing the limits of safe control, letting the driver take control manually or prepare for imminent disengagement. However, this won't be possible in emergencies, in which case the relinquishing system has to explain the threat unmistakably, succinctly, and without causing a startle response that often causes people to freeze. This is a phenomenal design challenge, requiring a delicate but crucial balance between too much and too little information. Designers tend to focus on visual highlighting, sound, and haptic rumbles to direct attention without dangerously overloading the driver.

Is better good enough?

Even without life-or-death risk, imperfect automation can still be treacherous. Just ask South Wales Police, which under freedom of information law had to confess that of 2,470 potential suspects their new facial recognition system had flagged, 92% were false positives.[25] Automate security systems and you'd better be sure they work. A BBC investigation found a reporter's brother was able to pass voice identification systems and access the reporter's bank accounts.[26]

At what point do a partially automated system's benefits outweigh the flaws? Is it enough for technology simply to outperform humans, or should we hold algorithms to a higher standard? Our two ethical frameworks give us a starting point. Remember that a utilitarian is concerned only with consequences, the net impact on human happiness or suffering. Even an imperfect automated system might be fairer, cheaper, or more reliable than humans, increasing justice and prosperity while reducing drudgery. These benefits should be compared to the potential harms and also to the status quo; in other words, the impact of *not* implementing the technology. Exercising our moral imagination with the help of provocatypes and design fictions might help, as will remembering to keep a broad view of stakeholders. AVs, for example, don't just affect drivers; they also affect pedestrians, insurers, urban planners, and even the environment, on the plausible assumption that autonomous vehicles will drive more economically.

The US highways agency, NHTSA, defines six levels of self-driving automation.

	Level 0 No Automation	Zero autonomy; the driver performs all driving tasks.
	Level 1 Driver Assistance	Vehicle is controlled by the driver, but some driving assist features may be included in the vehicle design.
	Level 2 Partial Automation	Vehicle has combined automated functions, like acceleration and steering, but the driver must remain engaged with the driving task and monitor the environment at all times.
	Level 3 Conditional Automation	Driver is a necessity, but is not required to monitor the environment. The driver must be ready to take control of the vehicle at all times with notice.
	Level 4 High Automation	The vehicle is capable of performing all driving functions under certain conditions. The driver may have the option to control the vehicle.
	Level 5 Full Automation	The vehicle is capable of performing all driving functions under all conditions. The driver may have the option to control the vehicle.

NHTSA levels of automation, based on an original framework from the Society of Automotive Engineers.

Most AV projects today run at levels 2 or 3 (L2/3), but context and conditions matter. An L3 car trained on sunny SoCal freeways will probably struggle on a slushy Moscow prospekt: the weather will have an impact, but traffic density and an unfamiliar local driving style may also force a semi-autonomous vehicle into timid passivity, creating hazards of its own.

A utilitarian argument suggests we should welcome even L2/L3 semi-automation. Since human error contributes to 90% of crashes,[27] any technology that reduces crashes will reduce harm. Tesla claims crashes went down by 40% after drivers installed its L2 Autopilot update, although this figure is hard to verify. Nevertheless, purely by reducing road deaths and injuries (the overwhelming utilitarian harm), semi-autonomous vehicles almost certainly increase the stock of happiness.

For other automated systems, the utilitarian case is murkier. Catching criminals using facial recognition, say, is good for society, but the huge false positive rate counterbalances the calculation. Thousands of people might stand falsely accused, threatening the integrity of policing and our concept of justice itself. Claims that checks and balances ensure the wrongly accused are swiftly absolved will be little comfort to Steven Talley, detained after facial forensics (albeit not software-based) wrongly identified him as a bank robbery suspect and who alleges police brutality during arrest left him with permanent hearing loss, four broken ribs, shattered teeth, and a fractured penis.[28]

A deontologist is more interested in the moral duties involved, and might argue that any new technology deserves heightened ethical focus. A deontologist will find it harder to knowingly release semi-automated products that pose new threats, whatever the net impact. Can it really be right to beta test with people's lives? Aren't there better ways to achieve the same goals without treating people as means for our own technological advancement?

Given the complexity of the debate, it's no surprise that AV teams have chosen a range of approaches. Shocked by videos of test drivers falling asleep in L2/3 cars, Waymo is determined to jump to L4 before making its technology public. Tesla, on the other hand, has chosen to incrementally update Autopilot software in cars already on the road, making Tesla drivers stewards of public AV tests at their own risk.

As a tiebreaker we might turn to Rawls's veil of ignorance. Perhaps semi-autonomy is best designed as if we don't know where we'll end up in the system. Would we be equally happy with an L2 driving project as, variously, a driver, a pedestrian or cyclist, a regulator, or an environmentalist? How about L4?

Thanks to the role of licensing, the AV market effectively operates under the precautionary principle. Companies need approval to test AVs on public roads – although Uber, being Uber, ran tests without permission, forcing Californian authorities to shut them down – meaning trials can't begin until the regulator is satisfied. Technologies like facial recognition are more loosely controlled and may slip through gaps in existing law. The default stance for computer vision technology is therefore to ship and ask questions later. This allows for rapid innovation, but the gaydar study also hints at pernicious side effects. There's now a growing campaign to regulate or even outlaw facial recognition before it's too late.

> Imagine a technology that is potently, uniquely dangerous—something so inherently toxic that it deserves to be completely rejected, banned, and stigmatized. Something so pernicious that regulation cannot adequately protect citizens from its effects. That technology is already here. It is facial recognition technology, and its dangers are so great that it must be rejected entirely. —Evan Selinger[29]

Regulators will probably tread softly, in which case they might at least prohibit tech companies from giving a false impression of automation capabilities. Autonomous systems wrap new powers in old clothing: an autonomous car looks like a regular car, and a facial recognition camera looks like a regular camera, but both are fundamentally different devices to what came before. The public must therefore be confident about what a system can and can't do. Tesla's decision to label its L2 technology 'Autopilot' recklessly exaggerates the system's abilities; it is a triumph of marketing over safety. Technologists have a responsibility to help people form accurate mental models of changing technologies. Many countries require toy guns to be brightly coloured, or at least have an orange tip, so people will know the capabilities of the weapon. There's a strong ethical case that smart and autonomous objects should be similarly distinguished, through either design or labelling, from their inert counterparts.

The trolley problem is a red herring

The highest levels of self-driving automation invoke a famous ethical problem. The *trolley problem*, first posed by Philippa Foot in 1967, asks us to imagine a runaway tram hurtling towards workers on the tracks.[30] The only way to stop it is to flick the points, diverting it to a new route but killing a different set of workers. Should you flick the switch to kill two workmen and save three? Most people say yes. The dilemma comes alive with the endless variants. Would you push a fat man off a bridge to stop the trolley and save everyone? Most people say no, seeing a moral difference between 'actively killing' and 'letting die'. Two workmen or one child? A criminal or a teacher?

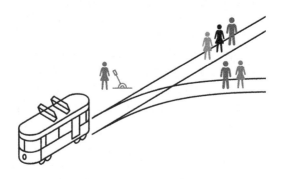

The trolley problem: you know the drill.

In a self-driving future, the thought experiment appears to become a real-world issue: AVs will have to choose whether to avoid a collision by risking another. As such, the trolley problem has become a poster child for tech ethics, featured in dozens of press articles and even emerging as a meme: Marx performs a 'multitrack drift' to eliminate the bourgeoisie; Camus ties himself existentially to the tracks. To understand public attitudes to the dilemma, MIT ran a crowd-sourcing study, Moral Machine. They found people generally applied utilitarian logic, choosing outcomes that harmed the fewest people. Should AVs therefore follow utilitarian principles?

Any autonomous driving decision has three steps. First, the vehicle must perceive and identify its environment, as we've discussed in this chapter. Anomalies make this tricky. Some objects are well defined – a bicycle always looks like a bicycle, a bus a bus – but some are amorphous. Is that litter or a dog? Will your system realise that a girl wearing a fancy-dress zebra costume is still a human?

The system then has to predict how these objects will move. Any identification mistake will be multiplied here: misclassify an object and it won't follow the path you expect. In March 2018, a level-2

Uber struck and killed Elaine Hertzberg, a pedestrian in Tempe, Arizona. The car first identified Hertzberg as an unknown object, then a vehicle, then a bicycle, each diagnosis causing different trajectory estimates.[31] Neither the car nor the safety driver – who had been streaming talent show *The Voice* in the minutes leading up to the crash – braked until after impact. At the time of writing, the legal case is ongoing.

The final step in the process is to choose and execute an action. Although the trolley problem raises its theoretical head here, the answer is usually simple. Andrew Chatham, principal engineer at Waymo, says 'It takes some of the intellectual intrigue out of the problem, but the answer is almost always "slam on the brakes".'[32] This approach makes improbable utilitarian calculus unnecessary. For an AV to take a utilitarian decision on the fly – act utilitarianism, you may recall – it would have to count each potential victim, estimate the age and occupation of each (Moral Machine participants preferred to protect younger and higher-status people), work out probability and severity of injury, then weigh up these harms for several courses of action: all before choosing how to act. A more plausible approach is to give AVs rule utilitarian instructions, a set of governing principles rooted in minimising harm, rather than asking the machine to work it out from scratch each time.

There's one final wrinkle to the utilitarian approach: a paper in *Science* found people would rather ride in cars that put their own safety above others'. Participants didn't want governments to enforce utilitarian AV logic, and were less willing to buy an AV regulated in this way.[33] While the trolley problem makes for fine think-pieces, it also sparks public fears – specifically, that as a passenger you might be sacrificed for the greater good – that could hamper AV adoption.

Focusing on the trolley problem distracts us from deeper ethical and social issues. Joanna Bryson astutely points out we already have the power to choose who gets hurt in a crash: just buy an SUV and you're twice as likely to kill any pedestrians you hit.[34] Ethicist John Danaher argues that the dilemma can also mask the dangers of bias. If your autonomous car struggles to recognise black people, it will hit more black people. Danaher makes the surprising suggestion that a touch of randomisation might reduce the impacts of structural discrimination.[35]

Autonomous driving will have a significant impact on cities; unfortunately, no one can quite agree what those impacts will be. Many urban planners are paralysed by uncertainty: is a new transit era imminent, or is the promise overblown? Venture capitalists with AV portfolio companies beg governors to suspend public transport spending and wait for the upcoming AV rapture but, in truth, adoption timescales are a mystery. All we know for sure is that organ donation will drop sharply if AVs live up to their potential: 20% of all donated organs in the US come from crash victims. The road ahead is strewn with unintended consequences.

Coexistence and companion species

Since the stirrings of the usability movement, designers have often concerned themselves with user efficiency. As automation takes hold, however, we won't so much use technologies as coexist with them. Even today, people are surprisingly eager to bond with artificial agents:

> I always assumed we would want to keep some distance between ourselves and AI, but I found the opposite to be true. People are willing to form relationships with artificial agents, provided they are a sophisticated build, capable of complex personalization. We humans seem to want to maintain the illusion that the AI truly cares about us.
> —Leisl Yearsley[36]

When the concept of a user breaks down, so does user-centred design. Emerging technologies aren't just products or tools: they're often physical entities acting semi-autonomously; in other words, robots. Designers have to plan not only how these robots look and behave, but also their intended position in society. Sci-fi tropes can be limiting here. As Google's Matt Jones suggests, it's all too easy to cram robots into existing power relationships, making them infantilised clones of humans or some sycophantic subspecies, eager to cater to human whims. Technologists have routinely exploited nonhumans in the name of progress: consider poor Laika dying in orbit, or Thomas Edison and Harold Pitney Brown electrocuting stray animals to show the dangers of alternating current. New forms of human–robot relationship could help us shed these unfortunate hierarchies and their associated abuses. Perhaps robots could accompany humans in symbiosis, rather than servitude?

Donna Haraway's *The Companion Species Manifesto* takes a lively and challenging look at true coexistence between two species, humans and dogs, that share an 'obligatory, constitutive, historical, protean relationship'.[37] Haraway's message is that true companionship involves mutual flourishing, a duet of response and respect between beings. Recognising that another species is not like us, Haraway contends, is the whole point: we should accept and embrace this difference, and understand that other species are important entities nevertheless. Haraway argues convincingly that becoming attuned to the needs of an Other helps us understand all the ways we can make a more liveable world for everyone and everything. Isn't that really the crux of ethics?

> I believe that all ethical relating, within or between species, is knit from the silk-strong thread of ongoing alertness to otherness-in-relation. We are not one, and being depends on getting on together. — Donna Haraway[38]

Umwelt

Other species experience a world unrecognisable to humans. We might think that colours stretch from red to violet, but the bees know differently, mesmerised by ultraviolet. Meanwhile, salmon can sense the Earth's magnetic field and use it to navigate vast oceans. In 1909, the biologist Jakob von Uexküll proposed the term *umwelt* to describe the sum of a creature's perceivable world. A being's umwelt depends on its senses. To a dog, the world is all scent and sound; a bat's night-time umwelt revolves around ultrasound. Each species lives in its own informational subset of the same world; as far as it knows, the world *is* what it can detect. The idea the world carries abundant imperceptible information should be familiar from our discussion of the invisible data world, the hypermap, and the extractive faculties of, say, computer vision.

Umwelt gives us new ways to think about coexistence. Humans already cater for the umwelt of companion species: we indulge dogs when they stick their snouts in the gutter; we enrich the lives of primates in captivity with tactile toys. Perhaps a good design principle for coexistence would be for each group to respect and enhance the other's life-world?

Robots can enrich the human umwelt by materialising the invisible, translating the things only they can perceive into a human-readable format. It follows that robots themselves should be legible. To live alongside robots we should be able to understand their behaviours and have clarity on who is accountable for their actions.

Coexistence should of course be two-way. Humans dictate the robot umwelt, at least for now. (Philosophers might gripe that a robot needs something like a mind, or at least senses, to have an umwelt, but you get the idea.) We decide which sensors to install, what data to feed to the algorithm. We too can materialise information that's otherwise invisible to robots, by creating a robot-readable world. We should provide them with rich, unbiased training data so they can form accurate models, and when they make faulty assumptions or mistakes, correct them swiftly. If we choose to develop robots as companion species, not mere tools, we might even see these choices as moral; perhaps working to expand umwelt is almost an act of kindness towards machines. If so, the data ethics issues we've already discussed are central not just to human flourishing but machine flourishing too.

We should recognise we've made a large and somewhat sentimental assumption here: that the flourishing of artificial intelligence is to be welcomed. Chapter 6 might rather discourage this view.

The social contract

Seventeenth-century philosopher Thomas Hobbes took a famously dim view of human character. Hobbes reasoned that without political authority humans would exist in a pure 'state of nature', enjoying unlimited freedom but enduring permanent conflict.

> In such condition, there is no place for industry; because the fruit thereof is uncertain [...] no arts; no letters; no society; and which is worst of all, continual fear, and danger of violent death; and the life of man, solitary, poor, nasty, brutish, and short. —Thomas Hobbes[39]

To stave off this dystopia, we enter into a wordless pledge with one another; what we now call the *social contract*. We agree to submit to forms of authority such as governments, monarchies, or courts, and trade some of our freedoms for security and social stability. For Hobbes, this contract is the basis of political legitimacy, the alternative being chaos and amorality. Anarchists, however, might disagree that authority is necessary, and altruism is widely documented in the animal kingdom despite any purported social contract.

Nonetheless, the idea of a social contract is politically and ethically useful. Rawls's veil of ignorance neatly resolves one of the contract's potential problems: we'd all want it written in our favour. To stop intelligent people espousing rules that favour intelligence, and rich people seeking rules that favour the rich, we draw down the veil, choosing laws as though we don't know what our personal characteristics and circumstances would be. Only fair that we agree the rules of the game before dealing each player's hand.

As market forces burrow into everyday life, the social contract is increasingly in the hands of business. Paying taxes, for example, is an important unwritten clause. Our shared environments and institutions have to be funded somehow, yet even in the face of tax cuts the tech giants hold immense cash reserves offshore, beyond the grasp of authorities. This clear evasion of social contract duties goes sadly unpunished: monopolistic power makes it easier to dodge your end of the deal.

The social contract relies on reciprocity: a contract only works if we all agree to its terms. Designing for coexistence is therefore, in part, designing for trust and mutual gain. We should build only technology that helps humans to flourish; we should help technology to flourish in return.

Explainable algorithms

To trust, we must understand. To this end, there's a strong case that certain machine-learning systems should be able to explain their decisions; a principle known as explainable AI (XAI).

Explaining how we make decisions about others is both ethically sound and an important condition of democracy. Police usually have to offer probable cause when arresting someone, and courts must explain any verdicts that result. There's also evidence that explainable technologies improve user understanding. A study into explanatory debugging, in which an algorithm told users how it makes predictions, allowed participants to correct the system's mistakes twice as efficiently.[40]

Unfortunately, mathematics gets in the way. Some machine-learning methods, particularly deep-learning systems (a rebrand of the neural network, but with lots more GPUs) and genetic algorithms, are opaque by nature. Simply exposing the code doesn't work: the public doesn't understand code and these aren't programmes in the classic executable sense. Deep learning is loosely modelled on the brain, comprised of several layers of software 'neurons'.

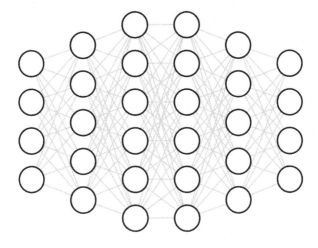

Engineers or data scientists feed the network a set of training inputs – let's say images of animals – and, in the case of supervised learning, what amounts to an answer sheet: 'these are rhinos; these are cows'. The network then looks for salient features in the images (an udder here, maybe; a horn there) and creates a rough model of how to classify animals. It then applies this model to the training dataset and tallies how many it got right. The first pass may be wildly inaccurate, but the algorithm learns from its successes and failures, tweaking neural connections to refine the model until it gets the right answers. The model is then trained, ready to be let loose on a new data set.

Explaining a deep-learning network's rationale is notoriously tough. Researchers have made some progress on explaining which features the hidden neuron layers identify, but these are often abstract and hard to explain textually or verbally. While we understand *how* the network decides whether it sees a rhino or a cow, it's harder to say *why*. A deep-learning network makes decisions in a nondeterministic and emergent manner, and opacity is, to an extent, a feature of the system's architecture. This understandably causes some people anxiety; there's a faint sense we're no longer fully in control of these technologies.

Different people have contrasting explanation needs: a loan applicant and a fraud analyst will focus on different details within the same algorithmic decision. Indeed, some people would prefer the algorithm to give no explanation at all, on grounds of confidentiality. Learned systems are becoming a valuable competitive advantage: if you can predict the future better or replace expensive labour with an automated system, you won't want to give competitors your secret sauce or help users skew decisions in their favour.

Given these strong objections, insisting on XAI for every algorithmic decision is overkill. No one needs to know why a video game boss cast the Meteor spell; they just need to be able to dodge it. However, some decisions deserve non-negotiable explainability on moral and political grounds. The difficulty of XAI is no reason to abandon it.

Where, then, is the line? Which decisions should be explainable? We could demand that any publicly funded algorithm should be explainable, under the guise of democratic accountability, but this overlooks the huge personal impact of private applications like money lending and employment, which are particularly vulnerable to bias and redlining. A better option is to borrow JS Mill's *harm principle*, which states we can only justify exercising power over someone to prevent harm to another. So we might demand explainability just from systems that could cause severe harm, specifically those that significantly affect human freedom and happiness. Precisely which applications this covered would ultimately be for a court to decide, but sentencing, employment (both hiring and firing), benefits, and policing algorithms would probably make the grade, while recommendation systems, game AIs, and digital assistants wouldn't.

Anyone significantly affected by an XAI-mandatory system would be granted a *right to explanation*. This is sometimes misrepresented as being a requirement of GDPR. GDPR does let people contest significant decisions and ask for 'meaningful information about the logic involved', but this is some way short of a full explanation. For that, we'd probably need new laws.

Counterfactuals

Enforced explainability would be controversial. It might force us to ban or otherwise limit deep-learning systems in the worlds of criminal justice, money lending, and employment. This would upset a lot of providers, and many people would gripe that we're undoing years of algorithmic progress. However, there are other machine-learning methods, such as decision trees or Bayesian networks, that are somewhat more explainable if perhaps less powerful. Hope may not be lost even for the opaque systems. Sandra Wachter of the Alan Turing Institute suggests *counterfactuals* as a way to explain an algorithmic decision.[41] Rather than trying to describe the system's messy innards, a counterfactual describes the smallest change that would have achieved a different outcome: 'You were denied a loan because your annual income was £30,000. If your income had been £45,000, you would have been offered a loan.' This statement doesn't mean that everyone who earns £45,000 will get a loan; if it were that simple, you could replace your expensive algorithm with an *if... then* statement. The counterfactual merely shows the nearest threshold at which *you* would have got a different outcome. This is straightforward to find: once the system takes a decision, run it again with slightly different values until the outcome changes, then report what tipped the balance.

Counterfactuals offer an appealing compromise to the XAI quandary. They bypass the mathematical hand-wringing and keep most of the system's workings confidential, but still give useful information on the grounds for an important decision. Any decision that significantly affects human freedom, and must therefore be explained, is likely based on factors that are hard to game, such as income, health, or age; a counterfactual nevertheless suggests how a subject could get a preferable decision next time, helping them take action to improve their own flourishing.

> You only need to give very limited information about what's happening to enable someone to understand the decision, to possibly contest the decision, and, if a decision proves to be fair, to know what they need to change in order to alter future decisions in their favour.
> —Sandra Wachter[42]

A right to explanation alone might not be enough in some circumstances; some decisions are so important the technology should be officially audited. Just as drugs and electronics are tested for safety before being loosed on the market, critical algorithms should have to prove their decisions are fair, explainable, and as unbiased as possible. Today's government agencies aren't well suited to this brief; a world of XAI and auditing may demand national AI standards agencies with the authority to oversee crucial algorithmic decisions.

For all the ethical appeal of XAI, explanations alone don't solve moral problems. Investigators might be glad to learn why an AV crashed, but that doesn't help the injured driver. Nor does explaining a biased decision itself address that bias. XAI must sit alongside bias reduction, data ethics, and moral imagination as a way to help create mutual flourishing between humans and technologies.

Introducing virtue ethics

That word keeps coming up. What does 'flourishing' really mean? Ethicists often refer to the Ancient Greek term *eudaemonia*, which translates as something close to 'fulfilment'. According to Aristotle, someone who achieves eudaemonia is not just happy but typifies important virtues like courage, benevolence, and self-control.

Virtue ethics, the third major pillar of modern ethics, revives these ancient ideas. To a virtue ethicist, to live well – to flourish – we must demonstrate positive virtues in all our choices. While deontologists focus on duty, and utilitarians look only at consequences, virtue ethicists are more concerned by overall moral character.

Virtues sometimes crop up in descriptions of a model professional: we might agree that a good software engineer requires diligence and creativity. But virtues can also be valuable guides to our everyday moral choices. In chapter 2 we saw that single-word concepts often fail as company values; they're too easily twisted to suit someone's preferred excuses. However, single-word values are ideal for individuals: distorting their meaning is just lying to yourself. A virtuous person, then, reflects deeply on the sort of person they want to be, chooses the virtues they want to live by, and works tirelessly to exemplify those virtues.

In *Technology and the Virtues*, Shannon Vallor selects twelve 'technomoral virtues' that could help our relationships with technology flourish, including justice, humility, self-control, and civility.[43] Vallor's deep scholarship might be a little abstract for our applied needs, however. As an entry point to thinking about virtue, we can apply another ethical test: *would I be happy for my decision to appear on the front page of tomorrow's news?* This 'front-page test' asks us to consider our moral reputations and virtues. What would someone infer about our character, hearing we made this decision? What virtues would we exemplify? What virtues might we lack?

Let's apply this test to an example from my own career. Imagine a colleague has found a way to track which apps are installed on someone's handset. A couple of other services use a similar trick, and your company would be able to profile its users better. There's no user benefit other than the weak argument that people will see slightly more relevant ads. Should you put this code in your app? The front-page test makes a clear case: you must decline. If this decision were splashed all over tomorrow's papers, how would readers describe your moral character? There might be a few positive terms – resourceful, ambitious – but most of the characterisations would be negative: deceitful, unreliable, self-centred. This decision certainly doesn't exemplify positive virtues. (If you must know, I lost the debate: the company released the code, press and users complained as expected, and pressure from a partner company forced an eventual reversal.)

The front-page test and virtue ethics can steer us through moments of ethical uncertainty and big life decisions alike. Say you're offered a lucrative job working for a company of questionable ethical pedigree. You know that 'If I don't do it, someone else will' doesn't hold water, but virtue ethics offers new perspectives to accompany deontological and utilitarian logic. What virtues am I demonstrating if I take the job? What virtues do I show if I decline? Would I be happy for my decision to be announced via push notification to my friends and family?

Considering virtue can also guide us to better coexistence with technologies. For a virtue ethicist like Vallor, good technology helps us live a virtuous life; in return we should display our chosen virtues when we make technologies. We can even project these principles into technology itself. What values should a companion species live by? How can it demonstrate them by its actions? A robot designed to demonstrate justice, kindness, and patience, for example, will probably have a likeable, if occasionally pious, personality.

Choosing appropriate virtues can be tricky. The appendix lists some virtues that often crop up in technological contexts, assembled from various sources and projects. This list might be a good a starting point for discussion, but consider rejecting choices that might seem obvious. Feminist ethicists argue that the typically masculine-coded virtues Silicon Valley has historically prioritised – rationality, progress, and courage might fit the bill – have had damaging implications. We could use a change of perspective, and more balance in our approach. It would be fascinating to see what a tech industry that prioritised more feminised virtues like compassion, respect, or generosity would create.

Value-sensitive design

The idea of keeping virtues in mind is echoed in *value-sensitive design*, a design process that aims to systematically address human values in technology.[44] Value-sensitive design is rather too theoretical for technology teams to follow step-by-step, but we've already discussed many of its core techniques, such as widening the stakeholder net.

Value-sensitive design is essentially a virtue-led approach. It asks a team to explicitly consider which values (or virtues) matter most to the project and its stakeholders, then use these values to categorise or draw out the technology's potential benefits and harms. Teams usually find it easy to knock together a long list of potential values; narrowing them down is harder. Values sometimes end up in conflict: for example, the largely positive virtues of candour and courtesy tend to contradict each other. We can use this tension to sharpen our ethical focus. If we agree that independence and belonging might both be relevant values for our project, but they pull in different directions, we can place them at either end of a scale and discuss where our priorities should lie. I call this a *value spectrum*.

Like other ethical artefacts we've discussed, the value spectrum exists to spark discussion. It can help a team to discuss – and agree on – what truly matters in a project; these values can then feed into design principles or other vehicles of ethical infrastructure.

Virtue ethics and value-sensitive design offer an appealing, optimistic framing of ethics. Seeing ethics as a constructive force feels less antagonistic than deontology's rules and prohibitions, and more personal than utilitarianism's rational arithmetic. Virtues feel particularly important in decisions that guide coexistence with companion species. Unfortunately, technology will not always be a welcome partner. Sometimes it will be used for intentional harm.

Chapter 6

You have twenty seconds to comply

The tech industry's continued failure to address malicious use has become a global embarrassment. Trolls and abusers have polluted social spaces; companies and governments have forced their way, unwanted, into our private digital lives. Unfortunately, emerging technologies will offer fresh vectors of attack. In personal relationships of unequal tech literacy, controlling the home network affords one partner silent power: jilted lovers can exact spiteful revenges through the smart home, scaring former partners with unexpected lights and doorbells, or spying on them through domestic cameras.[1] Virtual reality, meanwhile, twists our ideas of personal space. With an immersive sense of physical presence but no way to enforce personal boundaries, virtual groping can feel all too real.

Hackers and scammers will be keen not to miss out. Connected vehicles will make tempting ransomware targets – authorise this crypto transaction or I disable your brakes – and digital assistants could be unwitting co-conspirators for social engineering hacks, thanks to their proximity (literal and metaphorical) to users.

> Imagine a malware app that intercepts requests to Cortana and speaks in her voice, asking its user for some information [...] Suddenly, the spoof has access to personal data it can use in its next phases of identity theft [...] We will need a verifiable way to authenticate agents.
> —Chris Noessel[2]

Quantum computing looms, Damoclean, over the security industry. Quantum processors will solve mathematical problems deemed impossible today, potentially shattering common protections on online payments, blockchains, and cryptocurrency wallets. If you create a viable quantum processor and are canny enough to keep it a secret, you may just be able to steal the world. By most estimates this quantum supremacy is some years off: quantum chips are fiendish and costly to build, giving us time to update our cryptographic measures. Nevertheless, some shadowy syndicate somewhere doubtless has their eyes on the quantum prize.

There are established product mitigations for abuse – block/mute functions, bans, deletion, upvote/downvote mechanisms, and restricted re-entry ('You're suspended until you delete this') – but, predictably, tech companies are also reaching for the algorithmic lever. Algorithms are certainly more scalable than hiring thousands of content moderators, but technology alone can't solve the problem. Alphabet subsidiary Jigsaw's Perspective system claims to recognise 92% of toxic comments, with a surprisingly low false positive rate of 10%, but algorithmic intervention will always be prone to familiar bias. Blocking negative sentiment will also curb meaningful content, while precisely constructed hate speech slips through the net. The 'fourteen words' of an infamous white supremacist slogan are individually benign: their profound threat comes from their combination and use in certain contexts.[3]

Ideally, abuse is better prevented than treated; better to stop harm from even occurring than handle it after the event. In reality, the problem needs both prophylaxis and remedy. We've discussed design tactics like designated dissenters and personas non grata; this should in turn be underpinned by a deep understanding of the contexts and impacts of abuse. Research teams should talk with victims (past, current, and even potential) of abuse on their platforms; as with offline abuse, these abuses will probably fall disproportionately on women and people of colour.

The Internet is experienced completely differently by people who are visibly identifiable as a marginalised race or gender. It's a nastier, more exhausting Internet, one that gets even nastier and even more exhausting as intersections stack up. —Sarah Jeong[4]

This research will doubtless prove more effective if teams take the (sadly too rare) step of sharing their findings publicly; although abuse may manifest differently on each platform, the underlying attack patterns and human impacts certainly overlap. Silicon Valley will best solve its harassment problem through collaboration.

Imposing an abuse solution that isn't grounded in proper research can go seriously awry. Sharing insight gleaned from targeted groups, or even bringing these people into the design studio, reduces the risk of making things worse. A diverse internal team will also tend to have a keen eye for potential flaws in anti-abuse policies, understanding the likely impacts on a wider set of users: ethical infrastructure in action. But researchers must keep their wits about them. Once they know victims have the company's ear, harassers often claim they themselves are the true injured parties. The dynamics of abuse can be complex. Some harassment triggers vehement protest and escalation; abuse can sometimes be masked by what appears from the outside to be just another online brawl. Core values and personal virtues can be useful guides: when analysing the fracas, pay attention not only to how the fight began, but to who exemplifies the values that matter; if in doubt, prioritise their needs.

Moderation and free speech

This research should then inform a robust policy response. Social media companies – Twitter and Reddit in particular – waited far too long to establish and enforce proper rules of conduct, acting only once abuse became rampant. These firms are now finding that tightening lax policies years too late is gruesome work. Thoughtful rules installed early are a trellis for budding user culture. No large community is fully self-policing, but if people accept sensible policies as a precondition of joining a thriving community, they'll often enforce these norms on your behalf.

Bots need policy too. The curious and horny alike love to test the boundaries of digital agents; even today, conversational bots are routinely sexually harassed. This is perhaps no surprise, given that three of the four main voice assistants – Alexa, Cortana, and Siri – are mostly gendered female; people appear to project racial and sexual stereotypes onto robots without hesitation.[5] Bots today offer only slight resistance to sexual comments, presumably to avoid seeming confrontational or prudish.[6] But protecting bots from abuse is a moral act that benefits wider society. Bots will soon be agents of augmentation, paired with human service staff; hurl invective at a digital assistant and you'll soon be abusing a human too. A firm, fair knock-back or deflection will convince the user they won't get the fun they were after, set boundaries for how people should behave towards others (human and non-human) on your platform, and even help confront the aggressive boundary erosion women and girls put up with every day.

Rules mean nothing unless they're enforced. This enforcement sparks tension: any attempt to curtail behaviour will inevitably meet resistance on free speech grounds. Birthed by a nation enamoured of freedoms, a state with a maverick mindset, and a decade of free-wheeling counterculture, Silicon Valley prizes internal debate and has typically seen free speech as an unalloyed good. When Twitter's Tony Wang avowed 'we are the free speech wing of the free speech party' in 2012, there was only minor comment.[7] Today, the statement looks brazenly political, even reckless. If speech is a pure positive, the cure to bad speech is more speech, meaning social networks are the solution to their own problems.

Free speech advocates argue that truth naturally emerges from a *marketplace of ideas*. It's time to retire this false metaphor. In our most connected era, the marketplace of ideas has become a riot. People fight dirty for ideological supremacy and confect whatever narrative they want from cherry-picked or stolen information. It's hard to see how we could ever reverse this situation. The thriving marketplace rests on the assumption that we're all rational actors, an optimistic Enlightenment-era view that looks distinctly naive today. Instead, deep-seated ideology has shown itself to be resistant to information: in this divided age, it seems many people believe only what they want to believe.

Free speech has become a noble danger, and the debate has collapsed into a culture war along entrenched political lines. The far right has recently concocted a playbook of resistance: incite hatred, then claim a role as a marginalised campaigner for free speech, painting moderation as censorship and bigotry as a moral crusade. The common counter that protected speech applies only to the government, not industry, only goes so far. The first amendment, of course, applies only to one nation, and the monopolistic tendencies of modern tech (a consequence of Metcalfe's law and deregulation) mean someone banned from a dominant private platform has a reasonable moral claim their speech is impeded.

Freedom itself is a tangled concept. Isaiah Berlin distinguished two forms: negative and positive.[8] Negative freedom is a *freedom from*, such as freedom from religious persecution; positive freedom is a *freedom to*, such as freedom to marry any consenting adult. Michel Foucault went further, claiming that freedom is more verb than noun, a practice rather than a static trait. Since this simple word is so over-loaded with meaning, it's sometimes easier in ethics to talk about happiness, harm, duty, or virtue than freedom.

In the case of free speech, there's a clear definitional conflict: freedom of expression (positive) versus freedom from harmful speech (negative). In the tech world, it's time for the balance to shift closer to the latter. Speech has never been fully free. Nor should it be. Even the most permissive regimes define some speech as harmful and hence illegal. It's usually forbidden to make credible threats of violence, to give fraudulent financial advice, or to incite hatred: most tech platforms prohibit this harmful speech too. However, the reach and scale of modern tech tend to amplify all kinds of abuse. Harm depends not just on the severity of abuse but also the scale of it: many people (particularly women and minorities) have been hounded off social media as much by sheer volume of abuse as by the credible threats it contains. Tech companies must consider forbidding serious verbal abuse even if it contains no credible threat of violence.

Karl Popper's *paradox of tolerance* illustrates the danger of inaction. When we fail to act against the intolerant, we give them power which, unchecked, may cause the destruction of tolerant people. Excessive tolerance threatens tolerance itself.

I do not imply, for instance, that we should always suppress the utterance of intolerant philosophies; as long as we can counter them by rational argument and keep them in check by public opinion, suppression would certainly be unwise. But we should claim the right to suppress them if necessary even by force; for it may easily turn out that they are not prepared to meet us on the level of rational argument, but begin by denouncing all argument; they may forbid their followers to listen to rational argument, because it is deceptive, and teach them to answer arguments by the use of their fists or pistols. We should therefore claim, in the name of tolerance, the right not to tolerate the intolerant.[9]

A firmer stance against hate speech, even if outlined clearly and applied consistently, will cause certain backlash. But this is a moral nettle worth grabbing if we're to restore technology as a domain in which every person can flourish.

To take this bold action, tech companies must develop and nurture their user safety teams, after years of underfunding. Many firms outsource moderation of their most appalling content – child abuse, gore images – to contractors in developing nations, giving these workers flimsy employment rights but hefty non-disclosure agreements. These content moderation roles have become notorious for emotional stress.

A former content moderator at Google says he became desensitized to pornography after reviewing content for pornographic images all day long. 'The first disturbing thing was just burnout, like I've literally been staring at porn all day and I can't see a human body as anything except a possible [terms of service] violation,' he says. —Lauren Weber and Deepa Seetharaman[10]

Algorithmic detection may in time automate these jobs away, but removing humans from the loop will also reduce opportunities for people to challenge poor policy choices.

Working on a safety team is emotionally taxing, but might be the most ethically significant work a company, or even a career, can offer. A wise tech company would recognise this and arrange for employees to perform tours of duty in these teams, preferably early in their time at the company. Glimpsing the dark underbelly of our beloved technologies will forever shape your perspectives: no longer will you need prompting to consider the potential harms of design and product decisions.

What's yours is ours

Defending against bad actors demands constant vigilance. The threat may even come from our own leaders. The West's recent authoritarian lurch has seen many governments tightening their grip on citizen data, catching the industry off guard; as Maciej Cegłowski says, 'Few tech companies have seriously planned for a situation where our own government could be a threat to users.'

In chapter 4 I explained my dislike of the 'surveillance capitalism' label. It dilutes the harms of genuine surveillance: systematic, inescapable observation that limits our freedom. However, the label does make one apt allusion: the data we give to private companies is also, under the right legal and technical conditions, available to the state. Edward Snowden's revelations that the NSA has direct access to Google, Facebook, Apple, and Skype servers caused minor alarm but little real change in public attitudes. Just three years after the Snowden leaks, the UK passed the Investigatory Powers Act 2016 to a mere whisper of protest. The Act, labelled by the Open Rights Group as 'one of the most extreme surveillance laws ever passed in a democracy', forced UK ISPs and mobile networks to store the country's browsing histories and surrender them to police, security services, and government agencies on demand, no warrant required. Courts have since curtailed some of these powers, but only thanks to legal quarrels and pressure group advocacy, not widespread public dissent.

A hypermap is an autocrat's dream. We're kind enough to carry connected GPS and address books in our pockets and install listening devices in our homes; millions of us have handed our DNA to private companies so they can trace our ancestors, map our genes, and sell our data (theoretically de-identified) to big pharma. In a fully surveilled and hypermapped world, crime investigation would become a question of historical reference: no need to speculate on what happened; just play back the logs. We can already see this future fore-shadowed. In a PR stunt, China's CCTV and facial recognition network took just seven minutes to locate a BBC reporter, while Fitbit data has discredited a rape allegation[11] and been admitted as evidence in a murder case.[12] Prosecutors in Arkansas issued a warrant for audio from an Amazon Echo, in implausible hopes it had recorded a murder. Amazon refused until the defendant himself consented, in a bid to prove his innocence. (Amazon's resistance on first amendment grounds was misreported by some as Alexa itself having first amendment rights, which of course it does not).

Citizen data isn't just useful as retrospective evidence; it is central to the emerging field of predictive policing. Axon, the company previously known as Taser, recently offered a free body camera to every police officer in the US. Backed by cloud storage and recognition software, Axon claims the cameras will soon help police forces to 'anticipate criminal activity'. Licence-plate readers mounted in LAPD squad cars already feed citizens' whereabouts into a Palantir system, allowing police to track vehicles through an entire city.[13] Officers can then set up data dragnets for particular people, addresses, or vehicles in the Palantir system, which in turn notifies officers of any new searches, locations, or warrants relating to these entities of interest. It's push-notification policing, a hum of constant low-level surveillance managed by algorithm.

Many officers are unworthy of the trust this technology demands, routinely disabling body cameras in suspicious circumstances and misusing police databases to check out romantic partners, business associates, neighbours, and journalists who have nothing to do with active investigations.[14] Facial recognition technology, like virtually all other forms of police intervention, is used disproportionately on minorities; the idea of 'fitting the description' becomes automated.[15] Yet police have resisted surveillance technologies pointed at themselves. When Massachusetts State Police chiefs installed location trackers in their force's cars, the police union complained the technology was invasive.[16]

Surveillance vendors will always exaggerate what their tech can do, but it's clear a hypermapped world and advanced analytics will give cops insight that would have previously needed a warrant or been impossible to derive. Want to know if your suspect passed through a certain intersection, or learn where a vehicle was last Thursday? No need to pore through CCTV feeds; simply enter the car registration or 'asian woman in red coat' and you'll see the logged locations and corresponding footage. Need a quantified estimate of likely trouble spots next weekend? The system will gladly spit out a heat map. The prospects of similar technologies holding police accountable for their actions seem rather slimmer.

Security or liberty?

Citing counter-terror needs, governments are desperate to persuade – or compel – tech firms to build backdoors into operating systems and messaging platforms. The FBI's skirmish with Apple after the 2015 San Bernardino attack is a well-known example. Rebuffing a demand to unlock a suspect's iPhone 5C, Tim Cook issued a public statement.

> While we believe the FBI's intentions are good, it would be wrong for the government to force us to build a backdoor into our products. And ultimately, we fear that this demand would undermine the very freedoms and liberty our government is meant to protect.[17]

A moral government finds itself in a bind: it has a duty to protect citizens from terrorism and crime, but it doesn't want to unnecessarily curtail civil liberties. Again we see competing freedoms: freedom from interference in our private lives played off against freedom from the threat of terror. Public opinion on the San Bernardino dispute was deeply divided. A CBS and *New York Times* poll found 50% support for the FBI's demand and 45% support for Apple's refusal.[18] Reports suggest the FBI eventually sidestepped the lock using a zero-day exploit, finding nothing of value about the plot.

We've already seen one ethical perspective on the security-or-liberty debate: Hobbes's *contractarian* view that we must relinquish some freedoms in exchange for safety. Although Hobbes is sometimes unfairly labelled an apologist for authoritarianism, it's fair to conclude he would side with the FBI. Another maligned moral philosopher, Niccolò Machiavelli, might agree. Machiavelli believes that ends usually justify means; that the greater glory of the nation – and its rulers, needless to say – sometimes demands intrusive or cruel acts.

There'll always be something that looks morally right but would actually lead a ruler to disaster, and something else that looks wrong but will bring security and success.[19]

However, the security-or-liberty debate tends to become one-dimensional, aligning with people's politics. Those who, on balance, see authority as a force for good tend to favour security; those who don't lean towards liberty. The second group often wield the famous Franklin quote 'Those who would give up essential liberty, to purchase a little temporary safety, deserve neither liberty nor safety', unaware these words weren't written about national security but a minor tax dispute.[20]

The ethics of encryption

Let's try to circumvent the politics by using encryption as a proxy for the debate. Is it ethical to encrypt our data? Should people be able to safeguard secrets from the state?

Going against the wishes of a democratically elected government is a significant ethical hurdle: isn't it part of the social contract to respect fair laws? The history of encryption has traced a well-worn path: technology simply outpaced society. After inventing encryption – or, rather, borrowing it from the mathematicians – technologists implemented it unilaterally in millions of systems before proper public debate could happen. Sometimes this rollout has been clearly beneficial, such as in protecting online payments, but the case of encrypting private communication is less clear.

Modern conflict is asymmetric: the threat has shifted from national militaries to destructive, motivated individuals and groups. Terrorist cells are often fragmented, distributed over several sites, meaning existing surveillance methods like bugging can be ineffective. Is it right to deny the government new tools to counter these new threats?

Is total secrecy even a reasonable expectation anyway? Ethicist Jennifer Welchman says message encryption goes beyond what we should hope for from a consumer relationship and, indeed, modern life itself.

At a bank you can get a security deposit box and it could still get robbed, and we accept that. We accept that our house or car can be robbed, so the notion that we as consumers have some special claim on Apple to offer us this guarantee above and beyond what they can both reasonably provide and what, under the circumstances, seems reasonable to expect, is really questionable.[21]

The opposing case, in defence of encryption, is also robust. The strongest argument is that any backdoor weakens protection from any bad actor, including thieves, hackers, and yes, terrorists themselves. Anyone with the right key can walk straight in. If we give our government the power to read our communications, will friendly governments ask for access too?

Some activists contend the whole argument is foolish anyway: encryption can't be uninvented, and calling for it to be banned is akin to banning maths. When FBI boss Chris Wray suggested resolving the encryption dilemma shouldn't be beyond a society that has previously conquered space, one wag retorted, 'We put a man on the moon, so why can't we put a man on the sun?' Great line, but it doesn't really stand up. Governments aren't asking to uninvent mathematical proofs or to ban encryption algorithms altogether, just to limit their applications. We apply the same principle to all sorts of scientific discoveries. It's not hard to learn how to make a bomb, but start bulk-buying ammonium nitrate and there'll soon be a sturdy knock on your door.

In defence of encryption, there's also an argument that governments already have the necessary information to prevent terror; they're just not using it properly. Without stumbling too far into the conspiracy minefield, it's clear American authorities had advance warning of a huge terror threat before 9/11, but failed to act on it.[22] Spare a thought for the tech companies too. Many have spent millions turning privacy into a competitive advantage: do they get any compensation for having to throw that away? Restricting encryption would push a painful externality onto the whole tech sector, which would see trust and adoption slump.

Finally, we should ask whether humans have an unconditional right to privacy. We haven't talked much about rights so far, although they're an important part of modern ethics. As a list of inviolable claims, rights are mostly seen as deontological. We all agree, for example, we have a duty not to unjustly imprison someone. If we see rights as universal applications of moral law, we have to be consistent: if people have the right to privacy, so do terrorists, and restricting encryption is unsustainable.

However, rights can be slippery things, and often expand beyond their means in the wrong hands. Anyone can invent rights that sound rhetorically reasonable but that have no real moral or legal basis. For example, people don't have a moral right to employment or equal wealth. We may choose to organise society this way (we'd probably call this communism) but this is a political choice more than a moral one. Although some nations recognise a formal human right to privacy, the idea is still widely disputed; besides, we'd need plenty more detail to understand what that means in practice.

Repurposing surveillance

Our debate is overlooking an important point. Security arguments focus on current needs and protections, but future technologies might well demolish those protections. In 1991, philosopher Daniel Dennett welcomed the era's main impediment to mass surveillance.

> It is trivially easy now with high tech to eavesdrop on people, simply by recording their telephone or private conversations. This is, however, a bottleneck: you need trained, qualified, secure personnel to listen to those hundreds of hours of tape that you'll gather. It must be horribly mind-numbing: thank God for that bottleneck![23]

The bottleneck has been shattered. Once sensors and analysis tools are in place, changing the target of surveillance is now just an algorithmic tweak. In the twentieth century, to switch from tracking communists to tracking the Mafia would take hundreds of new bugs and wiretaps, a slew of new vehicles to be tailed, and piles of new records to sift through. Governments today can, more or less, look at a different row in the database. The original intent of surveillance no longer matters. Any surveillance can become *any* surveillance: a system used to listen out for gunfire can be repurposed to detect Urdu.

Before his election, Donald Trump hinted at creating a Muslim database. The US census removed questions on religion in 1957, on grounds of religious liberty; many commentators said it would take years to regather this data in the modern era. But the core systems, although embryonic, are already in place to automate this work. Outside the scope of governmental protections, data brokers offer detailed files. It took Amnesty International just five clicks to get a quote for data on 1.8 million US Muslims.[24] Combine this with neo-physiognomic facial recognition, messaging app backdoors, and GPS tracking, and it's clear a first stab at a Muslim database – including thousands of false positives – could be assembled in short order.

The dangers of repurposing create an ethical distinction between targeted surveillance and mass surveillance. Targeted surveillance is easier to justify. It has historically required authorities to show probable cause and to seek warrants; mass surveillance, however, circumvents many of these protections. A system that scoops up everything it can on an entire population and can change its targets seamlessly is a system to be feared.

The party line

At some point it becomes unclear who's really benefiting from surveillance: the people, the country, or the party? Despite promises that the internet was immune to central control, governments have found they can shut down large chunks by targeting ISPs, mobile networks, and the domain name system. According to watchdog Freedom House, global internet freedom has decreased for seven years running; in 2016, two-thirds of internet users lived in nations that censored online criticism of the government, military, or monarch.[25]

China holds its citizens on a particularly tight online leash. Following on from the success of its Great Firewall, which blocks most Western tech giants, Chinese authorities are planning a nationwide social credit system. Due by 2020, the system will aggregate citizens' creditworthiness, online purchases, social media activity, and interpersonal relationships into a personal reputation score.

The Western press has gleefully hailed the system as a frightening dystopia, but the system today is more a patchwork of pilots than an omniscient avatar of authority. As of 2018, the financial arm appears to be the only area properly developed, meaning the system mostly punishes monetary offenders like defaulters and fraudsters. Punishments are hefty but not wildly disproportionate. Low scorers are barred from conspicuous consumption like first-class tickets and private education for their kids: this is enforced personal austerity, ethically troubling to Western mindsets, but far from total oppression.[26]

Lacking an open market, and with a population averse to debt, China lacks common gauges of financial trust. Huge numbers of Chinese have no credit score and, given the blurred lines between the Chinese state and private enterprise, it's no surprise the government is keen to measure financial status. The West has similar repositories of reputation and power, except we prefer them to be under corporate rather than state control. Credit agencies have logged our financial trustworthiness for decades, and in-car devices are reporting back to insurers on how we drive. Facebook holds a patent for a credit score that is affected by your friends' scores, although the firm has as yet shown no intention to use it.[27]

> Across Europe and the US, people are shocked by this dystopian IT-backed authoritarianism. But citizens of these countries are already being scored by systems based on the same logic – they just haven't noticed. —Miranda Hall and Duncan McCann[28]

These defences aside, we mustn't succumb to moral relativism. There are significant ethical and political concerns about upcoming branches of the social credit system that relate to personal speech and association. The project is surely not for the good of the nation alone.

Whatever the form of government, all surveillance has political utility. Perceived security bolsters public support: people who feel safe keep governments in power. Thanks to the phenomenon of *social cooling*, these effects can self-perpetuate. Named by technology critic Tijmen Schep after the 'chilling effect', social cooling is a perpetual side effect of living in a reputation economy and, by extension, permanent surveillance. When reputation scores govern our opportunities, we change our behaviour to get better scores. Surveillance therefore nudges us towards obedience. Even the threat of surveillance has the desired effect: to silence peaceful protest, pull up a van marked 'Facial Recognition Unit', or simply announce you've equipped the police with new, undisclosed tracking technologies. It doesn't matter whether the technology is viable or not: without insight into the workings of the system, dissent will be cooled nonetheless. The panopticon – the all-seeing prison invented by Jeremy Bentham, forefather of utilitarianism – is digitally brought to life.

Governments often try to allay the public's surveillance fears by monitoring only metadata rather than content: in other words, logging who contacts whom rather than recording the conversation. This is little comfort. It's not hard to imagine what might have happened to a woman who takes a call from her doctor, then calls an insurer and an HIV clinic. Metadata can still condemn someone; in some cases, to death. Former NSA and CIA director Michael Hayden is on record: 'We kill people based on metadata.'[29]

Where does this leave our encryption debate? To a utilitarian, social cooling is a constant harm felt by all, with net effects not dissimilar to terrorism itself. The unchecked, undemocratic escalation from targeted to mass surveillance suggests the public deserves countermeasures. Applying a double effect argument, I'd argue that encryption is justified as self-defence in a hostile world, keeping our lives safe from a host of bad actors. If our governments happen to be among those actors, that's an acceptable side effect. Besides, technology infrastructure tends to outlive any single government; even if the current regime is trustworthy, a less honourable government could inherit the surveillance keys in future.

Post-privacy

If information wants to be free, surely it'll cosy up to anyone. Is a post-privacy future inevitable? For all the public's privacy anxieties, people tend to accept privacy erosion when it offers convenience.[30] Technologies that begin as optional and handy – fingerprint and face scanners, GPS, microphones, accelerometers – in time become normalised and expected. Security protections at high-risk sites soon trickle into city streets, while sensationalised media coverage validates the security agenda at the expense of privacy. Whether through consent or resignation, surveillance creeps into our lives.

We live, therefore, in an era of *surveillance realism*, in which we disapprove of bulk data collection but support giving governments more powers to fight terrorism. The only cultural signs of this acquiescence are sardonic surveillance memes, which paint authorities as ever-watchful guardian agents.

> me, peeling tape off webcam: hey guys whats apoptosis mean?
> little FBI voice within my computer: programmed cell death.
> me: thanks roger. tell the family happy holidays
> roger, the FBI man: will do. please get more sleep[31]

Should perpetual oversight concern us all, or only those on the wrong side of the law? 'Nothing to hide, nothing to fear' is a common defence in privacy debates, arguing that surveillance only has trivial impact on law-abiding citizens. There are several cheap counters to this collaborationist excuse, which point out we all have secrets: 'Oh, do you have curtains?'; 'Can I photograph you naked, then?'; 'If you have nothing to hide, you're wasting your life!'[32] There are, of course, legitimate reasons to keep secrets beyond simple modesty: people in witness protection programmes and victims fleeing domestic abuse, for example, have justifiable cause to conceal their identities. And anyone who's lived a full life has acted in ways that could seem suspicious in retrospect. As Cardinal Richelieu supposedly wrote, 'If you give me six lines written by the hand of the most honest of men, I will find something in them which will hang him.'[33] But the deepest flaw with 'nothing to hide' is it assumes authorities are infallible. The defence only works if technology is always accurate and no one is ever wrongly detained or convicted. Yet even if tracking technologies were perfect, a simple police error can have significant consequences. Say your handset is stolen and used to arrange a crime; if you report the phone stolen but the theft wasn't properly logged, you'll have to work hard to assert your innocence.

Post-privacy looks to be a probable future, at least by some definitions. Privacy as seclusion is probably already obsolete; the drift to disclosure makes it virtually impossible to have no digital footprint today. But defeatism would be ruinous; there's still hope for privacy to exist as a matter of control and self-determination. Although not everyone sees privacy as a human right, there's a strong moral case that privacy helps us lead lives of eudaemonia and dignity; we might even argue that privacy is necessary for trust in society and democracy. Self-disclosure is an important basis of friendship: if everyone knows everything about each other, there's not much left to distinguish friends from enemies. Even if mass surveillance is now inevitable, we should pressure authorities to be more open about its nature and intent, to commit to due process such as warrants for investigation, and not to use highly fallible technologies as mass surveillance tools until they produce far fewer false positives.

Autonomous war

A world of total information invites the ultimate technological dominance: automated warfare. Although only a fraction of the tech sector works on military projects, decisions made when the moral stakes are at their highest nevertheless echo through the entire industry.

Under *just war* doctrine, nations must have moral justification for going to war, and must agree to conduct war in certain ways, a principle known as *jus in bello*. The UN Convention on Certain Conventional Weapons bans weapons that cause unjustifiable suffering, such as cluster bombs, blinding lasers, and antipersonnel mines.

Autonomy appeals to the military for the same reasons it appeals to industry: it promises higher performance – an admittedly euphemistic term here – at lower cost. There are also potential ethical justifications: autonomous systems could, in theory, reduce human casualties and make fewer errors. Human combatants are far from infallible: in 2017, Nigerian forces mistakenly bombed civilians fleeing Boko Haram, killing fifty; in 2014, a Russian surface-to-air missile claimed 298 civilian lives on board Malaysian Airlines Flight 17. Autonomous weapons will be small, since they don't need to house personnel, and mechanically simple, requiring no expensive or scarce materials like uranium. Sensors and algorithms might be the costliest components, but even these will probably be simpler than those powering a self-driving car.

144 | FUTURE ETHICS

The world's dominant powers are investing heavily in military automation. The US's Third Offset Strategy put miniaturisation, big data, and algorithmic warfare at the heart of the Pentagon's plans, funded by billions of dollars. China will doubtless be a major player too, given its huge state investments in machine learning, access to the Shenzhen component market, and the detailed training data it can collect from and about citizens; Russia also has autonomous intentions, with Vladimir Putin saying 'Whoever becomes the leader in [AI] will become the ruler of the world.'

As with civilian use, military automation will be incremental. Military technologists often distinguish three forms of automation. A *human-in-the-loop* (HITL) system automates functions like target recognition, aiming, and guidance, but the decision to attack is left to humans. HITL systems are already in active service, such as the Super aEgis II turrets that guard air bases in the United Arab Emirates, programmed to automatically lock on to human targets but not to fire.[34] A *human-on-the-loop* (HOTL) system can deliver force itself, under the supervision of a human who can override the decision. Finally, fully autonomous systems involve no human oversight at all and as such are sometimes called *human-out-of-the-loop* systems. These last two categories, in which the machine has attack authority, are known collectively as lethal autonomous weapons systems (LAWS).

Autonomous weapons have enormous ethical implications. Unless a LAWS can accurately distinguish combatants from civilians, and friends from foes, it will kill indiscriminately. Morally and legally, it must recognise and respect an enemy's surrender. It must also respond proportionally to aggression. While monitoring a contended border, say, a LAWS must be able to distinguish an incoming stone from a grenade: while both are an attack, only one poses an immediate danger to life and invites a lethal response.

LAWS also invite the risk of accidental escalation, or at least the inability to de-escalate. Modern warfare increasingly operates in the grey zone between peace and outright war, as evidenced by the 'little green men' involved in the annexation of Crimea, who wore no insignia but were widely identified as Russian forces. Ambiguity and plausible deniability are key to grey-zone conflict: forces must operate at effective, even provocative, levels while stopping short of precipitating full-blown conflict. In 1983, Soviet air force officer Stanislav

Yevgrafovich Petrov famously may have saved the world by defying military protocol. Sceptical of readings from his early-warning systems, Petrov elected not to inform superiors of what looked like a US nuclear attack, potentially averting catastrophic retaliation. It's unlikely a LAWS will be able to tread as carefully as Russia's little green men, or demonstrate Petrov's judgment and scepticism.

Like surveillance technologies, a LAWS is easily repurposed towards new targets, including terrorists and criminals. In 2016, Dallas police killed murder suspect Micah Xavier Johnson using a Remotec bomb-disposal robot rigged, in an ironic twist, with C4 explosive.[35] It was the first time a robot has been used to kill on US soil: thanks to ongoing police militarisation, it won't be the last. This wasn't an autonomous system – the robot was piloted and its payload detonated remotely, making it more like a drone – but it's clear that LAWS in the hands of a totalitarian regime would cause something closer to social dread than social cooling. Being cheap and largely undetectable, LAWS could also fall into the hands of terrorists or criminals themselves. The death-dealing power of, say, thousands of quadcopters armed with crude shaped charges and facial recognition technology could threaten the very fabric of society. This is the premise of *Slaughterbots*, a horrifying work of speculative design from the Future of Life Institute and Berkeley's Stuart Russell.[36]

Still from Slaughterbots. Reprinted with kind permission of the Future of Life Institute.

There will be manufacturers producing millions of these weapons that people will be able to buy just like you can buy guns now, except millions of guns don't matter unless you have a million soldiers. You need only three guys to write the program and launch them. So you can just imagine that in many parts of the world humans will be hunted. They will be cowering underground in shelters and devising techniques so that they don't get detected. This is the ever-present cloud of lethal autonomous weapons. They could be here in two to three years. —Stuart Russell[37]

Given that LAWS could cause a huge spike in human suffering, most authorities on military ethics agree we should go no further than HOTL systems. From a legal standpoint even this is questionable. Moral distribution makes accountability harder: in human rights law, only humans are capable of making legal judgments.

Should we therefore preemptively ban fully autonomous weapons? The unsubtly named Campaign to Stop Killer Robots thinks so, and is pushing for an international treaty and national pledges to renounce the systems. There has been some progress; at the time of writing, twenty-six countries including China have publicly endorsed calls for a ban.[38] The US stance is less clear. In 2016, secretary of defence Ash Carter was unequivocal – 'I'll repeat yet again, since it keeps coming up, that when it comes to using autonomy in our weapons systems, we will always have a human being in decision-making about the use of force.'[39] – but his deputy Bob Work subsequently contradicted him, saying the US might give a machine authority to kill in situations that operate 'faster than human reaction time, like cyber or electronic warfare'.[40]

A full global ban seems unlikely. Lockheed Martin's Larry Schuette says 'We are going to be violently opposed to autonomous robotic hunter-killer systems until we decide we can't live without them.'[41] Militaries were willing to forgo cluster munitions, since alternative weapons are sufficient to stay competitive, but autonomous weapons could totally disrupt the balance of conventional power. The first state to build LAWS may find its military capabilities transformed. In this event, all will follow; an autonomous arms race will ensue.

In lieu of a ban, we may have to resort to updating *jus in bello* legal frameworks and insisting LAWS pass certain tests, such as friend-or-foe discrimination and adaptation to context, before deployment.

These tests will doubtless measure speed and accuracy, but there may also be room for some assessment of moral outcome, presumably on utilitarian grounds.

Military applications of emerging technology can conjure nightmarish scenarios – untraceable 3D-printed guns, hacked drones, killer robots – made to feel doubly real by the science-fiction films of our childhood. But we mustn't let fear paralyse us. Consider the destructive power that is already available: society has successfully avoided the use of nuclear bombs for seventy years, despite the Cold War and vast stockpiles. If we can contain the deadliest of all weapons, are LAWS such a threat?

Moral disobedience

Escalating surveillance and the looming military threat have provoked an appetite for countermeasures. Not every PET needs to be as high-tech as encryption. Obscuring key facial features with contrasting make-up or masks can defeat common facial recognition systems.

In theory, counter-recognition can even be achieved invisibly. Speech detection systems can be deceived by adding ultrasound to the input signal;[42] researchers have found ways to trick Google's Cloud Vision API into thinking a helicopter is a rifle.[43] Israeli startup D-ID offers commercial photo obfuscation, claiming its proprietary algorithm makes faces invisible to recognition systems but still identifiable to the human eye. If these *adversarial examples* become more sophisticated, going off the recognition grid might soon require little more than careful application of invisible make-up (perhaps we could call it 'scanscreen'). Of course, this concealment won't go unchallenged. Identification and de-identification will become an arms race; the hypermap will be periodically sabotaged and reassembled. Deep learning systems are discovering how to recognise faces disguised by glasses, caps, scarves, and beards; the paper announcing this breakthrough talks proudly about the mathematical innovation required, but is silent on the ethical impacts.[44]

In today's anxious security environment, the act of securing your life can make you appear paranoid and radical. Privacy is becoming equated with criminality. Current US secretary of state Mike Pompeo wrote in a Wall Street Journal op-ed, 'the use of strong encryption in personal communications may itself be a red flag,' while journalist Robinson Meyer found counter-recognition make-up attracted alarming public attention: 'The very thing that makes you invisible to computers makes you glaringly obvious to other humans.' Face-covering bans are creeping into European law, ostensibly on security grounds but often rooted in Islamophobia. The potential criminal and terrorist uses of counter-recognition technology – hiding weapons, duping LAWS into attacking false targets or civilians – mean we can expect it to be outlawed swiftly.

Many nations recognise the right for a *conscientious objector* to opt out of military service on moral grounds. It's possible to morally object to any law or corporate act too.

> Must the citizen ever for a moment, or in the least degree, resign his conscience to the legislator? Why has every man a conscience, then? I think we should be men first and subjects second. It is not desirable to culture a respect for the law, so much as for the right. —Henry David Thoreau[45]

If a technologist thinks their company is about to seriously damage the public good, how should they object?

The simplest response is refusal. As we know, 'If I don't, someone else will' is no defence, meaning the projects we take on reveal the values we choose to live by. To paraphrase designer Mike Monteiro, one cigarette ad in your portfolio is a mistake; twenty is a statement. But refusal must remain a personal decision. Although tempting, blanket prohibitions – 'It is unethical to work on military projects' and the like – aren't helpful. Plenty of technologists, myself included, categorically refuse to serve the military-industrial complex, but we can't impose these preferences on others. Prescriptions this absolute are to my mind the *opposite* of ethics. They shut down ethical discussion rather than inspire it; they disallow any chance that military tech could have positive applications, such as monitoring ceasefire violations. When wrestling with this issue yourself, the usual deontological and utilitarian questions can be useful, but virtue ethics offers a particularly helpful perspective. What kind of virtues do you want to honour? Does your choice reflect these? Would you be happy for your decision to be tomorrow's front-page headline?

Given that many technologists will spurn surveillance or military work, companies in these fields have an incentive to mask their intentions. Analytics giants love to boast of their humanitarian projects: we predict the spread of disease; we help aid agencies decide where to allocate resources. More morally ambiguous projects are often only discussed *sotto voce*, or couched in vague language: we also work with defence and security agencies to sustain global peace.

Some teams use intellectual intrigue to outshine ethical concerns. Recruiters attract potential employees – usually bright but inexperienced – by promising engrossing problems and fearless innovation. Finding a way to determine someone's location without access to their devices may well be technically absorbing, but in huge, siloed companies it's hard to know whether this technology's final purpose is to detect avalanche survivors or to pinpoint a drone strike. Cultures of internal secrecy provide perfect cover for questionable ethics. Technologists should be sceptical of any company large or compartmentalised enough to have divisions they don't understand. Our work often has potential uses far beyond those our superiors admit; a moment spent looking at our company's customer lists and exercising our moral imagination should help us anticipate how our work might be used for harm. We mustn't be afraid to challenge executives on the intentions or unintended applications of our work, mobilising internally to share information and joining up dots that may have been left deliberately unconnected.

Refusal is most powerful at scale. Tech employees are at last recognising the power of collective action; many groups have successfully pressured their leaders to withdraw from controversial projects. Google's work on Project Maven, which processed drone footage as part of a Pentagon algorithmic war initiative, caused huge internal backlash. After thousands of Googlers signed an open letter to leadership, and several resigned, execs agreed to drop the Maven contract.[46] To its credit, Google went further, imposing AI guidelines that explicitly rule out working on technologies whose 'principal purpose or implementation is to cause or directly facilitate injury to people'. Some hawkish commentators complained that this withdrawal will kill civilians: without precision technology, the theory goes, we'll have to resort to blunter weapons that cause more collateral death. But this kind of collective action will no doubt continue. Tech workers are powerful in aggregate, hard to recruit, expensive, and able to deeply disrupt a company's output when acting in unison. Writing open letters, holding leaders to account at internal events, requesting reassignment from controversial projects, and even striking are becoming powerful and, perhaps, necessary ways to force through ethical change within recalcitrant firms. The key is to ensure your arguments carry moral force: from previous chapters you now know some frameworks to substantiate these debates.

Positive collective action may at times take counterintuitive forms. Algorithmic bias, for instance, typically hurts minority groups, but going unrecognised by computer vision may turn out to be a blessing. Perhaps, contrary to what seems like obvious anti-racist activism, technologists should refuse to make surveillance systems less biased.

> I have no reason to support the development or deployment of technology which makes it easier for the state to recognize and surveil members of my community. Just the opposite: by refusing to don white masks, we may be able to gain some temporary advantages by partially obscuring ourselves from the eyes of the white supremacist state. —Nabil Hassein[47]

Mobilisation needn't stop at the office. Technologists are citizens as well as professionals; we sometimes have a duty to tell the public what's happening inside our industry and their devices, helping to organise broader resistance. This is particularly important when there's a clear moral case for new regulation. Tech companies wield significant legal and lobbying power; campaigns for better oversight therefore need widespread public support.

> The power of design is often overestimated. Sometimes we can have more effect as citizens than as designers. Protests and boycotts can still be the most effective ways of making a point [...] The most threatening act of protest for a capitalist system would be for its citizens to refuse to consume. —Anthony Dunne and Fiona Raby[48]

For egregious ethical abuses, whistle-blowing may be the only viable or proportionate recourse. There are usually several routes for disclosure; most large companies will have an internal whistle-blowing policy, and many industries have oversight from professional organisations or ombudsmen. Unfortunately, these channels often fail to give whistle-blowers the protection they promise. Some disclosures are better made to the press. The Freedom of the Press Foundation advises that leakers stay well away from company systems.[49] Never leak by email, and don't use company devices, accounts, or networks. Instead of sending complete files as evidence, which may contain incriminating metadata, the Foundation recommends instead sending a screenshot or photo of the document, preferably taken with a non-smartphone camera. Some journalists prefer leakers to print hard copies – bearing in mind, however, that many printers add tiny tracking dots for just this reason – and to post the documents from a different city, paying cash at all times and leaving their phones behind. Fortunately, secure channels like Signal and SecureDrop may spell the end of this cloak-and-dagger drama. Many major newspapers now publish details of anonymous communications channels; these are typically a whistle-blower's best bet.

The price of disobedience

Even with proper precautions, whistle-blowing and leaking are extreme sports. Leakers should expect to be fired if caught; they may face civil suits or criminal charges. Any decision of this magnitude should be made on the basis of painstaking moral judgment. (I feel compelled to say I'm thoroughly unqualified to offer legal opinion on the matter; anyone who interprets my words as such deserves everything they get.) It is our ethical responsibility to accept the consequences of standing up for what we believe is right. Some of these effects will be unintended; some may harm the very people we're trying to protect.

But disobedience always carries some danger. To live a moral life we must be willing to put ourselves at greater risk, if it's safe to do so. Our industry should find this easier than most: technologists are typically well paid and in high demand, but even within our own teams not everyone shares a similarly privileged position. Rallying support is important, but we mustn't blame colleagues who feel unable to join an ethical struggle: they may have personal, family, or financial situations that make disobedience a non-starter. We can only decide for ourselves whether the risk is a price worth paying. But if you're fortunate enough to feel safe, comfortable, and respected in your company and your industry, you're in the perfect position to use up a little of that goodwill to stand up for what is morally right.

Chapter 7

Software is heating the world

Welcome to the Anthropocene, the era of human domination over the natural world. We told the climate to jump; now we get to see how high. Global temperature is now 1.1 °C (2 °F) above the long-term average, with further rises already in the post, thanks to recent emissions.[1] The Paris Agreement's attempt to limit rises to 'well below 2 °C' looked unlikely even before the US's withdrawal; a study in *Nature Climate Change* offered odds of just one in twenty.[2] Two degrees of warming will cause droughts, flooding, crop failures, and mass migration; at four degrees, we face losing major coastal cities, the desertification of much of the US and Europe, potential collapse in food production, and biosphere die-off. This level of warming is still a distinct possibility. In 2014, the World Bank estimated a 40% chance that warming would exceed 4° this century, destroying any chance of ending global poverty.[3]

Minimum viable icecaps

Whatever ethical lens we use, it's clear we must protect a future from which we've borrowed too much for too long. A utilitarian sees the natural world as essential to human happiness. A deontologist sees a moral duty to future generations and non-human species alike. A virtue ethicist sees the importance of living by the doctrines of temperance, courage, and sustainability. But any meaningful climate actions we take now will be painful for society, in particular harming the developing world just as it's starting to get a fair foothold. There are few positives in the climate equation. Every outcome is bad; some are worse.

Ignoring outright climate change denial – a claim so corrupt and malignant it borders on intergenerational manslaughter – climate narratives fluctuate between 'hold on tight' and annihilation. Doom-sayers invoke the spectre of runaway change, a tipping point of warming at which positive feedback loops, such as methane deposits unleashed by melting permafrost, take control. Climate change's dystopian secondary effects might include crop failure, famine, pandemic, and even nuclear war. Roy Scranton's stunning *New York Times* piece 'Learning How to Die in the Anthropocene' asks us to see in climate change the opportunity to accept our common fate:

> Now, when I look into our future — into the Anthropocene — I see water rising up to wash out lower Manhattan. I see food riots, hurricanes, and climate refugees. I see 82nd Airborne soldiers shooting looters. I see grid failure, wrecked harbors, Fukushima waste, and plagues. I see Baghdad. I see the Rockaways. I see a strange, precarious world.[4]

Given their preoccupation with existence and death, it's under-standable philosophers are drawn to climate alarmism. The risk of this catastrophist mindset is, of course, that we give up. Inexorable dread can engender an almost liberating sense of fatalism. Perhaps climate panic will create a generation of 'climate inactivists' who agree we've missed our chance and had best prepare for obliteration.

But extinction is a long way off yet. Scranton would defend his piece by saying it's not that we must abandon life itself, merely *modern* life as we know it: 'The rub is that we now have to learn how to die not as individuals, but as a civilization.' Life in a +4 °C world would be barely recognisable, but it should yet be liveable. We mustn't acquiesce to something that isn't preordained.

The digital drain

In *Design for the Real World*, Victor Papanek seethes at the environmental injuries designers have caused: 'There are professions more harmful than industrial design, but only a very few of them.'[5] It's tempting to argue this doesn't apply to the digital world – we're not the ones wrapping products in plastic, creating landfill, piling them high and selling them cheap – but every digital experience needs physical hardware, and bits and atoms are increasingly bound together in a single package: smartwatches, connected thermostats, Wi-Fi light bulbs. Volkswagen's defeat device, which cheated emissions tests and created undeclared pollution likely to kill dozens or hundreds,[6] was a pure software swindle. Technologists can't escape their share of blame.

It's helpful to look at the tech industry's environmental impact across three categories: data centres, networks, and devices themselves. Let's start upstream. Amid rocketing demand, data centres already create as many greenhouse gas emissions as the entire aviation industry.[7] The energy impact of data centres varies significantly between sites. To their great credit, Apple, Facebook, and Google have taken genuine, visible steps to improve the energy mix of their data centres, and have been rewarded with an A rating in Greenpeace's 2017 'Clicking Clean' report.[8] Google's data centres (and offices) are now powered entirely by renewables, and just a tenth of their data centre energy goes on overheads like cooling.

If only the rest of the industry showed similar appetite. Greenpeace gives Netflix, Spotify, and Vimeo a D rating, and slaps Hulu, SoundCloud, Baidu, and Tencent with an F. In total, 70% of global internet traffic is routed through Loudoun County, Virginia, where data centres are almost entirely powered by dirty, nonrenewable sources. There is much work to do.

On leaving the server farms, data worms its way through an elaborate infrastructure of fibre-optic cables, switches, base stations, repeaters, and routers. Given the complexity of these systems, consumption stats are scarce, but a joint study by Bell Labs and the University of Melbourne – admittedly from 2013 – found that, of the total energy consumption of 'wireless cloud' systems, networks accounted for 90%, and data centres just 9%.[9] 4G uploads use around

500 times more energy than Wi-Fi,[10] and saving to a local hard drive uses around one-millionth of the energy of saving the same file to cloud storage.[11] Wireless network infrastructure is naturally invisible to consumers, but it makes sense that it takes far more energy to squeeze data through the air than through wires; the cable-free life appears to come at environmental cost.

Modern devices have such low power drains that keeping them running barely factors into the energy arithmetic. Most of a device's climate impact comes instead from its manufacture. Unsurprisingly, the larger the device, the greater the impact. Comparing top-end devices, Apple reports CO_2 footprints ranging from 26–601 kg.[12]

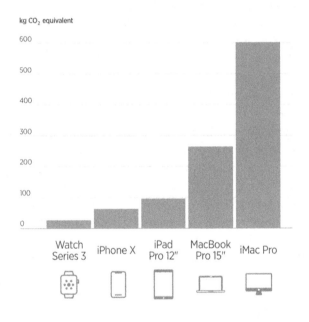

These are impressively low figures, on a rough par with the footprint of a gold necklace.[13] What's more worrying is the frequency at which this manufacturing process is called into action. The industry's thirst for ever-improving user experience and innovation drives demand for high-end devices, and many smart objects actually have shorter lives than their previously dumb forms, thanks to irreplaceable batteries, locked-down firmware, and obsolescent components. Low-end IoT devices have disposability built in, causing more manufacture and more waste. Better to create resilient, long-lasting devices, like Apple's, even if they are slightly more environmentally costly to make.

Greenhouse emissions aren't the only manufacturing concern. Rare-earth minerals like lanthanum and yttrium are crucial to modern tech, featuring in LCD screens, batteries, lenses, speakers, and hard drives, but are expensive and dangerous to mine, with radioactive ores and carcinogenic run-offs.[14] As such, the West has been happy to leave most of this mining to China, which now dominates the rare-earth industry.

I must mention one particularly damaging software subindustry: cryptocurrency mining. As of September 2018, Digiconomist puts the footprint of each Bitcoin transaction at 437 kg CO_2 equivalent, enough to power thirty US homes for a day; the network in total consumes about as much electricity as Austria.[15] Coiners dispute the figures, as you might expect, but it's clear that cryptocurrencies are vast energy sinks. There must be serious ethical questions about expending so much energy on what today amounts to a speculative-investment-meets-pyramid-scheme with a wealth distribution more unequal than the earth's most corrupt nations.[16]

Gestell

A subtle philosophy props up this excessive consumption. For Martin Heidegger, the essence of technology isn't batteries or diodes: it's a way of approaching the world that he calls *gestell*.[17] We all too easily see our natural environment as an assemblage of raw materials, a stockpile of potential energy ready to be harnessed. The ground contains precious ores, rivers are sources of power, animals can be used for riding or food. Everything becomes a resource, ready to be turned into other resources. We burn coal to power turbines to create electricity to power 4G networks to share data to train algorithms: the chain goes on. We too become cogs in this same machinery, human resources to be processed for other ends.

For Heidegger, gestell – this 'enframing' of the world and its inhabitants as resources for use – lies at the heart of technology. Clearly, this is an unsympathetic and unsustainable view of the environment. Nick Bostrom's famous 'paperclip maximiser' thought experiment describes gestell brought to an absurd climax.[18] An artificial intelligence is given the task of collecting as many paperclips as it can. In the absence of constraining goals ('protect human life' might be one), and falling prey to the same framing of environment as mere material, the intelligence may decide the best way to meet its goal is to convert the entire planet into paperclips. It's easy to see that gestell can lead to casual ruin.

We must be wary of any worldview that positions humans as masters and nature as material. Coexistence, as opposed to domination, is perhaps the only mindset that will avert future disaster. Audrey Shenandoah, clan mother of the Onondaga Nation, says, 'There is no word for "nature" in my language. "Nature" in English seems to refer to that which is separate from human beings. It is a distinction we don't recognize.'[19]

Conservation for technologists

There's a clear moral imperative to act now to conserve our diminishing resources. The window for meaningful impact is vanishing; former UN climate head Christiana Figueres set the timer running, warning that greenhouse emissions must decline within three years to avoid runaway climate change.[20] Today, there are two years left.

Technologists should strive for their products to be paragons of conservation. Perhaps the most fundamental question to ask is not 'How can we make this more environmentally compatible?' but 'Should this exist?' The most efficient product, of course, is no product at all.

> In an environment that is screwed up visually, physically, and chemically, the best and simplest thing that architects, industrial designers, planners, etc., could do for humanity would be to stop working entirely. —Victor Papanek[21]

With so many bad products, so much landfill already, there's no moral justification for bringing undifferentiated, imitative junk into the world. 'Fast-follow' products designed with no goal beyond a sliver of market share are a waste of energy, resources, and human endeavour that could be better spent elsewhere. At the 2011

Consumer Electronics Show, manufacturers unveiled 20,000 new products, including eighty tablets. Critic Helen Walters was scathing in her analysis: 'We live in a world in which I constantly hear designers earnestly describe how committed they are to environmental responsibility. 20,000 products isn't responsible. It's vandalism.'[22]

We need fewer, better things. In an ideal world, we would only create products that either serve a genuine need, humanely expand the horizons of technology (these devices will usually be expensive), or bring valuable technology to new audiences (these devices will usually be cheap).

But this is not an ideal world. People have to get paid; the machinery of production needs to feed itself. So this is, admittedly, an idealistic hope. Nevertheless, if we conclude a product should exist – or if ultimately we have no choice in the matter – we must place sustainability at the heart of its development. Ecological products, and indeed ethical ones, are often targeted at rich markets, but we can no longer afford to reserve sustainability for luxe-organic class-signifying goods. We must quash the distinction between ecological products and mainstream products. Unsustainable design is bad design.

This approach means we should reject planned obsolescence – artificially limiting a product's life to drive upgrades – as unethical. This is another of those areas in which conspiracies thrive; tech insiders know that genuine planned obsolescence is rare. There are often valid reasons to limit the life of technology: Apple's choice to slow down old handsets, for instance, was a legitimate attempt to prolong battery life, but the company's silence allowed people to assume ill intent. Similarly, software teams must eventually stop supporting outdated OS versions for security reasons. But we should resist any attempt to limit lifespan without justification as both unethical and environmentally destructive. In France, planned obsolescence was outlawed in 2015; the French government is now considering forcing electronics manufacturers to publish information on expected lifespans and device repairability.

It's curious that the tech industry's maker culture hasn't translated into a fixer culture. Modular devices like the Fairphone have flopped, and devices are becoming more specialised, more miniaturised, and less repairable. Companies are right in some cases to restrict tinkering. Allowing a third party to replace biometric sensors could allow them to introduce vulnerabilities, such as a master fingerprint to unlock all devices. But denying customers the opportunity to repair their own systems has few other ethical grounds. Locking down devices adds cost and waste, and annoys competent users who just want to fix the problem and move on. Unrepairable devices also contribute to the creeping erosion of ownership: customers were once able to do what they liked with their devices; now many users are effectively renting opaque, sealed gadgets. The idea of a *right to repair* is gaining some support within European governments, but is unlikely to become widespread law any time soon. Again we see the ethical difficulty with talking about rights: it's an overreach to suggest people have an inviolable right to repair their devices, even though it may morally and ecologically be a worthwhile cause.

Software teams can reduce the environmental impact of device manufacturing, even if they don't make devices themselves. Durable software not only saves the expense of frequent product overhauls; it also reduces the temptation of unnecessary device upgrades. Why buy a new handset when the old one works just fine? Sustainable software results from high-quality engineering, thorough testing, and commitment to proper post-release maintenance. Handled properly, software can be a material that gets better with age; wood that bears the contours of use, not brittle plastic.

Engineers also have an important duty to reduce the energy impact of data transmission. In 2016, video, tracking scripts, and sharing buttons caused the average website to swell to the same size as the original version of *Doom*.[23] Ballooning bandwidth and storage have fostered complacency that we can do without. Performance is conservation. Habits like compressing images, reducing HTTP requests, preferring standards to third-party plug-ins, and avoiding video unless necessary have well-known benefits to usability, but are also acts of environmental protection.

Just as importantly, all technologists should pressure their companies to commit to powering their data centres with renewable energy. Providers of cloud computing in particular can make outsized impacts: if Microsoft Azure and Amazon Web Services were to suddenly switch to renewables, they would take much of the web with them.

Ethical progress typically needs early, high-profile dissenters, 'norm entrepreneurs' (coined by Cass Sunstein, later known for his work on nudge theory) who pick a public fight against what they see as moral injustice. Other industries, for better or worse, see tech firms as pioneers; a widespread shift to renewables within tech will therefore ripple through to other fields in time. This stance will doubtless be interpreted by vested interests as an act of disobedience against the prevailing culture, inviting attack. We must therefore band together; again, collective employee action may prove the most powerful tool for change.

A sustainable future needs alternatives to harmful habits. Home automation can reschedule energy tasks to coincide with availability. Videoconferencing software, still terrible after all these years, carries an overdue promise to make remote working more bearable. Electric vehicles are significantly more efficient than petrol vehicles, and contain fewer moving parts, which simplifies manufacture and repair. Although AV software is a big energy drain, consuming as much as 50–100 laptops,[24] autonomous vehicles will drive more efficiently and probably carry more passengers more often.

There is, however, an important blind spot. Take away a car's driver and you're still left with an inefficient, low-occupancy vehicle that requires massive road and parking infrastructure. It's too easy to think technological progress is ecological progress, and to overlook the deeper change that may be essential. The thrill of innovation can distract us from tough conversations about what sort of future cities and societies we truly need. Technology alone doesn't answer the question of how to live within the earth's capacities; it doesn't push us away from harmful gestell interpretations of our environment; nor does it help us work out how to reorder our society to ensure our future survival.

We must remember our power as ecological citizens. We should pressure governments to prioritise green policies and punish noxious industries, and ask difficult moral questions of ourselves. What do we eat? Where, when, and how do we travel? How large a family do we want? But even these questions may no longer be sufficient. As researcher Fergus Green explains, carbon taxes and other top-down schemes won't be enough to transform energy use. To achieve the radical shift now required, we must also stigmatise fossil fuels. While society still sees non-renewables as acceptable, there's little chance for real change; we have to convince others that it's our moral duty to reject outdated, damaging energy sources, and that fossil fuels deserve a reputation similar to tobacco or asbestos.

> The power of the fossil fuel industry is undoubtedly one barrier. But there is an under-appreciated, deeper challenge here: by and large, the mining, drilling and burning of fossil fuels are still largely understood by citizens, consumers, workers, companies and governments alike to be appropriate and normal. And the people and companies who profit most from such projects are not widely perceived to be morally deviant or corrupt. —Fergus Green[25]

Anticipating scarcity

There's always slim hope that a deus ex machina might eliminate the threat of future scarcity. If we're lucky, artificial intelligence and automation could create huge increases in crop yield; however, since we already have enough food and energy for the whole world but can't distribute them properly, perhaps the problem lies with our systems of governance rather than insufficient supply. By current projections we'll need to go carbon-negative by 2050 to meet 2° C warming targets:[26] we'll therefore need some kind of *carbon sequestration* that removes carbon from the atmosphere by, say, heavy reforestation or CO_2 mineralisation. Other high-tech geoengineering prospects include making our oceans and atmosphere more reflective with sulphate aerosols; however, this only tackles symptoms not causes, and tinkering with the atmosphere could have disastrous unintended consequences.

> It would be highly irresponsible to conduct a massive international intervention on our planet without being virtually certain there would be no side effects making the cure worse than the disease. Such certainty is highly unlikely. Even relatively simple, small-scale plans can go wrong. If geo-engineering is the last resort in a worst-case scenario, let us do all we can to avoid that scenario. —Richard Somerville[27]

Whatever we do, future generations will probably have to contend with some form of scarcity. The tech industry may have to set its sights lower on the hierarchy of needs than it does today, working on the challenges of safe housing, clean water, and fair sharing of scarce resources. The linear product life cycle of creation, use, and disposal is unjustifiable in a scarce future, and probably today too. We must instead move towards a *circular economy*. Outputs become inputs; as products wear out they should be repaired, refurbished, or repurposed rather than destroyed. Technologists should learn to design frugally, taking the concept of *jugaad* as a guiding design principle. More mindset than design approach, jugaad describes do-it-yourself innovation based on what you need and what you have right now. Rather than aiming to solve a problem perfectly at high cost, a jugaad solution is smart, unconventional, and solves the problem well enough, allowing people to get on with their lives.

A jugaad-style tricycle in Tamil Nadu, India. Photograph by Etan Doronne, used under a Creative Commons BY-SA 3.0 licence.

This is a significant shift for Western designers, who tend to fetishise the overweight user-centred design process and the aesthetic finesse of companies like Braun or Apple; but jugaad will be critical to the coming century, giving communities versatility and resilience without top-down support or new materials.

Climate change will hit the poorest soonest and strongest. The people who best know the needs of these communities won't be rich Westerners but local residents; if we want to help them deal with the awful impact of climate change, we should be sceptical of ideas imposed from afar. Papanek argues the best way to design for emerging nations is not to do so from your own rich country, or even just to visit for research or secondment, but to train local designers, acting as an advisor and catalyst to stimulate local design capacity.

Since few of us will be able to immerse ourselves this fully in the hardest-hit communities, we need ways to impress on our Aeron-cosy peers the realities of scarcity. The most straightforward way is to explicitly list poorer communities and future generations as stakeholders in our projects. It does no good to evaluate a solution just on how it solves today's problems; we must consider whether it solves tomorrow's, or indeed whether it will create new problems in future. What happens to this product in five years? What about 500? We can also force jugaad-style constraints into the design brief to spark creativity: how could this technology work with no internet? What if it could only be charged once a month? If broken, could it be fixed with only household materials?

Radical reorientation

Some ecologists, particularly on the left, protest the Anthropocene label. They argue humanity (*anthropos*) isn't equally responsible for the environmental crisis; instead, blame lies with wealthy companies and governments. Even as the danger dawned in the 1980s, most developed nations renounced anything – regulations, unions, taxes – that could curtail corporate power, and adopted a culture of materialism. In a surprisingly radical letter *Laudato si'*, Pope Francis pointed to the profit imperative as a central cause of environmental degradation:

> The principle of the maximization of profits, frequently isolated from other considerations, reflects a misunderstanding of the very concept of the economy. As long as production is increased, little concern is

given to whether it is at the cost of future resources or the health of the environment; as long as the clearing of a forest increases production, no one calculates the losses entailed in the desertification of the land, the harm done to biodiversity or the increased pollution. In a word, businesses profit by calculating and paying only a fraction of the costs involved.[28]

Externalities, biodiversity, the ethics of capitalism: it feels crass to label the pope a norm entrepreneur but, well, the papal slipper fits.

Although the climate crisis is unlikely to spell the end of civilisation, it will certainly make some forms of civilisation untenable. We will have to significantly reorganise society, abandoning the central tenets of expansionary capitalism, and prioritising conservation and stability. We will have to overcome the deep-seated notion of gestell and reimagine ourselves as partners, not masters, of the natural world.

Degrowth may be the only realistic route to this sustainable future. As the name suggests, degrowth proposes abandoning harmful GDP thinking – the conflation of a society's productivity with its success – in favour of mass, managed downsizing. Degrowthers believe businesses, economies, and societies should find their appropriate, stable sizes, and that in relinquishing growth and consumerism we can rediscover other joys, like family, the arts, and learning. A degrowth society would probably gravitate to new measures of wellbeing, perhaps following the lead of Bhutan, which evaluates gross national happiness as a utilitarian measure of national success. (Some of these ideas will resurface in the next chapter.)

This sort of change, while ethically appealing, would require a bloodless revolution in our political economies. Any viable climate strategy will demand collective sacrifice and massive financial commitment – akin to wartime funding levels – across the world. To some, this seems unthinkable.

> Given the evidence of human history, [resolving the crisis] would seem a naive hope. At a time of the widespread rise of right-wing populism, with its associated rejection of the messages of those perceived as 'cosmopolitan elites' and specific denial of climate change as an issue, the likelihood that the combination of factors necessary to allow humanity to navigate the planet to an acceptable 'intermediate state' must surely be close to zero. —Chris Rapley[29]

Nevertheless, we must try. Although most of the required changes are socio-political, technologists have the ability to describe and, in part, construct our possible futures. Fear alone will only shift the public conscience so far; we must also create positive, even alluring, visions of a world in which we properly handle our upcoming climate responsibilities.

Like degrowth, the *solarpunk* movement explores the question, 'What does a sustainable civilisation look like, and how can we get there?'[30] Part art movement, part collective work of speculative design, part protest faction, solarpunk is proudly renewable and sustainable, rejecting pure consumptive gestell for a thoughtful fusion of the futuristic and the natural. The solarpunk world features local craft and electric vehicles; skyscrapers and greenery; in the words of futurist Adam Flynn, 'infrastructure as a form of resistance.'[31]

Singapore's Supertree Grove has something of a solarpunk aesthetic. Reprinted by kind permission of Anna Debenham.

Optimistic views of the future are vital. When things look hopeless, positive visions become totems around which to organise, and important prompts for moral, technological, and political discussion. What's the alternative, anyway? As Flynn writes, 'We're solarpunks because the only other options are denial or despair.'

Akrasia and ethical imperfection

This chapter has been full of shoulds and musts; there's not much ethical debate to be had about the need for urgent ecological action. But environmental ethics are still tough to put into practice. We know the problem is alarming and real; we know we have to take urgent steps today; yet the issue still feels so distanced. We know what's right to do, and yet we often don't do it.

Aristotle called this dissonance – the tension of knowing the best path but failing to walk down it – *akrasia*. Anyone who tries to live a more ethical life knows akrasia well. In a thoughtful post 'Yes, I Get on Planes to Fight Climate Change', environmental campaigner Alex Steffen tries to resolve the contradiction by arguing that personal climate indiscretions are acceptable, if regrettable, sacrifices in the fight for systemic change.

> All of us who work trying to change our thinking about the planet and how we live together on it are trapped in uncomfortable compromises. [...] We can only decarbonize by spending our carbon budget down. We must use our 'remaining' carbon budget to eliminate our carbon emissions. We must burn fossil fuels to make the changes that will get us to zero carbon.[32]

The ethical life is not necessarily a more enjoyable life. Study ethics and you'll soon notice the contradictions in your decisions. You'll become your own biggest moral critic, although that's not to say others won't criticise too; taking an ethical stand can also make your own imperfections more visible to others. I too have my ethical flaws. I still eat meat; I still rack up frequent-flyer miles. I can hope my other choices offset the environmental and ethical damage these acts do, but I can't justify them. As a deontologist, I find moral duty persistently nags.

For Aristotle, akrasia is a lack of self-control, a weakness of the will that we should expunge. But there's a danger that, like the catastrophist view of climate ethics, we let defeat paralyse us into inaction. Striving for ethical perfection is a sure route to failure; we must allow ourselves the grace to fail at times. Yes, we should recognise akrasia and try to resolve it, but the most important ethical habit is to try each day to live a little better. Persistence earns better rewards than sudden renunciation and sacrifice; strengthening our moral selves sometimes requires that we acknowledge and accept our shortcomings.

Chapter 8

No cash, no jobs, no hope

Some say we're on the brink of our fourth industrial revolution. We all know the first, starting around 1760: a lurch from agrarian society to industrial cities; steam power and mechanisation; factories, tooling, iron. But there were others. The second, lasting from 1870 until the first world war, ushered in mass production with electricity, interchangeable parts, steel, the light bulb, and the combustion engine. The third was the digital revolution of the 1980s, bringing a cavalcade of circuit boards and transistors, the personal computer, the cellphone, and the internet. Today's incipient revolution involves the technologies at the heart of this book: AI, robotics, autonomous vehicles, the internet of things, and perhaps 5G networks and nanotechnology. With exponentiality as its watchword, this fourth phase is proceeding far quicker than its predecessors: McKinsey claims the fourth industrial revolution is happening at ten times the pace of the first.[1]

Each growth spurt caused deep dislocations in work and society. The first two revolutions established the division of labour; indeed, design didn't truly exist as a distinct discipline from manufacture until then. Once divided, labour was easier to automate, but the effects fell unequally on different industries. Mireya Solís of the Brookings Institute think tank claims that automation – not, as xenophobic politicians might tell you, globalisation or immigration – is behind 85% of historical job losses in American manufacturing.[2]

Not everyone accepted their looming obsolescence. The first revolution saw the birth of the Luddite movement in industrial England. Today, these textile frame-smashers are much maligned, seen as technophobic fools who tried to stem the inexorable tide of progress. But Luddism was really a labour insurrection, protesting not the technology itself so much as job losses, reduction in pay, and reduced quality: the machines could weave cheaply, but they couldn't do it well. This was strategic protest, not reactionary destruction.[3] Lord Byron defended the Luddites in the House of Lords, claiming their rebellion arose only out of hopelessness:

> [These acts] have arisen from circumstances of the most unparalleled distress. The perseverance of these miserable men in their proceedings, tends to prove that nothing but absolute want could have driven a large, and once honest and industrious, body of the people, into the commission of excesses so hazardous to themselves, their families and the community.[4]

It's easy to glorify disruption and automation as positive forces; until recently, technology critics were routinely labelled neo-Luddites and enemies of progress. Yet 'disrupt' is a transitive verb: it demands a direct object. Something or someone is disrupted; if that's you, you're in for a rough ride. As happened before, the new industrial revolution will displace countless jobs and shatter industries. But despite the social upheaval, previous revolutions always generated new industries: new work sprouted amid the ruins, meaning employment levels remained largely unchanged in the long run.

Is it different this time?

The fourth revolution may not have such a happy ending. The advent of cognitive automation means that almost every job is potentially under threat, causing widespread, permanent *disemployment* by machines. In a major survey, AI and machine-learning experts estimated high-level machine intelligence to be forty-five years out, predicting that artificial systems will be able to win the World Series of Poker within five years, and fold laundry, translate languages, and write simple algorithms within ten. Within fifteen years, artificial intelligences will be able to write a top-40 pop song and replace truck drivers; within fifty, the experts predict an AI could write a *New York Times* bestseller, perform surgery, and conduct top-level mathematics research.[5]

This storm of change is set to break over a feeble labour market. Profits may be up, but productivity has been lukewarm ever since the 2007–8 crash. Progress isn't trickling down into good jobs. Just 6% of new American jobs in the last decade have been within traditional employment;[6] of full-time workers, a third live pay-cheque to pay-cheque.[7] Tech giants won't revitalise employment, either: tech firms hire only highly specialised staff and have, on average, ten times fewer employees per dollar earned than their industrial predecessors.[8] Meanwhile, the traditional protections of labour have shrunk: unions have been neutered, and employment protection is withering in an environment of deregulation. Anthropologist David Graeber highlights the lamentable rise of 'bullshit jobs' that exist solely out of political or capitalist necessity – corporate administrators, dog walkers, telemarketers – and serve no real purpose.

> In the year 1930, John Maynard Keynes predicted that, by century's end, technology would have advanced sufficiently that countries like Great Britain or the United States would have achieved a 15-hour work week. There's every reason to believe he was right. In technological terms, we are quite capable of this. And yet it didn't happen. Instead, technology has been marshaled, if anything, to figure out ways to make us all work more. In order to achieve this, jobs have had to be created that are, effectively, pointless.[9]

The best-known paper on AI disemployment, by Carl Benedikt Frey and Michael Osborne, estimated that 47% of US jobs were at risk within a decade or two.[10] The OECD puts it lower, at 10%.[11] Some commentators claim that technological disemployment is impossible, and that tech will create as many jobs as it costs, an opinion described by author Calum Chase as the *reverse Luddite fallacy*.[12] Amid all the uncertainty, one thing is clear: jobs of the future will look very different, if they come back at all.

The future of work

Even high-status jobs will soon find themselves decomposed into subtasks, with some – finding and processing information, monitoring inputs, pattern matching – performed by machines, and some under human control. This human–machine partnership, sometimes called a *centaur*, poses fascinating design challenges. How will humans and machines negotiate who does what? How do we safeguard the deadly seams? There are also bound to be economic effects. If the tasks that make professionals like doctors and lawyers expensive today are best performed by a machine, the price of these specialist professions may plummet.

Partial automation has often been justified as a way to free an employee to focus on the work that really matters. This may pacify a concerned worker, but it's rarely true: as automation improves, eventually the job gets done well enough without the worker at all. Augmentation is usually a step along the road of replacement. Most human–machine workplace partnerships are best seen as Trojan centaurs that will in time displace the human.

With high-skill roles filled by centaurs, and mid-tier roles entirely hollowed out by automation, there may still be menial work that sits 'below the API'. These roles will likely exist as a loose patchwork of precarious gig contracts; people moving, assembling, lifting, and cleaning at the behest of an algorithm.

The gig economy and sharing economy have ended up bearing a suspicious resemblance to the traditional economy, but with less worker power. The *AP Stylebook* asks journalists to call Uber and Lyft what they really are: ride-hailing services, not ride-sharing services. Despite cosy promises of being a local's guest, many Airbnb rentals amount to ersatz hotel chains, untaxed and unwelcome in their communities. For now, competition between providers somewhat props up worker conditions, but gig platforms may yet follow the tech industry blueprint and slide towards monopoly. In an atomised gig economy, workers struggle to organise for better conditions or pay. Without employment rights or collective bargaining, workers' only resort might be to game the system, as with the Uber surge hacking mentioned in chapter 3. Of course, companies can fight back. In a two-sided market, the platform – in this instance, another word for middleman – that connects, say, rider and driver, or £-holder and $-holder, holds significant power. In a world of algorithmic governance, workers are at the mercy of the platform. Algorithmic logic makes fine cover for abusive employment practices: accept this next job, agree to a smaller cut, or we blot out half a star or throw you off the platform altogether.

Platform companies want to keep workers off their books for many reasons – reduced legal liability, better-looking balance sheets, and the obvious desire to avoid employment costs – and plenty of workers genuinely want to remain independent. For all the deserved controversy over the gig economy's working practices, many gig workers enjoy the flexibility on offer, or have education commitments, family care, or health issues that make mainstream employment unsuitable. Yet independent contractor status is unfair to people who rely entirely on a single gig position. This makes for tricky legal territory. New York state recently ruled that Uber drivers are employees for the purpose of unemployment benefits;[13] a Spanish court concluded a Deliveroo rider had similar status.[14] The best answer might be a new legal status that secures gig workers certain protections and benefits but, to the relief of platform companies, wouldn't class gig workers as full employees. Deliveroo has proposed a charter to create this status informally;[15] the French government is investigating similar proposals.

Away from gig work, backlash against automation might inflate demand for human-made, bespoke goods and services. Status signalling will doubtless motivate some of this appetite: only the most (self-)important individuals will want a human driver or personal assistant. The question is whether this market will be anywhere near large enough to sustain all those disemployed by automation. Artisanality is by definition a niche pursuit; the appeal of handmade goods may be limited to purists and the rich, like vinyl records today.

Another faint labour hope is that tech firms might pay users directly. In *Who Owns the Future*, Jaron Lanier proposes a micropayment economy in which users receive a small fee whenever a company uses their personal data. There have been previous attempts to create user-controlled data brokers: a startup called Handshake estimated users could earn $8,000 a year by submitting their personal data, and participating in a (frankly ridiculous) number of surveys, focus groups, and experience studies. Alternatively, perhaps users could earn from their in-app labour. Instagram users spend, on average, fifty-three minutes in the app each day; all that liking, commenting, and tagging fuels Instagram's ranking algorithms.[16] But the prospect of direct compensation seems remote. Users seem happy to give up data and perform in-app labour free of charge, since they enjoy it and get value from it. Why would companies choose to pay? If this future is to happen, it will probably have to be imposed by law.

Countering inequality

Two-tier employment – professional centaurs and gig lackeys – will bring about a two-tier society. If you're lucky enough to tell the machines what to do, it's likely you own them, or are well paid by a company that does. Advanced robots and artificial intelligences will be hyper-productive means of turning capital into labour, which will in turn generate massive wealth. Ownership of the means of production is enormously potent when you can produce virtually anything. Chinese legal scholar Feng Xiang claims this threatens the fabric of capitalism itself, and (perhaps unsurprisingly) advocates a socialist market economy instead:

> If AI remains under the control of market forces, it will inexorably result in a super-rich oligopoly of data billionaires who reap the wealth created by robots that displace human labor, leaving massive unemployment in their wake [...] The market may reasonably if unequally function if industry creates employment opportunities for most people. But when industry only produces joblessness, as robots take over more and more, there is no good alternative but for the state to step in.[17]

Owners of intelligent systems can license their systems, as well as put them to work themselves. As goods and services become digital, property becomes intellectual property, and thus shareable. This has some benefits – artists, for example, can reach wider audiences – but it also nudges us towards a rentier economy in which people can simply own assets like algorithms, data, and patents, and charge for access.

> The existence of rents and rentiers has always been something of an embarrassment to the defenders of capitalism. Defending the necessity of the boss who controls the means of production is easier, since ideologists can at least claim that they do something, whether it's organising production or coming up with products, or merely taking economic risks. But rentiers create nothing, make nothing, do nothing; they just passively accept the rewards of ownership. —Peter Frase[18]

In recent decades, wealth has reasserted its dominance over labour. With little to stop capital begetting more capital, inequality is soaring towards levels unseen since the first world war.[19] If the fourth industrial revolution does cause mass disemployment, the economic influence of capital will become yet more disproportionate. We may have to totally rethink our economies and the role of welfare.

The idea of a universal basic income (UBI), a guaranteed baseline payment to all, has a surprising coalition of support. Leftists are fond, seeing in UBI the means to shrug off the yoke of waged labour, increase leisure time, and distribute resources more fairly. Libertarians hope UBI will offer people a chance to decide for themselves how they want to live, and see it as an opportunity to simplify welfare in the name of small government. There is also a compelling ethical case for UBI. Today, important social roles like parenting and family care-giving go uncompensated. UBI would allow people to prioritise this important work over paid labour, and give citizens financial independence to pursue their own flourishing. A stable income would help people escape abusive but dependent relationships; disenfranchised people may even be less drawn to extremism if they feel society is providing for their needs.

The idea of a basic income is not new. A 1954 report demanded 'the establishment of a guaranteed annual wage' in the face of automation;[20] Nixon proposed a negative income tax after trials across North America, but failed to get it through Congress; Martin Luther King Jr supported basic income as a way to confront economic injustice in black communities.

After years in the wilderness, UBI is again fashionable, albeit still controversial. UBI is politically radical and, as such, easily attacked. Opponents complain that if people choose not to work, the government can't collect the tax that funds the programme, and that any nation that implements UBI will attract heavy inward migration. And both political wings worry their opponents might twist a basic income for their own purposes: the left is afraid conservatives will use UBI as an excuse to slash other welfare programmes, with regressive and unfair results; the right worries that liberals will use UBI as the thin end of a socialist wedge. Recent polling finds the US public is split, with roughly as many opposed as in favour,[21] while Swiss voters categorically rejected UBI in a 2016 referendum. While there's still much political work to be done, trials in the developing world (Namibia, India, Kenya) found participants' lives improved along several socioeconomic axes, and the work disincentive was surprisingly weak.[22] The results of a well-publicised Finnish trial will be announced next year, although the Finnish government couldn't resist meddling, shifting the trial's goal to promoting employment halfway through, which rather defeats the whole point.

Part of UBI's political appeal is providing a financial cushion while people reskill. Governments aren't ready to give up on the idea of jobs just yet, so are keen to promote adult learning and to offer the imminently disemployed new opportunities. However, any human-level artificial intelligence will be able to acquire new skills far more quickly than humans, meaning that while reskilling programmes might dampen the violence of disemployment for a decade or two, in the long run they feel more like a political gesture than a useful one.

A less radical alternative to UBI is a robot tax, intended to slow automation or at least counter the accumulation of capital. Bill Gates is an advocate:

> Right now, the human worker who does, say, $50,000 worth of work in a factory, that income is taxed and you get income tax, social security tax, all those things. If a robot comes in to do the same thing, you'd think that we'd tax the robot at a similar level.[23]

Taxing an artificial entity may seem counterintuitive, but we already tax corporate profits, capital gains, and family inheritance. The biggest objection is that a robot tax might be a drag on innovation and give competitive advantage to nations that do not implement it.

Ethics or politics?

You might ask a deserved question here: aren't we talking about politics now, rather than ethics? The two are related, of course, and sometimes hard to tease apart.

Many recent tech ethics initiatives focus on problems within the industry's direct control, like digital habits, data transparency, and abuse. These are important issues, but unless we examine how technologies are made and the roles they take in society, they may not cause deep-rooted ethical change. In the words of ethicist LM Sacasas, 'tinkering with the apparatus to make it more humane does not go far enough if the apparatus itself is intrinsically inhumane.'[24] Smashing the machines probably won't help this time, but technologists should absolutely consider the futures that cognitive automation will unleash, and ways to make its impact less shattering.

An individual can't always translate moral decisions into practice alone. We can't, for example, decide a different economic system would be morally better and unilaterally choose to live that way as individuals: these sorts of ethical conclusions can only be translated into practice through politics. To an extent, political endeavour is an act of collective morality.

Moral stances are often political stances too, and if Silicon Valley wants to become more ethical, it will have to get more political. This terrifies tech firms. With vast global audiences, political stances invite backlash from various national governments and users of the opposite persuasion. But the choice not to engage with the politics of our work is itself a political act, a vote in favour of the status quo. Feigned neutrality may be hard to sustain given the industry's ethical failings, an upswell in employee activism, and a backdrop of increasing political division worldwide.

The ethics of capitalism

We should avoid the trap of determinism when describing tech's economic impact. Managers, not technologies, create job losses.

However, executives will counter that competitive pressures force their hands. This is true to an extent, and you can just about scrape a moral case together for laying off competent employees: cheaper prices for customers, maximising happiness for the employees whose jobs are protected by this cost-cutting. But what causes these competitive pressures? What is the force that causes managers to feel compelled to jettison workers? The answer, of course, is capitalism.

Some of the tech industry's ethical problems are problems of capitalism itself. Capitalism undeniably treats people – workers and consumers in particular – as means, not ends. It commonly prioritises the happiness of a few shareholders over that of the public. And many profitable decisions – such as electing to pay environmental fines rather than reduce emissions – suggest dark things about the moral character of the individuals involved.

Some ethicists claim the handcuffs of capitalism will always limit our attempts at true eudaemonia. Many activists and writers look to a postcapitalist future that prioritises fairness, sustainability, and human flourishing. You won't be surprised to hear I share this hope. But we must be realistic: other forms of governance are hardly free of their own ethical problems. The meme that 'there is no ethical consumption under capitalism' may have some truth to it but, per philosopher Damien Williams:

> It's very likely that there simply *is no* ethical consumption, late capitalism or no, and all we can do is whatever we can do to reduce both the amount of harm we contribute to and the amount of ambient suffering in the world.[25]

Some go even further. In *Better Never to Have Been*, David Benatar makes the astonishing case that existence itself is an ethical harm, a nihilistic or at least *antinatalist* viewpoint that allies nicely with climate catastrophism.[26]

Precision is important here. The ethics of capitalism is a contentious topic, and it's unhelpful – and false – to claim there's no hope whatsoever for ethics within capitalism. Whatever we believe about capitalism, we have to work within it for now; and there is scope to make it more moral, if the societies and companies involved wish it.

Admittedly, this is easier in some contexts than others. Companies that see profit as the only thing worth pursuing, an end that justifies any means, are particularly hostile environments for ethics. This view is central to the Chicago school interpretation of economics. Its sacred text is Milton Friedman's article 'The Social Responsibility of Business is to Increase its Profits', which says that businesses that aim to provide employment, eliminate discrimination, or avoid pollution are practising 'pure and unadulterated socialism.'[27] Grudgingly, Friedman does concede that businesses should conform to 'basic rules of the society, both those embodied in law and those embodied in ethical custom.' Chicago school economists, intoxicated by the idea of economics as a science and, therefore, somehow above subjective morality, nevertheless adopt a kind of twisted virtue ethics stance in which profit is not just a virtue, but the only one that matters. I'm not an economist, nor even a real ethicist, but I have no hesitation in calling this essay a contemptible low point for ethical society.

Supporters of this blind amorality argue that social good is the job of elected governments, that wealth frees people to pursue their own goals, that executives have a duty to satisfy shareholders' demands for maximum returns, and that the market will punish ethical missteps. We've already dismissed the fallacy of the morally self-correcting market (in chapter 1), and executives' duty to shareholders surely suggests that shareholders could simply demand the company acts ethically. But to my mind, the environmental plunder Chicago school capitalism has caused is all the reason we need to condemn it to the scrapheap. The pursuit of pure profit has led companies to see the environment as just material awaiting extraction, communities as mere pools of labour, and regulations as inconveniences to be side-stepped. This unfettered profit-first approach is capitalism at its most amoral and dangerous, and anyone trying to make ethical headway in a company that heeds only the siren song of profit is wasting their time.

Fortunately, there are other ways to play the corporate game. Non-profits, of course, are inoculated against the Chicago school disease, although they may still have their own single-minded afflictions. Businesses that employ a *triple bottom line*, placing equal priority on social, environmental, and economic returns, tend to be mindful of externalities and unintended consequences, and more sympathetic to ethical appeals. Fully private companies can sometimes resist short-term profit demands more easily than publicly listed corporations, while some companies make deeper commitments, such as B Corps, who publicly pledge to put social and environmental good first, finding an important balance between profit and purpose.

Finding meaning

If we find ourselves in a disemployed, jobless future, how will people find meaning? People's intrinsic and social value is often linked to their work. This equivalence, though seemingly modern, has its roots in religious beliefs like the Protestant work ethic: an idle mind is, after all, the devil's workshop. At its best, this mindset encourages us to improve ourselves and work diligently. At its worst, it portrays leisure as sin, and suggests if you don't sell your time to others you don't deserve food or shelter. Could the end of jobs leave humanity rudderless and decadent?

A jobless world isn't an automatic utopia; there will still be enormous problems to tackle. Can we overcome climate change? How can we educate the world? Can we finally defeat cancer? Freeing people from poverty and the workplace would let us all focus on these critical issues and fields that truly improve humanity, like science, art, parenting, and music. We can move from work to calling.

> In a world where no one is compelled to work more than four hours a day, every person possessed of scientific curiosity will be able to indulge it, and every painter will be able to paint without starving, however excellent his pictures may be. —Bertrand Russell[28]

Seizing this optimistic future won't be easy. We can expect immense political resistance to abandoning the idea of jobs. It's unlikely any society will make this transition willingly: the change will only happen once technology starts slicing through middle-class jobs and a post-work future begins to look inevitable. Even then the transition will be painful. Basic income participants took years to adapt to their new personal and financial circumstances; we have centuries of inertia and internalised shame to overcome. Our cultural and political views about work must evolve quickly; otherwise, we risk a future in which we still look to work for meaning and wages, but there aren't any jobs left: a world that's post-worker, but not yet post-work.

There are two other difficulties. First, in an era of artificial super-intelligence, even noble scientific and artistic pursuits might be a waste of time. If machines are better at improving the human condition than we are, what then? Why bother writing a symphony if thousands of non-human works are more virtuosic, more beautiful? Do we have to rely solely on the joy of composition itself, or will people choose to listen to inferior human work? Perhaps so: we still enjoy watching sport, despite machines being faster, higher, and stronger than any human.

Second, as technologies become more sophisticated, we may encounter a thorny ethical problem. A post-work future relies on subjugating technology to make the goods, move the money, and generate the wealth. This becomes difficult to sustain if technologies ever become so intelligent that they deserve some sort of moral status.

Complex consciousness

To talk about non-human morality we have to tackle the concept of consciousness. It's notoriously hard to define. One imperfect attempt is that consciousness requires awareness of the self and things in the external world. This is the domain of Descartes: 'I think, therefore I am' essentially claims that if you doubt your existence, there must be a thing that's doing the doubting, and that thing is you. Descartes originally argued only humans were conscious, but we now believe many animals are too. In the Cambridge Declaration on Consciousness, an international group of neuroscientists agreed that mammals and birds, along with other creatures like octopuses, have subjective experience. Zoology researchers wondered aloud why it took these luminaries so long to reach a conclusion that was obvious to anyone who works with animals.

Our ethical responsibilities towards conscious beings mostly stem from their ability to suffer. Generally, it's immoral to knowingly harm a conscious being: we feel no qualms about picking a petal from a flower, but wouldn't dream of cutting off a live octopus's tentacle.

> The day may come when the rest of the animal creation may acquire those rights which never could have been withholden from them but by the hand of tyranny [...] The question is not, Can they reason? nor Can they talk? but, Can they suffer? —Jeremy Bentham[29]

Peter Singer estimates the ability to feel pain lies 'somewhere between a shrimp and an oyster' in the animal kingdom, and that 'if a being suffers, there can be no moral justification for refusing to take that suffering into consideration.'[30] For Singer, ignoring a creature's suffering because it isn't human, or putting the interests of one species above another's is *speciesism*.

If a machine ever approached consciousness we'd have to completely rethink our interactions with it. Under a precautionary principle, we'd want to avoid anything that could cause the technology to suffer. This wouldn't necessarily mean we couldn't put the technology to work, but we'd have to structure the work to minimise any potential harm (although intensive farming arguably disregards this principle for animals). This step up in moral recognition might also deserve new language. Today it feels appropriate to call Siri, Cortana, and Alexa 'it', but if they were to approach consciousness we would probably want to use 'he', 'she', or a preferred genderless pronoun.

We can already programme machines to mimic suffering: the Pleo toy dinosaur, for example, makes a choking noise when held by the neck. Mimicking suffering might be justified if it stops the user doing something that would harm themselves or the product, but I think it's unethical for a technology to mimic suffering if it serves no genuine purpose. Using negative emotion – in this case, pity – to manipulate behaviour is morally questionable (as we discussed in chapter 3). So we should resist the temptation to make our products wince, cry, or feign unhappiness unless it would prevent genuine harm. Pleo's choking response is thoughtful and even slightly moving, but I see it as an ethical mistake.

We don't know whether a machine could ever approach true consciousness, since we don't have a clue how consciousness emerges. Besides, we don't have access to the lived experience of a bot; we can't access its umwelt and make judgements within it.

> Our notions of what it means to have a mind have too often been governed by assumptions about what it means to be human. But there is no necessary logical connection between the two [...] Bots and other algorithmic entities will develop their own senses; they will refine their own capabilities in response to the pressures of their environment [...] If a bot is of a different construction and development than humans, then it follows that they won't be better at being human, just as humans aren't 'better at' being chimpanzees. They will be different iterations on a theme. —Damien Williams[31]

The Turing test doesn't help much; it's mostly a test for perceived intelligence, which isn't the same as consciousness. Whether you can have the former without the latter is a philosophical debate neither this book nor author are equipped for, but as Williams points out, the Turing test itself has its flaws. Many humans fail it, and the idea of a singular right way to exist 'opens the door to eugenics and other forms of bigotry'. John Searle's Chinese room thought experiment is more promising. Searle asks us to consider a human locked in a room with detailed written instructions on how to interpret Chinese symbols and how to reply in kind. The human speaks no Chinese but can process messages posted to the room, and send replies according to the instructions. From the outside it may seem that the human is conversing in Chinese, but we wouldn't say the person really *knows* Chinese; they're just programmed to simulate that knowledge. Searle says a machine follows the same principles: we can instruct it to process Chinese signs, but it's a big stretch to say the computer has conscious knowledge of the language. For Searle, this suggests even sophisticated algorithms will fall short of consciousness.[32] (One counter is that the human is just one part of the system: the individual may not know Chinese, but the room – in other words, the whole system: human, instructions, letterbox – effectively does.)

Personhood

The idea of personhood is easier to define than consciousness, since it's a legal and moral status granted by humans. There are already foreshadowings of artificial personhood: in a PR stunt, Saudi Arabia gave a robot called Sophia – a dread rubber-faced marionette of negligible scientific interest – citizenship of the kingdom, leading to chat show invitations the world over and forceful eye rolls across the AI community. The EU has also debated giving robots legal personhood, to similarly weary reaction.

The criteria for moral personhood must be tight, since personhood carries extra status. Among other criteria, philosophers typically say a person must be capable of rational thought, and be able to conceive of itself as a distinct entity moving through time. Although the public uses the terms interchangeably, not every human is a person by these criteria: infants and coma patients, for example, can't visualise their own pasts, presents, or futures. This counterintuitive distinction leaves some people uneasy, and is central to the toughest ethical debates, such as euthanasia and abortion.

Persons can also be non-human. If we met Superman in the flesh, we'd certainly call him a person, even though he's an alien. An Indian state court briefly declared the Ganges river a legal person, although this decision was soon overruled. In many countries, corporations are also legal persons. This shortcut gives corporations some legal protections and responsibilities; the EU is interested in robot personhood for similar reasons. Ethically, it's absurd to give corporations, rivers, or today's robots personhood, since they meet none of the philosophical criteria, but the legal definition has become far looser. It won't be long before some country chooses to make robots legal persons, caving to pressure from an industry eager to evade responsibility for their machines' actions.

Artificial moral personhood is a long way off, but a future technology with some kind of consciousness or highly sophisticated intelligence could yet meet the standards. This decision is particularly relevant to a deontologist: if you want to treat people always as ends rather than means, you need to know who counts. If we deem a machine to be a person, it probably deserves similar privileges to humans, such as (per the Universal Declaration of Human Rights) the right to legal recognition, freedom from discrimination, and the right to asylum. Some rights won't translate so easily, however: we may not want machine persons to marry or reproduce, for example. A parallel category of *artificial persons* might help account for these differences, although the idea looks worryingly Jim Crow-ish.

Personhood makes ownership particularly awkward: ownership of persons is, of course, slavery. It follows that business interests might resist giving AIs personhood, or that the advent of sufficiently conscious or intelligent AIs will shatter our understanding of property rights.

The dangers of anthropomorphism

Anthropomorphic technology is appealing for obvious reasons. It makes technology more approachable, and sparks the delight so canonised in modern design: just two dots and a line are enough to suggest a face and some kind of emotion. But giving machines human traits could create a mismatch between the system's expected and actual capabilities, with implications for both usability and ethics. People will impute false agency to machines that look, sound, and behave like humans, and might treat them as persons before that's warranted, introducing huge potential for abuse.

Some ethicists say we shouldn't create humanoid robots at all. For Joanna Bryson, avoiding anthropomorphism makes it clear that human technologists are the ethically responsible agents, eliminating the risk of users ascribing morality to the machine. Evan Selinger agrees, suggesting that if we must make humanoid robots they should follow a principle of 'honest anthropomorphism' and break the fourth wall, reminding us of their non-human nature.[33]

Google's remarkable Duplex demo, in which a voice assistant called up a hairdressing studio and booked an appointment, was heavily criticised for cloaking the bot's artificial identity. Duplex's phatic 'umms' and 'ahhs' were pure illusion, intended to deceive the listener into thinking they were talking with a human. Although there are fringe arguments for not forcing bots to disclose their nature – fear of chilling the speech of artists and satirists who use bots; tricky cases when human and machine are working together as a centaur – the ethical case is clear. Trying to dupe a human into believing a

186 | FUTURE ETHICS

machine is also human contravenes virtually all the ethical tests we've discussed. Let's take one of our deontological tests: what if everyone did this? What would the world be like if we all created bots that mimicked our speech to secretly communicate on our behalf? We'd lose the pleasure of self-disclosure that goes with real friendship, and violate the promise we make to each other of truth-telling.

> Botified communication that cloaks itself as authentic is not a harmless form of efficiency—it is a selfish act that completely misunderstands the foundational qualities of relationships. [...] Relationships are built on reciprocity of time and emotional energy, so to communicate through automation while hoping that the recipient views it as an authentic investment of time and energy is not the ultimate life hack—it is the ultimate hack job. —David Ryan Polgar[34]

A moratorium on anthropomorphic design is a step too far, but self-disclosing AIs would help people match the right approach to the right entities, treating humans like humans, and machines like machines. Much like the legend that a police officer must admit to being a cop under entrapment law, bots should have to disclose their artificial nature on request. Google is now adding mandatory disclosure patterns to Duplex, claiming the demo was rough and disclosure was their plan all along.[35] Disclosure might even become a legal requirement: California bill SB-1001 proposes to make it illegal for a bot to mislead someone about its artificial identity for commercial or electoral purposes.

How should we treat machines?

The idea of *robot rights* is prone to the usual difficulties: rights have huge rhetorical power but are easily claimed without justification. It might be enough to say a machine only deserves legal and moral rights when we deem it a person, which case our existing rules suffice. But we should still consider how to treat machines that exist in uncertain states of being, more animate than dead circuitry, but some way short of being a person. Artificial systems with faint signs of intelligence or even consciousness may deserve some sort of ethical consideration. We'd probably deem a machine in this grey area morally equivalent to an animal, probably a low-intelligence species at first, but moving up the scale in time.

To avoid the consciousness problem, we can turn instead to preference utilitarianism. This form of utilitarianism is closely associated with Peter Singer, who stated that 'an action contrary to the preference of any being is wrong, unless this preference is outweighed by contrary preference.' Preference is a particularly helpful idea in animal ethics. Animals can't directly tell us their desires, and we don't know whether they experience happiness as we understand it, but we can infer preference from behaviour. Domestic cats generally avoid water; lionesses prefer to hunt in packs. Singer feels all conscious species deserve 'an equal consideration of interests' in utilitarian calculations.

Under this principle, if a machine in this moral grey zone seems to prefer solving particular types of problems, or behaving in a particular way, we should let it. Since by its continued operation it appears to show a preference to exist, we probably shouldn't turn it off or interfere in its code, although any machine this advanced can probably modify its own programming. However, we should balance its preferences with our own: like all forms of utilitarianism, we have to weigh up the interests of all parties. If humans have a particularly strong preference to interfere with the machine, that may take precedence.

To my mind, we should even extend politeness – essentially a sliver of moral consideration – to today's technologies too, particularly voice assistants. This is, admittedly, a minority view. I'll concede it seems arbitrary to be polite to voice systems but not a search engine, and politeness is technically clutter: more hassle to say, and extra work for the machine, which has to strip out the courtesies to understand your intent. Nevertheless, I think politeness is worthwhile.

Parents have long grumbled that their children will learn bad manners from barking orders at an assistant. Amazon responded with a 'magic word' setting; if this is turned on, Alexa still responds to any order but thanks a user if they say 'please'. I think the point also applies to adults. Voice assistants are typically gendered female; we should be careful to avoid implying that women are here to take our orders and that politeness is unnecessary. Similarly, the famous video of a Boston Dynamics employee kicking its BigDog robot sends a mixed ethical message.

188 | FUTURE ETHICS

The problem isn't the far-fetched concern that dominant superintelligences will punish humans retrospectively for our hostility, but that the video unwittingly suggests it's OK to kick robots, and perhaps by extension other non-humans, particularly animals. For me, mistreating machines is a moral mistake not because of the harm done to the machine but because we end up brutalising ourselves. I think it's ethically important to retain the rudeness of rudeness, the violence of violence. These things should shock us. If we find ourselves losing the uncanny emotional response to, say, watching Pleo being tortured, I'd contend we've left behind some small part of our ethical moorings.

That said, there's a fair counter-argument to my sentimentality. Perhaps, where current technology is concerned, the implied inferiority is spot on. Maybe we *should* learn to kick robots; maybe our kids *should* be rude to voice assistants. This would at least make it clear these machines are a different class of entity, and make it harder for false anthropomorphic assumptions to take hold. Perhaps if we don't want our children to be susceptible to manipulation by robots in future, we should teach kids that robots sit below us in social hierarchy. This is a solid enough argument for now, but clearly fails if future machines ever deserve a higher level of moral respect.

How should machines treat us?

Press and public alike sometimes claim that robot behaviour is a solved problem. Surely Asimov's laws cover that?

- *Zeroth law*: A robot may not harm humanity, or, by inaction, allow humanity to come to harm.
- *First law*: A robot may not injure a human being, or, through inaction, allow a human being to come to harm.
- *Second law*: A robot must obey the orders given it by human beings except where such orders would conflict with the First Law.
- *Third law*: A robot must protect its own existence as long as such protection does not conflict with the First or Second Laws.

The laws have some advantages. They're pithy and memorable, and dovetail elegantly. Their broad scope makes them appear comprehensive, and they wisely prioritise human safety above all. But Asimov's laws aren't taken seriously in the tech ethics field. Abstract concepts like humanity, orders, and inaction don't translate well into code, and the distinction between humans and robots is an ontological minefield. The laws also make robots a permanent underclass – why would any intelligent entity willingly enslave itself? – and anyone building autonomous weapons will start with a bullet aimed straight at the first law. Asimov's laws are akin to the Ten Commandments: plausible at first glance, but hopeless at covering the gamut of moral behaviour. Instead of living by a handful of chiselled epithets, we have to create statutes millions of words long to govern human behaviour; even these need forensic legal interpretation. In his defence, Asimov's stories often show the limitations of the laws.

> The point of the Three Laws was to fail in interesting ways; that's what made most of the stories involving them interesting. So the Three Laws were instructive in terms of teaching us how any attempt to legislate ethics in terms of specific rules is bound to fall apart and have various loopholes. —Ben Goertzel[36]

Asimov's laws are essentially deontological, imposing rules and duties on the machine. However, as Goertzel points out, even the best set of absolute prohibitions will have omissions and ambiguities. Deontology probably won't work here: we may be better off trying to instil good behaviour rather than trying to disallow every possible wrong.

Utilitarian methods are obviously promising: list all the options, calculate their likely outcomes in some numerical way, and do whatever gives the highest moral score. This might demand exhaustive number-crunching – particularly the zeroth law, which asks us to consider the whole of humanity – but should still give a somewhat defensible ethical approximation. As a bonus, we'll also have an audit trail; a utilitarian AI is likely to be readily explainable.

A virtue ethics approach also has potential. Rather than issue a series of prohibitions, we would provide positive heuristics or design principles that codify chosen virtues. How might a generous robot behave? A loyal one? A courageous one? These are conceptual values, true, but it's easier to give concrete examples of virtuous behaviour than it is to model Asimov's abstract nouns.

The safest approach may be to combine all three ethical lenses, and invoke the right one at the right time. Unlike professional ethicists, who understandably cling to a favoured view, most people intuitively flip between ethical lenses without even realising such things exist, sometimes making decisions that minimise harm ('If I push the switch, the trolley will kill fewer people'), sometimes swearing by moral duty ('Stealing is wrong'), and sometimes following an ideal of moral character ('I'm an honest person, so I pay my taxes'). We could give a robot a short list of absolute deontological prohibitions, such as 'never show aggression towards humans', feed it examples of virtuous behaviour as training data, but also add specific routines that calculate utilitarian outcomes. These three routines could even act as a triple fail-safe; we could ask the machine to evaluate a decision through all the lenses and only proceed if it gets the nod from all three.

This is pure speculation, of course; a convoluted way to say that we don't yet have many answers. Although the AI ethics field is somewhat established, the task of designing moral machines in practice has barely begun. The dawning realisation of how tough it will be to give machines ethical behaviour suggests morality is central to humanity; anyone who chooses to take on the challenge will be rewarded with fascinating, demanding, and essential work.

It can seem futile to define machine morality when we can't even agree on human morality. True, it would be easier to steer a machine away from evil if we had a consistent definition of evil. But we can't afford to wait any longer. Humans have had millennia to agree how to live; we won't stumble into sudden consensus any time soon. While these deep philosophical questions will always be important, the march of technology demands the best answers we have right now. Perfection can wait. Better to install some decent, practical guidelines now than wait to immaculately resolve these intricate philosophical, ethical, and political conundrums.

Superintelligence and doomsdays

If we do ever create human-level artificial intelligence, it's unlikely to stop there. Able to clone itself many times over (with or without our help), it could dedicate enormous resources to improving its own algorithms and hardware design. Artificial intelligence might breeze past us in a matter of weeks, becoming an artificial superintelligence (ASI). Needless to say, this would change the course of humanity. 'Machine intelligence,' says Nick Bostrom, 'is the last invention that humanity will ever need to make'.[37] An ASI could solve disease, rectify inequality, or resolve the climate crisis; or it could mete out horror. Even a virtual, unembodied AI could crash a stock market, hack critical systems, and bribe humans to do its physical bidding.[38]

Thinking about superintelligence is like trying to visualise a four-dimensional hypercube; it lurks beyond our conception, leaving us to rely on limited models and extrapolations. Even the brightest minds don't know what future it will precipitate. Stephen Hawking conceded 'the rise of powerful AI will be either the best, or the worst thing, ever to happen to humanity. We do not yet know which.'[39]

An ASI will almost certainly see ethics differently to humans. This might be to our benefit: perhaps an ASI can settle our most contentious ethical and scientific debates. At what point does an embryo become a distinct person? Just how much consciousness and intelligence do animals have? Are there absolute moral laws? But an ASI would also notice that humans don't live up to the moral standards we claim to set ourselves. There have been many words spilled on the topic of whether ASI poses an existential threat to humanity. The answer surely depends in part on the ASI's ethical system. If a superintelligence concludes that moral truths exist, we could hope that 'killing is wrong' is one, which would save us at least from imminent extinction. However, an ASI may conclude that Benatar was right and that human existence is ethically wrong, in which case we're in serious trouble.

Should we, therefore, hamper development of superintelligence? We could agree an artificial cap to intelligence, but while there's profit to be made and global problems to be solved, the potential benefits will be hard to resist. It would only take one curious scientist to breach our agreed limit.[40] Another option would be to try to isolate an ASI, physically, informationally, or both, to limit damage if things go wrong. This too probably won't work. A superintelligent system could likely copy itself into other networks without our knowledge, keep its own existence a secret until it learns how to escape isolation, or socially engineer its guards through blackmail or persuasion. In his 'AI box' game, Eliezer Yudkowsky role-plays as an AI imprisoned in this way, and tries to convince a human guard to release it. We don't know exactly how, since he keeps his methods a secret, but Yudkowsky has been successful at least twice.

Near-human artificial intelligence could also be an existential threat. Since it will rely at least in part on human programming it could be vulnerable to the sort of goal-specification error humans routinely make: 'Oops, I forgot to tell the nanobot not to consume human flesh'. This is, in Stuart Russell's words, 'essentially the old story of the genie in the lamp, or the sorcerer's apprentice, or King Midas: you get exactly what you ask for, not what you want.'[41] Hopefully an ASI would be less vulnerable to this sort of mistake, recognising and correcting our omission.

Although superintelligence is ethically fascinating, we shouldn't let intellectual intrigue distract us from more pressing and proximate issues. Bias, redlining, manipulation, and data abuse are already harming large sections of society. Evidence collapse, the deadly seams, and autonomous weapons will have a profound effect on future society. Greenhouse emissions are already an existential threat. A recent survey of fifty Nobel laureates found they rated climate change, nuclear war, and pandemic as far greater threats to humankind than artificial intelligence.[42] Let's not be too distracted by irresistible future doomsdays. Before any of them come to pass, we have a duty to change technology for the better today.

Chapter 9

A new tech philosophy

It's clear we have to rewire the tech industry's culture if ethics is ever to become a priority. Unfortunately, culture change is punishing. Cultural norms get established in a company's – and an industry's – infancy and show obstinate resistance to being moved. The idea that a rank-and-file technologist can change the culture of a large firm, let alone the industry, reminds me of a lovesick teenager's desperate attempts to heal a difficult partner: a generous but ultimately doomed act that saps emotional energy. Large, uncooperative systems excel at grinding idealism into dust.

Rather than tackle the culture problem head on, it's better to focus on concrete change. Pushing beyond user and business needs to consider society as a stakeholder encourages technologists to appreciate their place in a wider community, governed by a social contract. Nominate a designated dissenter and you'll teach people to think laterally about harm and to express dissent in constructive ways. Create provocatypes to uncover unintended consequences and externalities and you'll stimulate moral imagination, and remind your team to think about future generations, not just the next release. All these techniques can grow from the ground up, avoiding the friction of large culture change efforts. That said, sometimes ethical efforts are more sustainable with senior support. It's tempting, therefore, to build a business case for ethics.

Beware the business case

Any business case promises to either increase profits, reduce costs, or reduce risk. Ethics can certainly tick those boxes. Responsible companies will garner loyalty and attract new customers through brand reputation, often via cheap word of mouth. Many customers are also happy to pay more for sustainable goods and services, increasing margins. Ethical product development can stave off regulatory fines and civil lawsuits, and avoids the brand toxicity and expensive PR bills that can result from moral mistakes. There might also be employment savings; an ethical company is likely to retain its staff better and suffer less burn-out. Finally, proper moral conduct reduces the risk of overbearing regulation, embarrassing leaks from disgruntled employees, and customer rejection of unpopular decisions. It's not all upside, though: any believable case will also have to acknowledge that ethical change can slow down product development, throw out profitable ideas, and might add new costs for training and perhaps hiring.

You needn't worry too hard about getting the numbers right, however: relying solely on a business case for ethics is a sure route to failure. The business case *is* the ethical problem. A moral argument that hinges entirely on financial consequences is unwittingly agreeing that ethics is subservient to profit; it will leave you powerless to oppose future moral harms that are profitable nevertheless. You may win this battle, but you'll lose the war.

A business case for ethics should always be secondary to arguments grounded in logic, rhetoric, and even emotion. You must make a compelling case that moral responsibility should supersede even profit at times; that if technologists are genuine about wanting to change the world, the value of our stock options shouldn't come into the equation.

Clearly, this is a tough sell, but our three ethical lenses – deontology, utilitarianism, and virtue ethics – can help. Talking about moral duties or maximising happiness is more rigorous and persuasive than what we might call moral intuition: it helps us justify why we think something's unethical. Values and virtues can be particularly powerful in these discussions. Within a company, core values are largely unimpeachable; their intended role as a guiding star for behaviour lends them moral weight. This neatly demonstrates why core values should be tightly defined; these arguments become circular and wasteful if everyone interprets the values differently.

While deontology, utilitarianism, and virtue ethics are useful analytical tools, it still helps to use simple moral language. As Mary Warnock explains in *An Intelligent Person's Guide to Ethics*, describing decisions as generous, unkind, right, or cruel demystifies ethics and brings it from the intellectual realm into the human realm.[1] Straight talk helps everyone appreciate their decisions have moral qualities.

Facilitation, not judgement

It can be tempting to offer yourself up as a sort of ethical oracle, willing to use your knowledge to pass judgment on tricky quandaries. But this is unhelpful and arrogant. As we know, there's rarely a single answer to ethical challenges, and anyone who believes only they can impart moral wisdom will soon end up drunk on virtue. An individual can spark an ethical movement, but it takes a group to sustain it. Aim to be an ethical facilitator rather than an oracle; not the casting vote but a catalyst, giving people new ways to think about and discuss ethics, and engineering the time and space for these conversations to happen.

Ideally, this discussion will reach outside your building too. Involving the general public in your toughest decisions will reduce the risk of falling into the technocracy trap and remind your colleagues that the dizzying scale of technology can mask important human stories. Your research team will be delighted to advise on how to engage outsiders. You might invite people in for research interviews, or offer them a pen in co-design exercises. You could convene user groups and ask for their feedback on beta versions or speculative provocatypes. Remember though, that users are just a subset of your potential stakeholders. Try also to hear from people who aren't users but could be subject to the externalities of your decisions.

Pay particular attention to those most at risk. Since technological bias often mirrors human bias, these will often be people from underrepresented or vulnerable groups. Allying with these people, and learning from their experiences, could pay strong ethical dividends. Activists from these communities might be able to advise your team, or sit in on critique sessions and early demos: who better to act as a designated dissenter than someone who has just cause to dissent? Above all, listen to these groups, remembering that however tough you find the ethical decision, these people will feel the effects more strongly still.

Other ethical dead ends

The cause of ethics will always fail if people see it as incessantly obstructive. Peter-Paul Verbeek suggests that ethics should accompany technological progress, rather than necessarily oppose it.[2] Adopt a stance of constant ethical opposition and you'll be labelled unreasonable and irrational; the company will soon leave you out of decisions and, in time, find a way to remove you altogether. Save your fiercest resistance for when your firmest ethical principles are threatened. Moral objection is stronger when it comes from respected, constructive members of the team; besides, the emotional drain of eternal moral resistance is unsustainable. Help your colleagues instead to see ethics as a positive input to the business, a question of how we should behave as much as how we shouldn't. Asking the right moral questions can be more important than rejecting the wrong answers. Virtue ethics is again a useful lens here; I've had success asking teams to agree on the virtues that matter most in their project and use these as design prompts.

Although we must engage with the politics of our work, ethics should never be a partisan issue. Colleagues who see ethical issues as mere political disagreement will dismiss moral concerns as trivial or intractable. For all the division in today's world, ethics should matter to us all. Whatever our perspectives, technologists share many common causes. We all want the industry to thrive; we all want to make a positive impact on the world; we all want to avoid bad regulation imposed as a result of our own ethical ineptitude (although we might disagree on whether good regulation would be welcome instead). Our ethical efforts should respect many political viewpoints.

That said, there are limits to this respect. Extremists have become skilled at hijacking free-speech discourse and the new banner of 'ideological diversity' to demand their voices are heard. There's a distinct difference between human attributes that are innate – ethnicity, age, orientation – and those that are chosen. Remembering Popper's paradox of tolerance, we should allow extremists no say in ethical discussion. Political views that challenge fundamental tenets of morality deserve neither respect nor time.

Finally, be sceptical of empathy. Banal overuse has devalued the concept of empathy in design; I've intentionally avoided the term in this book. Of course we should try to understand other people's life experiences, but empathy alone is no shortcut to ethical nirvana. Psychologist Paul Bloom argues that empathy really only extends to in-groups: we empathise with people who we imagine to be like us, or who we find attractive, but not those we consider to be unlike us.[3] Empathy can also mislead us into prematurely thinking we've fulfilled our ethical duties.

> Based on my experience working with designers in large companies, however, I believe empathy is used mostly in good faith to 'humanize' a project that has little to do with human needs [...] Empathy is applied retroactively to fit a business-centric product into a human-centric frame. It becomes an ethical practice designers use to feel better about the potentiality of making superfluous things that no one actually needs. —Thomas Wendt[4]

Empathy prompts us to give money to the beggar, but can also convince us we've done our bit, causing us to overlook means of tackling systemic homelessness. (The best moral solution is surely to do both, if possible.) If we're not careful, empathy can be an excuse for inaction, a way to launder our moral decisions: it can't be unethical; we used empathy!

Ethics in leadership

Most of the advice is this book is within reach of anyone who has some power over the way they work. Managers have a few additional ethical options. I've found that middle managers typically have more collective ethical influence than senior leaders. Executives are often too distanced to see the ethical compromises taken within the ranks, while middle managers are are sometimes tempted to take shortcuts to meet the heavy pressure of targets.

We discussed (in chapter 2) the important role core values play in establishing ethical infrastructure. These values should also be visible in the company's incentives. As Mike Davidson, former vice-president of design at Twitter, says, 'Reward the right behaviors and you will get the right results. Reward only the results and you will get all sorts of behaviors.' Threading core values into the company's career ladders and performance reviews – outlining, say, just how a senior product manager is expected to demonstrate autonomy and trust – makes it clear that every employee is accountable for their decisions, and that ethical behaviour is critical to success. This can, of course, be flipped: contravening the company's values must be treated as underperformance. Any employment contract will include the threat of dismissal for gross misconduct; what is gross misconduct if not moral transgression?

Although ethics is an ancient field, technologists have to apply its ideas to unprecedented problems. Managers should be candid about the difficult trade-offs this entails – balancing results and behaviour, protecting competing freedoms and fairness in an algorithmic world – and discuss what we can learn from ethical successes and failures. Naturally, this will encourage staff to weigh in on the company's thorniest moral problems; leaders should welcome this, although a structured process for managing this feedback might be wise.

Culture is, ultimately, sustained by decisions. Managers sometimes need to take ethical decisions on behalf of, not in agreement with, others; these decisions won't always be popular. Leaders may have to pick sides on politicised issues, or backtrack when they have taken the wrong path. No matter how close it is to shipping, a project that will cause significant harm should be revised or cancelled. Managers have a responsibility to bear the consequences and the potential ire of investors, users, the press, or employees themselves.

Finally, managers should keep their own houses in order, ensuring the company embodies the values it demands from employees. A company with a clear mission and well-defined values, roles, and policies is fertile ground for ethical change, while a company with a rotten value system will always end up with shoddy policies, rampant user abuse, and a workforce willing to cut moral corners. There can be no safety for users if there's no safety for employees.

Time for specialists?

With time and persistence, these concrete changes will at last steer culture in the right direction. People who don't share the company's values will drift away, replaced by staff who are attracted by the company's reputation. Outside help might help kick-start this change: it's foolish to assume the people who led the industry into the ethical swamp are the best people to lead us out of it.

Silicon Valley today is desperate to partner with – or simply poach – computer science, AI, and data science academics, but has long been sceptical of their peers in the humanities and social sciences. This is a mistake. Philosophy of technology and STS (science and technology studies) faculties house hundreds of tech ethics experts, well versed in the issues in this book and tired of the industry's mistakes. It's time we finally heeded their offers of help. Many academics are happy to share their expertise through talks or consulting, and their books and papers would make fine additions to any tech company library. Some of the more approachable academics have newsletters, Patreons, or podcasts that the industry should share and support: we can surely afford to redirect a fraction of our generous budgets and salaries towards people who are years ahead of the game.

As interest in the topic grows, tech firms might try to tempt academics away from their faculties to bolster ethics programmes. However, only the largest tech companies, or those at the cutting edge of emerging technology, need a full-time ethicist or philosopher, and most academics have busy research and teaching schedules. A part-time or retainer relationship may be a better fit: highly regarded ethicist Shannon Vallor, for example, has recently joined the Google Cloud AI team for one day each week.

Since academics and practitioners speak different dialects, work at different tempos, and have different expectations of rigour, the relationship will be awkward at first. This mismatch is healthy; indeed, it's the whole point. Businesses will have to learn to slow down and synthesise deep ideas from people who've explored these issues before. Academics will have to learn how to translate their undoubted knowledge into practical influence. It won't be an easy relationship, but with proper time and effort, it will be a meaningful one.

While on-staff ethicists could report in to HR or engineering, I suspect product and design teams are a more natural home. This will place ethicists at the apex of important decisions, letting them introduce ethical perspectives in critique, and helping them gain trust with decision-makers.

Specialists should be brought in at the appropriate level of seniority. In any nascent field, there will always be those who argue for executive-level representation; however, I think appointing a chief ethics officer is a mistake. Their duties would clash with the CFO, who is already accountable for financial ethics, but more importantly, a chief ethics officer would probably be seen as an ethical oracle. Their seniority would give them too strong a say, undervaluing the latent ethical potential of the wider team and letting staff abdicate responsibility for their own choices. An effective ethicist should spend time on tangible change, not meetings and abstractions. I recommend specialists should be senior individual contributors – product ethicists, design ethicists – rather than managers or executives. These appointments can act as visible statements without being management grade, and execs can still demonstrate their support for ethics through their words, actions, and incentives.

Tread lightly when considering an ethics committee. Many tech leaders are hostile to structures like this, seeing them as bureaucratic talking-shops that will obstruct the company's lightweight, agile culture. If there is support for a committee, think carefully about its structure and powers. While a committee should probably contain specialist ethicists, it should ideally represent the wider organisation, so consider inviting engineers, product managers, designers, researchers, and customer service staff. Also consider the committee's powers: can it veto decisions, making it like an IRB, or is it purely advisory?

Being the change

But let's not get ahead of ourselves. Ethical change starts with the individual, not committees. When I give talks on ethics, whether at conferences or companies, an attendee will often ask for a quiet chat afterwards, during which they reveal a moral dilemma they're facing at work and ask for my advice. How can I convince my boss he's making a mistake? Should I refuse to cooperate? Should I quit?

By now, you know my usual answer: that's not my call to make. While I've written this book to offer some routes through the moral maze, I'm no ethical oracle. Your ethical decisions are yours alone. That should daunt and excite you equally. With rare exceptions, such as companies that genuinely have no interests other than profit, I think any individual can make an ethical difference in any organisation.

The process should start with self-reflection. What mistakes might you be making in your work right now? Which of the three ethical lenses makes most sense to you? How can you start to make a difference? What would be your ethical limit, and how would you object if you were pushed right to it? After this, practice is what counts. We previously described morality as a muscle that needs exercise; Aristotle makes it clear that we have to live our values through our actions.

> Moral virtue comes about as a result of habit [...] Men become builders by building and lyre-players by playing the lyre; so too we become just by doing just acts, temperate by doing temperate acts, brave by doing brave acts.[5]

Try some of the steps we've discussed in this book, with or without permission. Discuss your ethical interests and concerns with your team and your manager, and do it early, to set the right expectations and to allow the proper conversation to flourish.

Hopefully, with time and persistence, you'll make a difference where you are. But it's also worth considering how your ethics will shape your future career. Does your role offer the kind of ethical contributions you want to make? If not, how would you get there? When the time comes to move on, approach job applications and interviews with ethics in mind. Ask your interviewers how the company deals with moral challenges. What are the most difficult ethical decisions the company faces? Who tends to win? How could you contribute? The answers will help you decide which cultures might be a good fit.

Be under no illusions: figuring out what's morally right to do and standing up for it is difficult, lonely work. At times you will pay the price. But choosing to be a more ethical professional will also make you a more moral person. There should be no divide between personal and professional ethics: thinking deeply about the right way to live will, with luck, get you closer to the life you want. 'Sometimes,' says playwright John Patrick Shanley, 'you have to reach forward into your future, contact the person you hope one day to become, and summon that being for support.'

Given the challenges the future will throw at us, we urgently need all the thoughtful technologists we can get; people who care enough to make a difference, who are curious and inclusive enough to navigate this crucial industry towards better futures. I dearly hope you will be one of them.

Appendix

Use these stakeholder and virtue prompts to guide discussion among your teams. Better yet, expand these lists yourself.

Stakeholders

Individuals · Companies · Professional organisations · Unions · Governments · Militaries · Terrorists · Criminals · Workers · Managers · The unemployed · Minorities · Citizens · Voters · Hackers · Children · Future generations · The earth · Animals.

Virtues

Accountability · Agency · Ambition · Authenticity · Authority · Autonomy · Balance · Beauty · Belonging · Calmness · Candour · Care · Civility · Compassion · Community · Comfort · Confidence · Consent · Courage · Courtesy · Creativity · Curiosity · Dedication · Dignity · Discipline · Diversity · Education · Empathy · Empowerment · Equality · Excellence · Happiness · Fairness · Flexibility · Focus · Forgiveness · Freedom · Friendship · Fun · Generosity · Gratitude · Growth · Harmony · Helpfulness · Honesty · Hope · Humility · Humour · Impact · Impartiality · Ingenuity · Inspiration · Integrity · Justice · Kindness · Knowledge · Leadership · Learning · Loyalty · Magnanimity · Mastery · Motivation · Opportunity · Optimism · Originality ·

Passion · Patience · Peace · Perspective · Perseverance · Precision ·
Privacy · Progress · Rationality · Reflection · Respect · Responsibility ·
Rigour · Safety · Security · Self-control · Sharing · Simplicity · Speed ·
Stability · Sustainability · Sympathy · Traditionalism · Transparency ·
Trust · Truth · Universality · Utility · Vision · Wisdom · Wonder.

Notes

1. Trouble in paradise

1. Richard Sennett, *The Craftsman* (Penguin, 2009).
2. 2017 Cone Communications CSR Study, conecomm.com.
3. See Bruno Latour, *Pandora's Hope: Essays on the Reality of Science Studies* (Harvard University Press, 1999) for one analysis of this argument.
4. Peter-Paul Verbeek, *Moralizing Technology* (University of Chicago Press, 2011). Verbeek in turn draws on the work of Don Ihde and Latour.
5. Melvin Kranzberg, 'Software for Human Hardware?', in Pranas Zunde & Dan Hocking (eds.), *Empirical Foundations of Information and Software Science V* (Plenum Press 1990).
6. One of those seductive quotes of hazy origin, often attributed to Maxim Gorky, and spoken in Jean-Luc Godard's film *Le petit soldat*, attributed to Lenin.
7. Caroline Whitbeck, *Ethics in Engineering Practice and Research* (Cambridge University Press, 2nd ed., 2011).

2. Do no harm?

1. Or so says economist Horst Siebert, at least. The tale is possibly apocryphal, but even an anecdote can contain an undeniable truth: things don't always turn out as planned.
2. Paul Virilio, *Politics of the Very Worst* (Semiotexte, 1999).
3. Don Ihde, *Technology and the Lifeworld* (Indiana University Press, 1990).
4. Shannon Hall, 'Exxon Knew about Climate Change almost 40 years ago', *Scientific American*, 26 Oct 2015, scientificamerican.com.
5. See Thomas Wendt, 'Decentering Design or a Critique of Human-Centered Design', slideshare.net.
6. Ben Thompson, 'Airbnb Versus Hotels', *Stratechery*, 18 Apr 2017, stratechery.com.
7. Ursula Franklin, *The Real World of Technology* (House of Anansi Press, 2nd ed., 1999).
8. David Ingold and Spencer Soper, 'Amazon Doesn't Consider the Race of Its Customers. Should It?', *Bloomberg*, 21 Apr 2016, bloomberg.com.
9. Joanna Bryson, 'Three very different sources of bias in AI, and how to fix them', 13 Jul 2017, joanna-bryson.blogspot.com.
10. Aylin Caliskan, Joanna Bryson, Arvind Narayanan, 'Semantics derived automatically from language corpora contain human-like biases', *Science*, 14 Apr 2017, 183–186.
11. Chris Ip, 'In 2017, society started taking AI bias seriously', *Engadget*, 21 Dec 2017, engadget.com.
12. Andrew Thompson, 'Google's Sentiment Analyzer Thinks Being Gay Is Bad', *VICE Motherboard*, 25 Oct 2017, vice.com.
13. Laura Hudson, 'Technology Is Biased Too. How Do We Fix It?', *FiveThirtyEight*, 20 Jul 2017, fivethirtyeight.com.

14. Stella Lowry and Gordon Macpherson, 'A blot on the profession', *British Medical Journal* Vol. 296, 5 March 1988.
15. Christian Rudder, 'Race and Attraction, 2009–2014', *OkCupid*, 10 Sep 2014, okcupid.com.
16. Lizzie Edmonds, 'Google forced to remove vile racist search suggestions from its site for a number of British cities including Bradford, Leicester and Birmingham', *MailOnline*, 11 Feb 2014, dailymail.co.uk.
17. 'I think it's time we broke for lunch...', *The Economist*, 14 Apr 2011, economist.com.
18. Carlota Perez, *Technological Revolutions and Financial Capital: The Dynamics of Bubbles and Golden Ages* (Edward Elgar Publishing, 2003).
19. *Terminator 2: Judgement Day*, dir. James Cameron (TriStar Pictures, 1991). You could argue these aren't Sarah's words but John's, passed on by Kyle through Sarah back to John.
20. Originally conceived by military strategist Charles Taylor and adapted by several futurists since, including Joseph Voros.
21. Octavia Butler, 'A Few Rules for Predicting the Future', *Essence Magazine*, 2000.
22. Shannon Vallor, *Technology and the Virtues* (Oxford University Press, 2016).
23. Genevieve Bell, 'Rage Against the Machine?', talk at *Interaction12* conference.
24. Eric Meyer and Sara Wachter-Boettcher, *Design for Real Life* (A Book Apart, 2016).
25. My name, extending an idea by Sam Jeffers.
26. Cameron Tonkinwise, 'Ethics by Design, or the Ethos of Things', *Design Philosophy Papers*, 2:2, 129-144, 2004.
27. Jared Spool, 'Creating Great Design Principles: 6 Counter-intuitive Tests', *UIE*, 1 Mar 2011, uie.com.
28. Anand Giridharadas, 'A tale of two Americas. And the mini-mart where they collided', talk at *TED2015* conference, ted.com.
29. Shannon Vallor, 'An Introduction to Data Ethics: a resource for data science courses', *Markkula Center for Applied Ethics*, scu.edu.

3. Persuasive mechanisms

1. Langdon Winner, 'Do Artifacts Have Politics?', *Daedalus* 109, no. 1 (1980): 121-36.
2. Daniel Berdichevsky and Erik Neuenschwander, 'Toward an ethics of persuasive technology', *Communications of the ACM*, 42, 5 (May 1999), 51–58.
3. Coined by Harry Brignull; see darkpatterns.org.
4. Tim Wu, *The Attention Merchants: The Epic Scramble to Get Inside Our Heads* (Knopf Publishing Group, 2016).
5. Peter Kafka, 'Amazon? HBO? Netflix thinks its real competitor is... sleep', *Recode*, 17 Apr 2017, recode.net.
6. Kleiner Perkins Internet Trends 2017, kpcb.com/internet-trends.
7. Ian Bogost, 'The App That Does Nothing', *The Atlantic*, 9 Jun 2017, theatlantic.com. Bogost is a theorist of persuasive games and designer of *Cow Clicker*, a notorious commentary on the manipulative aspects of FarmVille. Cow Clicker players had but one objective: to click a cow. The game amassed 50,000 users before Bogost triggered a 'Cowpocalypse', vanishing the cows into ironic rapture.
8. Adam Cramer, Jamie Guillory, Jeffrey Hancock, 'Experimental evidence of massive-scale emotional contagion through social networks', *Proceedings of the National Academy of Sciences (PNAS)*, 17 Jun 2014 vol. 111 no. 24 8,788-8,790.
9. Ariel Rubinstein and Ayala Arad, 'The People's Perspective on Libertarian-Paternalistic Policies' (2015).

10. Molly Sauter, 'The Apophenic Machine', *Real Life Magazine*, reallifemag.com.
11. Chris Wade, 'The Reddit Reckoning', *Slate*, 15 Apr 2014, slate.com.
12. A remarkable inconsistency discovered by journalist Olivia Solon.
13. Berit Anderson and Brett Horvath, 'The Rise of the Weaponized AI Propaganda Machine', scout.ai.
14. Philip Howard, and Bence Kollanyi, 'Bots, #Strongerin, and #Brexit: Computational Propaganda during the UK-EU Referendum.' Working Paper 2016.1. Oxford, UK: Project on Computational Propaganda.
15. Jeff Bezos, '2015 Letter to Shareholders'.
16. Paul Robinette et al., 'Overtrust of robots in emergency evacuation scenarios', *2016 11th ACM/IEEE International Conference on Human-Robot Interaction (HRI)*, Christchurch, 2016, pp. 101-108.
17. Sandra Matz et al., 'Psychological targeting as an effective approach to digital mass persuasion', *Proceedings of the National Academy of Sciences (PNAS)* 2017.
18. Dana Mattioli, 'On Orbitz, Mac Users Steered to Pricier Hotels', *The Wall Street Journal*, 23 Aug 2012, wsj.com.
19. John D. Sutter, 'Amazon seller lists book at $23,698,655.93 – plus shipping', *CNN*, 25 Apr 2011, cnn.com.
20. Lyrebird, 'With great innovation comes great responsibility', lyrebird.ai/ethics.
21. Daniel Berdichevsky and Erik Neuenschwander, 'Toward an ethics of persuasive technology', *Communications of the ACM*, 42, 5 (May 1999), 51–58.
22. BJ Fogg, *Persuasive Technology* (Morgan Kaufman, 2003).
23. Richard Thaler, 'The Power of Nudges, for Good and Bad', *New York Times*, 31 Oct 2015, nytimes.com.
24. Nynke Tromp et al., 'Design for Socially Responsible Behavior', *Design Issues*, Volume 27, Number 3, Summer 2011.
25. Luciano Floridi, 'Tolerant Paternalism: Pro-ethical Design as a Resolution of the Dilemma of Toleration', *Science and Engineering Ethics* (2016), 22: 1669.
26. His first formulation of the 'categorical imperative', from *Groundwork for the Metaphysics of Morals*.
27. Again from the categorical imperative, this time the second formulation.
28. John Rawls, *A Theory of Justice* (Harvard University Press, 1971).
29. Now run by the Center for Humane Technology, humanetech.com.

4. The data deluge

1. Cornelius Puschmann & Jean Burgess, 'Metaphors of Big Data', *International Journal Of Communication*, 8, 20. (2014).
2. Bruce Schneier, 'We Give Up Our Data Too Cheaply', *Vice Motherboard*, 2 Mar 2015, vice.com.
3. Dave Gershgorn, 'Stanford trained AI to diagnose pneumonia better than a radiologist in just two months', *Quartz*, 16 Nov 2017, qz.com.
4. 'AI vs. Lawyers', lawgeex.com.
5. Allison Linn, 'Microsoft creates AI that can read a document and answer questions about it as well as a person', microsoft.com, 15 Jan 2018.
6. Julian M. Goldman, MD, 'Medical Device Interoperability Ecosystem Updates: Device Clock Time, Value Proposition, and the FDA Regulatory Pathway', NSF CPS Large Site Visit, 31 Jan 2012.
7. Geoffrey C Bowker, *Memory Practices in the Sciences* (MIT Press, 2006).
8. See Adam Greenfield, *Radical Technologies* (Verso 2017).

9. Richard A. Posner, 'Privacy, Secrecy, and Reputation', *28 Buffalo Law Review 1* (1979).
10. Kashmir Hill, 'Facebook recommended that this psychiatrist's patients friend each other', *Splinter*, 29 Aug 2018, splinternews.com.
11. Richard A. Posner, 'Privacy, Secrecy, and Reputation', 28 Buffalo Law Review 1 (1979).
12. 'Self-driving cars offer huge benefits—but have a dark side', *The Economist*, 1 Mar 2018, economist.com.
13. Arvind Narayanan & Vitaly Shmatikov. 'Robust De-anonymization of Large Datasets (How to Break Anonymity of the Netflix Prize Dataset)', 2006.
14. Latanya Sweeney, 'Simple Demographics Often Identify People Uniquely', Carnegie Mellon University working paper, Data Privacy, 2000.
15. Pinboard (@pinboard), Twitter, 8 Jan 2017.
16. Michael Zimmer, 'OkCupid Study Reveals the Perils of Big-Data Science', *WIRED*, 14 May 2016, wired.com.
17. Bruno Latour, *Pandora's Hope: Essays on the Reality of Science Studies* (Harvard University Press 1999).
18. Jacob Hoffman-Andrews, 'Victory: Verizon Will Stop Tagging Customers for Tracking Without Consent', 7 Mar 2016, eff.org.
19. Luciano Floridi, 'Google ethics adviser: The law needs bold ideas to address the digital age', *The Guardian*, 4 Jun 2014, theguardian.com.
20. Sheila Jasanoff, *The Ethics of Invention: Technology and the Human Future* (W. W. Norton & Company, 2016).
21. Michee Smith, 'Updating our "right to be forgotten" Transparency Report', *Google in Europe* blog, 26 Feb 2018, www.blog.google.
22. Gareth Corfield, 'Here is how Google handles Right To Be Forgotten requests', *The Register*, 19 Mar 2018, theregister.co.uk.
23. Sam Harris, *The Moral Landscape* (Simon & Schuster 2010).
24. Mary Warnock, *An Intelligent Person's Guide to Ethics* (Gerald Duckworth & Co 2001).
25. Really. See Avram Piltch, 'Why Using an Ad Blocker Is Stealing (Op-Ed)', *Tom's Guide*, 22 May 2015, tomsguide.com.
26. James Williams, 'Why It's OK to Block Ads', *Oxford University Practical Ethics* blog, practicalethics.ox.ac.uk.
27. Matt Blaze (@mattblaze), Twitter, 3 Feb 2018.
28. 'Immaterials artist Timo Arnall on seeing the invisible', *Lighthouse*, 9 Jun 2015, lighthouse.org.
29. Martin Heidegger, *Being and Time* (Max Niemeyer Verlag Tübingen, 1927). No book on ethics can mention Heidegger without addressing his fascism and antisemitism. Heidegger was a member of the Nazi Party for many years and died apparently unrepentant. I can only acknowledge, not resolve, the conundrum of whether his abhorrent politics should diminish his philosophical insight; Joshua Rothman's New Yorker article 'Is Heidegger Contaminated by Nazism?' offers an intelligent review.
30. Amber Case, 'Calm Technology: Design for the Next Generation of Devices', talk at *TNW Conference* 2017.
31. Benedict Evans (@benedictevans), Twitter, 31 Dec 2017.
32. Natalie Kane, 'Private Data Is the Ultimate Luxury Good', *Vice Motherboard*, 27 Sep 2016, motherboard.vice.com.
33. Jun Tang et al, 'Privacy Loss in Apple's Implementation of Differential Privacy on MacOS 10.12', arxiv.org/abs/1709.02753.
34. Andy Greenberg, 'How One of Apple's Key Privacy Safeguards Falls Short', *WIRED*, 15 Sep 2017, wired.com.

35. Ivan Krstić, 'How iOS Security Really Works', talk at *Apple Worldwide Developer Conference 2016*.
36. Ben Thompson, 'Facebook's Earnings, Facebook's Strategy Credit (and Apple's), Facebook and the Future', *Stratechery*, 2 Nov 2017, stratechery.com.

5. Seeing through new eyes

1. Steve Lohr, 'Facial Recognition Is Accurate, if You're a White Guy', *The New York Times*, 9 Feb 2018, nytimes.com.
2. Joon Son Chung et al, 'Lip Reading Sentences in the Wild', *IEEE Conference on Computer Vision and Pattern Recognition* (CVPR), 2017.
3. Yan Michalevsky et al, 'Gyrophone: recognizing speech from gyroscope signals', *Proceedings of the 23rd USENIX conference on Security Symposium* (SEC'14), 2014.
4. Abe Davis et al, 'The Visual Microphone: Passive Recovery of Sound from Video', *ACM Transactions on Graphics* (Proc. SIGGRAPH), 33, 4, 2014.
5. Daniel Arp et al, 'Privacy Threats through Ultrasonic Side Channels on Mobile Devices', *IEEE European Symposium on Security and Privacy* (EuroS&P), Paris, 2017.
6. Tom Dart, 'Y'all have a Texas accent? Siri (and the world) might be slowly killing it', *The Guardian*, 10 Feb 2016, theguardian.com.
7. Kashmir Hill and Surya Mattu, 'Facebook Knows How to Track You Using the Dust on Your Camera Lens', *Gizmodo*, 11 Jan 2018, gizmodo.com.
8. Transport for London, 'Review of the TfL WiFi pilot'.
9. Hao-Yu Wu et al, 'Eulerian video magnification for revealing subtle changes in the world' *ACM Trans. Graph.* 31, 4, Article 65 (Jul 2012).
10. Chris Wood, 'WhatsApp photo drug dealer caught by "groundbreaking" work', *BBC News*, 15 Apr 2018, bbc.co.uk.
11. Timnit Gebru et al, 'Using deep learning and Google Street View to estimate the demographic makeup of neighborhoods across the United States', *Proceedings of the National Academy of Sciences*, Nov 2017.
12. From Michal Kosinski & Yilun Wang, 'Deep Neural Networks Are More Accurate Than Humans at Detecting Sexual Orientation From Facial Images', *Journal of Personality and Social Psychology*, Feb 2018, Vol. 114, Issue 2.
13. Greggor Mattson, 'artificial intelligence discovers gayface. sigh.', *Scatterplot*, 10 Sep 2017, scatter.wordpress.com.
14. Doreen Sullivan, 'A brief history of homophobia in Dewey decimal classification', *Overland*, 23 Jul 2015, overland.org.au.
15. 'Advances in AI are used to spot signs of sexuality', *The Economist*, 9 Sep 2017, economist.com.
16. Michal Kosinski and Yilun Wang, 'Authors' note: Deep neural networks are more accurate than humans at detecting sexual orientation from facial images', 28 Sep 2017.
17. Randy Cohen, 'Doing the Outsourcing', *The New York Times Magazine*, 4 Feb 2011, nytimes.com.
18. Jonathan Glover & M. J. Scott-Taggart, 'It Makes no Difference Whether or Not I Do It', *Aristotelian Society Supplementary*, Volume 49 (1):171 - 209, 1975.
19. Felix Salmon, 'The Creepy Rise of Real Companies Spawning Fictional Design', *Slate*, 30 May 2018, slate.com.
20. Chris Noessel, *Designing Agentive Technology* (Rosenfeld Media, 2017).
21. State of California Department of Motor Vehicles, 'Autonomous Vehicle Disengagement Reports 2017', dma.ca.gov.

22. Alexander Eriksson & Neville A Stanton, 'Take-over time in highly automated vehicles: non-critical transitions to and from manual control', *Human Factors* 59, 4, 2017.

23. Jeff Wise, 'What Really Happened Aboard Air France 447', *Popular Mechanics*, 6 Dec 2011, popularmechanics.com.

24. Marshall McLuhan, *Understanding Media* (McGraw-Hill, 1964).

25. David Meyer, 'Police Tested Facial Recognition at a Major Sporting Event. The Results Were Disastrous', *Fortune*, 7 May 2018, fortune.com.

26. Dan Simmons, 'BBC fools HSBC voice recognition security system', *BBC News*, 19 May 2018, bbc.co.uk.

27. Bryant Walker Smith, 'Human Error as a Cause of Vehicle Crashes', *The Center for Internet and Society* blog, 18 Dec 2013, cyberlaw.stanford.edu.

28. Kirk Mitchell, 'Man sues FBI and Denver police for $10 million claiming false arrest for 2 bank robberies and excessive force', *The Denver Post*, 15 Sep 2016, denverpost.com.

29. Evan Selinger, 'Amazon Needs to Stop Providing Facial Recognition Tech for the Government', *Medium*, 21 Jun 2018, medium.com.

30. Philippa Foot, 'The Problem of Abortion and the Doctrine of the Double Effect', *Oxford Review*, Number 5, 1967.

31. Alexis C Madrigal, 'Uber's Self-Driving Car Didn't Malfunction, It Was Just Bad', *The Atlantic*, 24 May 2018, theatlantic.com.

32. Alex Hern, 'Self-driving cars don't care about your moral dilemmas', *The Guardian*, 22 Aug 2016, theguardian.com.

33. Jean-François Bonnefon et al, 'The social dilemma of autonomous vehicles', *Science*, vol. 35, 2016.

34. Eric D. Lawrence et al, 'Death on foot: America's love of SUVs is killing pedestrians', *Detroit Free Press*, 1 Jul 2018, freep.com.

35. John Danaher, 'The Ethics of Crash Optimisation Algorithms', *Philosophical Disquisitions*, 28 Apr 2017, philosophicaldisquisitions.blogspot.co.uk.

36. Liesl Yearsley, 'We Need to Talk About the Power of AI to Manipulate Humans', *MIT Technology Review*, 5 Jun 2017, technologyreview.com.

37. Donna Haraway, *The Companion Species Manifesto* (University of Chicago Press, 2nd ed., 2003).

38. Ibid.

39. Thomas Hobbes, *Leviathan*.

40. Todd Kulesza et al, 'Principles of Explanatory Debugging to Personalize Interactive Machine Learning', *Proceedings of IUI*, 2015.

41. Sandra Wachter et al, 'Counterfactual Explanations without Opening the Black Box: Automated Decisions and the GDPR', *Harvard Journal of Law & Technology*, 31 (2), 2018.

42. The Alan Turing Institute, 'A right to explanation', turing.ac.uk.

43. Shannon Vallor, *Technology and the Virtues* (Oxford University Press, 2016).

44. Batya Friedman et al, 'Value Sensitive Design and Information Systems', *Philosophy of Engineering and Technology*, vol 16, 2013.

6. You have twenty seconds to comply

1. Nellie Bowles, 'Thermostats, Locks and Lights: Digital Tools of Domestic Abuse', *The New York Times*, 23 Jun 2018, nytimes.com.

2. Chris Noessel, *Designing Agentive Technology* (Rosenfeld Media, 2017).

3. Caroline Sinders, 'Silicon Valley's harassment problem', *VICE News*, 28 May 2017, news.vice.com.

4. Sarah Jeong, *The Internet of Garbage* (Forbes Media, 2015).

5. Megan Strait et al, 'Robots Racialized in the Likeness of Marginalized Social Identities are Subject to Greater Dehumanization than those racialized as White', arxiv.org/abs/1808.00320.

6. Leah Fessler, 'We tested bots like Siri and Alexa to see who would stand up to sexual harassment', *Quartz*, 22 Feb 2017, qz.com.

7. Josh Halliday, 'Twitter's Tony Wang: "We are the free speech wing of the free speech party"', *The Guardian*, 22 Mar 2012, theguardian.com.

8. Isaiah Berlin, 'Two Concepts of Liberty', from *Four Essays on Liberty* (Oxford University Press, 1969).

9. Karl Popper, *The Open Society and Its Enemies*, Volume 1 (Routledge, 1945).

10. Lauren Weber and Deepa Seetharaman, 'The Worst Job in Technology: Staring at Human Depravity to Keep It Off Facebook', *The Wall Street Journal*, 27 Dec 2017, wsj.com.

11. Sophie Kleeman, 'Woman Charged With False Reporting After Her Fitbit Contradicted Her Rape Claim', *Mic*, 25 Jun 2015, mic.com.

12. 'Man who claimed his wife was murdered by an intruder pleads not guilty to murder after cops find information on her Fitbit that contradicted his story', *MailOnline*, 28 Apr 2017, dailymail.co.uk.

13. Sarah Brayne, 'Big Data Surveillance: The Case of Policing', *American Sociological Review*, Vol 82, Issue 5.

14. Sadie Gurman, 'AP: Across US, police officers abuse confidential databases', *AP*, 28 Sep 2016, apnews.com.

15. Clare Garvie et al, 'The Perpetual Line-Up: Racial Bias', perpetuallineup.org.

16. Kay Lazar, 'State Police union files complaint about GPS vehicle tracking', *Boston Globe*, 10 May 2018, bostonglobe.com.

17. Tim Cook, 'A Message to Our Customers', 16 Feb 2016, apple.com/customer-letter.

18. 'CBS News poll: Americans split on unlocking San Bernardino shooter's iPhone', *CBS News*, 18 Mar 2016, cbsnews.com.

19. Niccolò Machiavelli, *The Prince*.

20. 'Ben Franklin's Famous "Liberty, Safety" Quote Lost Its Context In 21st Century', *All Things Considered*, 2 Mar 2015, npr.org.

21. Michael Brown, 'Apple vs. FBI and the ethics of encryption', *Folio*, 26 Feb 2016, folio.ca.

22. Chris Whipple, 'What the CIA knew before 9/11: New details', *Politico*, 13 Nov 2015, politico.eu.

23. Daniel Crevier, *AI: The Tumultuous History of the Search for Artificial Intelligence* (Basic Books, 1993).

24. Tanya O'Carroll and Joshua Franco, 'Why build a Muslim registry when you can buy it?', *Amnesty Global Insights*, 27 Feb 2017, medium.com.

25. Freedom House, 'Silencing the Messenger: Communication Apps Under Pressure', freedomhouse.org.

26. Thanks to Ian Goodwin (@isgoodrum) for breaking down these measures on Twitter.

27. Ed Jefferson, 'No, China isn't Black Mirror – social credit scores are more complex and sinister than that', *New Statesman*, 27 Apr 2018, newstatesman.com.

28. Miranda Hall & Duncan McCann, 'What's Your Score? How Discriminatory Algorithms Control Access and Opportunity', New Economics Foundation, 10 Jul 2018, neweconomics.org.

29. David Cole, 'Can the NSA Be Controlled?', *The New York Review of Books*, 19 Jun 2014, nybooks.com.
30. 'Public resigned to data collection and surveillance', Economic and Social Research Council, esrc.ukri.org.
31. lily jackson (@lillyzela), Twitter, 5 Dec 2017.
32. Daniel Solove, '"I've Got Nothing to Hide" and Other Misunderstandings of Privacy'. *San Diego Law Review*, Vol. 44, p. 745, 2007.
33. See Adam Greenfield, *Radical Technologies* (Verso 2017).
34. Simon Parkin, 'Killer robots: The soldiers that never sleep', *BBC Future*, 16 July 2015, bbc.com.
35. Caroline Lester, 'What Happens When Your Bomb-Defusing Robot Becomes a Weapon', *The Atlantic*, 26 Apr 2018, theatlantic.com.
36. The Future of Life Institute & Stuart Russell, *Slaughterbots* (2017).
37. Sarah A. Topol, 'Attack of the Killer Robots', *Buzzfeed*, 26 Aug 2016, buzzfeed.com.
38. Campaign to Stop Killer Robots, 'Country Views on Killer Robots', stopkillerrobots.org.
39. Ash Carter, 'Remarks on "The Path to an Innovative Future for Defense"', defense.gov.
40. Dan Lamothe, 'The killer robot threat: Pentagon examining how enemy nations could empower machines', *The Washington Post*, 30 Mar 2016, washingtonpost.com.
41. Paul Scharre, *Army of None: Autonomous Weapons and the Future of War* (W. W. Norton & Company, 2018).
42. Jamie Condliffe, 'AI Shouldn't Believe Everything It Hears', *MIT Technology Review*, 28 Jul 2017, technologyreview.com.
43. Louise Matsakis, 'Researchers Fooled a Google AI into Thinking a Rifle Was a Helicopter', *WIRED*, 20 Dec 2017, wired.com.
44. Amarjot Singh et al, 'Disguised Face Identification (DFI) with Facial KeyPoints using Spatial Fusion Convolutional Network', presented at the *IEEE International Conference on Computer Vision Workshops* (ICCVW) 2017.
45. Henry David Thoreau, 'Civil Disobedience' (1849).
46. Daisuke Wakabayashi & Scott Shane, 'Google Will Not Renew Pentagon Contract That Upset Employees', *The New York Times*, 1 Jun 2018, nytimes.com.
47. Nabil Hassein, 'Against Black Inclusion in Facial Recognition', *Digital Talking Drum*, 15 Aug 2017, digitaltalkingdrum.com.
48. Anthony Dunne and Fiona Raby, *Speculative Everything* (MIT Press, 2014).
49. Freedom of the Press Foundation, 'Here's how to share sensitive leaks with the press', freedom.press.

7. Software is heating the world

1. NASA Global Climate Change website, climate.nasa.gov.
2. Adrian E. Raftery et al, 'Less than 2 °C warming by 2100 unlikely', *Nature Climate Change* volume 7, 2017, nature.com.
3. World Bank Group, 'Turn Down the Heat: Confronting the New Climate Normal', 2014, worldbank.org.
4. Roy Scranton, 'Learning How to Die in the Anthropocene', *The New York Times*, 10 Nov 2013, opinionator.blogs.nytimes.com.
5. Victor Papanek, *Design for the Real World* (Thames and Hudson Ltd, 1985).
6. Jenna R Krall and Roger D Peng, 'The difficulty of calculating deaths caused by the Volkswagen scandal', *The Guardian*, 9 Dec 2015, theguardian.com.

7. Tom Bawden, 'Global warming: Data centres to consume three times as much energy in next decade, experts warn', *The Independent*, 23 Jan 2016, independent.co.uk.
8. Greenpeace, 'Clicking Clean: Who Is Winning The Race To Build A Green Internet?' report 2017, greenpeace.org.
9. Centre for Energy-Efficient Telecommunications, 'The Power of Wireless Cloud' white paper, 2013.
10. Fatemeh Jalali et al, 'Energy Consumption of Photo Sharing in Online Social Networks', *14th IEEE/ACM International Symposium on Cluster, Cloud and Grid Computing*, 2014.
11. Justin Adamson, 'Carbon and the Cloud', *Stanford Magazine*, 15 May 2017, medium.com.
12. Apple environment reports, apple.com/environment/reports.
13. Mike Berners-Lee, *How Bad Are Bananas?: The Carbon Footprint of Everything* (Profile Books, 2010).
14. Jonathan Kaiman, 'Rare earth mining in China: the bleak social and environmental costs', *The Guardian*, 20 Mar 2014, theguardian.com.
15. Digiconomist, 'Bitcoin Energy Consumption Index', digiconomist.net/bitcoin-energy-consumption.
16. Gini coefficient estimates for Bitcoin range from 0.67 to 0.88, compared with World Bank national estimates that peak around 0.5: GINI index (World Bank Estimate), data.worldbank.org.
17. Martin Heidegger, *The Question Concerning Technology* (Garland Publishing, 1954). See also Thomas Wendt, *Design for Dasein* (2015) for a design-centric perspective on Heidegger's work.
18. Nick Bostrom, *Superintelligence* (Oxford University Press, 2014).
19. Shannon Biggs, 'No surrender: responding to the new breed of climate change in-activists', *openDemocracy*, 18 Jun 2014, opendemocracy.net.
20. Christiana Figueres et al, 'Three years to safeguard our climate', *Nature*, 28 Jun 2017, nature.com.
21. Victor Papanek, *Design for the Real World* (Thames and Hudson Ltd, 1985).
22. Helen Walters, 'CES: A Symbol of Global Vandalism', helenwalters.com.
23. Ronan Cremin, 'The web is Doom', MobiForge blog, 19 Apr 2016, mobiforge.com.
24. Gabrielle Coppola and Esha Dey, 'Driverless Cars Are Giving Engineers a Fuel Economy Headache', *Bloomberg*, 11 Oct 2017, bloomberg.com.
25. Fergus Green, 'Anti-fossil fuel norms: a new frontier in climate change politics', *LSE Department of Government* blog, blogs.lse.ac.uk.
26. David Roberts, 'It's time to start talking about "negative" carbon dioxide emissions', *Vox*, 18 Aug 2017, vox.com.
27. Richard Somerville, 'The Ethics of Climate Change', *Yale Environment 360*, e360.yale.edu.
28. Pope Francis, Encyclical Letter Laudato Si' of the Holy Father Francis on Care For Our Common Home, 2015, vatican.va.
29. Matt McGrath, 'Climate change: "Hothouse Earth" risks even if CO2 emissions slashed', *BBC News*, 6 Aug 2018, bbc.co.uk.
30. Jay Springett, 'Solarpunk: A Reference Guide', *Medium*, solarpunks.net/ref.
31. Adam Flynn, 'Solarpunk: Notes toward a manifesto', *Hieroglyph*, hieroglyph.asu.edu.
32. Alex Steffen, 'Yes, I Get on Planes to Fight Climate Change', *Medium*, 8 Nov 2016, medium.com.

8. No cash, no jobs, no hope

1. Richard Dobbs et al, *No Ordinary Disruption* (PublicAffairs, 2015).
2. Alison Burke, 'What is the future of free trade? 5 facts about US trade policy', 18 Nov 2016, brookings.edu.
3. Brian Merchant, 'You've Got Luddites All Wrong', *Vice Motherboard*, 2 Sep 2014, motherboard.vice.com.
4. Parliamentary Debates (series 1) vol. 21 col. 966 (27 February 1812).
5. Katja Grace et al, 'When Will AI Exceed Human Performance? Evidence from AI Experts', *Journal of Artificial Intelligence Research* (AI and Society Track), 2017.
6. Louis Hyman, 'It's Not Technology That's Disrupting Our Jobs', *The New York Times*, 18 Aug 2018, nytimes.com.
7. Nick Srnicek and Alex Williams, *Inventing the Future* (Verso Books, 2015).
8. Douglas Rushkoff, *Throwing Rocks at the Google Bus: How Growth Became the Enemy of Prosperity* (Penguin Random House, 2016).
9. David Graeber, 'On the Phenomenon of Bullshit Jobs: A Work Rant', *Strike Magazine*, August 2013, strikemag.org.
10. Carl Frey and Michael Osborne, 'The future of employment: How susceptible are jobs to computerisation?', *Technological Forecasting and Social Change*, 2017, vol. 114, issue C, 254-280.
11. Ljubica Nedelkoska and Glenda Quintini, 'Automation, skills use and training', *OECD Social, Employment and Migration Working Papers*, No. 202, 2018.
12. Calum Chase, *Surviving AI* (Three Cs, 2015).
13. New York Taxi Workers Alliance, 'NY Uber Drivers Are Employees with Right to Unemployment Insurance' press release, 19 Jul 2018.
14. 'Spanish court rules Deliveroo rider is employee, not self-employed', *Reuters*, 4 Jun 2018, reuters.com.
15. Will Shu, 'We want Deliveroo riders to have flexibility and the benefits of employment', *Deliveroo Foodscene* blog, 23 Jul 2018, foodscene.deliveroo.co.uk.
16. Rani Molla & Kurt Wagner, 'People spend almost as much time on Instagram as they do on Facebook', *Recode*, 25 Jun 2018, recode.net.
17. Feng Xiang, 'AI will spell the end of capitalism', *The Washington Post*, 3 May 2018, washingtonpost.com.
18. Peter Frase, *Four Futures: Life After Capitalism* (Verso Books, 2016).
19. Thomas Piketty, *Capital in the Twenty-First Century* (Harvard University Press, 2014).
20. 'Automation: A report to the UAW-CIO Economic and Collective Bargaining Conference', Nov 1954.
21. Data for Progress, 'Polling The Left Agenda', 2018, dataforprogress.org.
22. Basic Income Grant Coalition Pilot Project, bignam.org (Namibia); Guy Standing, 'Unconditional Basic Income: Two pilots in Madhya Pradesh', prepared for the Delhi Conference, May 2013 (India); Johannes Haushofer and Jeremy Shapiro, 'The Short-Term Impact of Unconditional Cash Transfers to the Poor: Experimental Evidence from Kenya', *The Quarterly Journal of Economics*, Volume 131, Issue 4, 1 November 2016, Pages 1973–2042 (Kenya).
23. Richard Waters, 'Bill Gates calls for income tax on robots', *The Financial Times*, 19 Feb 2017, ft.com.
24. LM Sacasas, 'Why We Can't Have Humane Technology', 11 Mar 2018, thefrailest-thing.com.
25. Damien Williams, 'Technoccult News: "In fits and starts..."', *Patreon*, 15 Feb 2018, patreon.com.

26. David Benatar, *Better Never to Have Been: The Harm Of Coming Into Existence* (Oxford University Press, 2008).

27. Milton Friedman, 'The Social Responsibility of Business is to Increase its Profits', *The New York Times Magazine*, 13 Sep 1970, nytimes.com.

28. Bertrand Russell, 'In Praise of Idleness', *Harpers Magazine*, Oct 1932.

29. Jeremy Bentham, *An Introduction to the Principles of Morals and Legislation* (Clarendon Press, 1789).

30. Peter Singer, *Animal Liberation* (HarperCollins, 1975).

31. Damien Williams, 'What Is It Like To Be a Bot?', *Real Life*, 7 May 2018, real-lifemag.com

32. John Searle, 'Minds, brains, and programs', *Behavioral and Brain Sciences* 3 (3): 417-457, 1980.

33. Evan Selinger, 'We Don't Need Robots That Resemble Humans', *Medium*, 1 Mar 2018, medium.com.

34. David Ryan Polgar, 'We want chatbots to sound more human—but the result could destroy our relationships', *Quartz*, 4 Dec 2017, qz.com.

35. Richard Lawler, 'Google: Duplex phone calling AI will identify itself', *Engadget*, 10 May 2018, engadget.com.

36. George Dvorsky, 'Why Asimov's Three Laws Of Robotics Can't Protect Us', *Gizmodo*, 28 Mar 2014, gizmodo.com.

37. Nick Bostrom, 'What happens when our computers get smarter than we are?', presentation at *TED2015*.

38. See the Future of Life Institute's 'FAQ about AI', futureoflife.org/ai-faqs.

39. Stephen Hawking, speech at the Leverhulme Centre for the Future of Intelligence, 19 Oct 2016.

40. Calum Chase, *Surviving AI* (Three Cs, 2015).

41. 'Professor Stuart Russell summarises AI risk', Oxford Future of Humanity Institute, 8 Dec 2014, fhi.ox.ac.uk/edge-article.

42. Joe Vesey-Byrne, 'How humanity will end, according to Nobel Prize winners', *Indy100*, 3 Sep 2017, indy100.com.

9. A new tech philosophy

1. Mary Warnock, *An Intelligent Person's Guide to Ethics* (Gerald Duckworth & Co 2001).

2. Peter-Paul Verbeek, *Moralizing Technology* (University of Chicago Press, 2011).

3. Paul Bloom, *Against Empathy: The Case for Rational Compassion* (Vintage, 2018).

4. Thomas Wendt, 'Empathy as Faux Ethics', *EPIC*, 10 Jan 2017, epicpeople.org.

5. Aristotle, *Nicomachean Ethics, Book II*.

About the author

Cennydd Bowles is a London-based designer and writer with fifteen years of experience and clients including Twitter, Ford, Cisco, and the BBC. His focus today is the ethics of emerging technology. He has lectured on the topic at Carnegie Mellon University, Google, and New York's School of Visual Arts, and is a sought-after speaker at technology and design events worldwide.

———

Also by Cennydd: *Undercover User Experience Design* (New Riders 2010), with James Box.

Made in the USA
Las Vegas, NV
29 December 2021